HARVARD HISTORICAL STUDIES

PUBLISHED UNDER THE DIRECTION
OF THE DEPARTMENT OF HISTORY
FROM THE INCOME
OF THE PAUL REVERE
FROTHINGHAM BEQUEST

VOLUME LXXIX

THRONE
AND MANDARINS

CHINA'S SEARCH
FOR A POLICY DURING THE
SINO-FRENCH CONTROVERSY
1880–1885

Lloyd E. Eastman

HARVARD UNIVERSITY PRESS

Cambridge, Massachusetts

1967

For my parents

EVELYN S. EASTMAN
HARRY R. EASTMAN

PREFACE

When France in the early 1880's began to extend its control in Vietnam from Cochin China in the south to Tongking in the north, Chinese policy makers sensed a threat to the Chinese empire itself. Peking, however, reacted to the French advances with caution and hesitation. The Chinese recognized that if they did not intervene in Vietnam against the French aggressions, the frontiers of the empire would be exposed, and the French might thrust into the rich provinces of Southwest China. On the other hand, imperial armies might be no match for the modern forces of the French. The weakness of the empire would then be revealed to the lustful eyes of the British, Russians, Japanese, and other potential aggressors. *Throne and Mandarins* records the dramatic process by which this dilemma of Chinese policy was ultimately resolved.

By studying this process, we are able to gain an insight into the tortuous workings of decision-making in China. The power of the throne is seen to have been drastically limited by the mandarins, i.e. the officials, who had their own sources of power vis-à-vis the throne. And, as a result of the analysis, it is possible to challenge the widely accepted hypothesis that there was an historical tendency toward untrammeled autocracy in China since the Sung and Ming dynasties. The study also helps to explain the workings of regionalism during the late nineteenth century, for it shows how provincial authorities were able repeatedly during the crisis to safeguard their own interests against dictates of the central government.

The most significant contribution of the study may be the light it throws on the role of low-ranking, conservative officials in policy formation. It is curious and unfortunate that most students of this period of Chinese history have focused their attention upon men who were relatively amenable to change within China. But these proponents of reform were a minuscule minority; most Chinese deplored changes in the status quo. As a consequence, our knowledge of the late Ch'ing period is distorted and sorely out of balance. The conservatives, reactionaries, and obscurantists have not been given their due, for it was they, not the progressives and modernizers, who were ultimately responsible for China's modern fate. This study will, I hope, partially redress the balance.

More than eighty years have elapsed since the events discussed in the following chapters. Yet the Sino-French confrontation bears striking similarities to the American involvement in Vietnam in the 1960's. In the 1880's, the French did not understand or sympathize with Chinese interests in northern Vietnam. They failed to comprehend that not merely Chinese pride drove China into the controversy. More compelling from the standpoint of Peking was the conviction that Chinese territorial integrity depended upon the maintenance of a regime in northern Vietnam that was friendly to, if not necessarily subservient to, the Ch'ing dynasty. Nor did the French adequately analyze the political forces in Peking; as a consequence, they repeatedly miscalculated Chinese reactions to their demands and actions. Similarly, the French did not successfully communicate to the Chinese the extent and limitations of French aspirations in Vietnam, thereby creating fears and misunderstandings among those who formulated Ch'ing policy.

China has undergone enormous changes since the 1880's; the Ch'ing dynasty has vanished and the People's Republic of China now wields supreme authority in Peking. Can one, then, educe lessons from this study that are applicable to American policy in the twentieth century?

I am convinced that one can, for the Chinese Communists have inherited not only the geopolitical, or "objective," conditions in South China that did much to shape Chinese policy toward Vietnam during the imperial period. They were also bequeathed a view of the world, and particularly of China's proper place among the peoples of the world, that has merged neatly with the world outlook of Marxism and Leninism. This is not the place for a tract on the China policy of the United States. Nevertheless, I trust that this volume will add an historical dimension to the reader's understanding of the current problems in Vietnam and of Communist China's involvement there.

This study has benefited from the knowledge and efforts of many persons. I am indebted particularly to two. Professor John K. Fairbank's part in a research undertaking is not easily told, as each of his students knows. His encouragement has been crucial; he has read each of the several revisions of the manuscript, and has made valuable suggestions regarding matters of concept, fact, and organization. Margaret M. Y. Eastman has assisted unstintingly in the multiple roles of research assistant, secretary, and cheerful spouse. Other friends and scholars whose criticisms, suggestions, and intellectual stimulation have contributed directly to the work are Samuel Chu, Brians Evans, Hao Yen-p'ing, Hsiao Kung-ch'üan, Immanuel Hsü, Kuo T'ing-i, Lü Shih-ch'iang, David T. Roy, Nathan Sivin, and Wang Erh-min. The editors of *The Journal of Asian Studies* have kindly given permission to include here portions of my article, "Ch'ing-i and Chinese Policy Formation during the Nineteenth Century," that was published in volume XXIV, number 4, August 1965.

Lloyd E. Eastman

Cambridge, Massachusetts
July 14, 1966

CONTENTS

CONTENTS

CONTENTS

Illustration

THRONE AND MANDARINS

ABBREVIATIONS

CFCC: *Chung Fa chan-cheng*

CFCS: *Ch'ing Kuang-hsü ch'ao Chung Fa chiao-she shih-liao*

Ch'ing-shih-lu: Ta-Ch'ing li-ch'ao shih-lu

CSTL: Chung Fa Yüeh-nan chiao-she tzu-liao

HR: Cordier, Henri, *Histoire des Relations de la Chine*

ISHK: Li Hung-chang, "I-shu han-kao" (Correspondence with the Tsungli Yamen)

LJC: Li Tz'u-ming, *Yüeh-man-t'ang jih-chi*

PLHK: Li Hung-chang, "P'eng-liao han-kao" (Private correspondence)

TK: Li Hung-chang, "Tien-kao" (Telegrams)

WCSL: *Ch'ing-chi wai-chiao shih-liao*

WJC: Weng T'ung-ho, *Weng Wen-kung Kung jih-chi*

YNT: *Chung Fa Yüeh-nan chiao-she tang*

All translations, unless otherwise noted, are the author's own.

NOTE ON DATES

Chinese documents were dated according to the year of the emperor's reign and the lunar calendar. In the notes, these have been translated to the Gregorian calendrical notation. However, to assist scholars who may wish to consult an original source, the Chinese notation of all Chinese documents referred to is also given. As an example of a Chinese notation, the 26th day of the intercalary 5th month of the 10th year of the Kuang-hsü Emperor would read "KH10/*jun* 5/26." That is, the order is from year to month to day.

Dates of documents signify, wherever possible, the date of dispatch. However, documents addressed to the throne or to the Tsungli Yamen, that are in the *Ch'ing-chi wai-chiao shih-liao* and the *Chung Fa Yüeh-nan chiao-she tang*, bear the date of arrival.

I

INTRODUCTION:
POLICY AND POWER

The most striking fact encountered while doing research on the policy-making process during the Sino-French controversy was the enormous gap that separated the ideal from the reality of Chinese politics. In theory, harmony pervaded or ought to have pervaded relationships in government. In practice, there was conflict, or at least tension. The Chinese desired that the throne and the officials would strive together for the common good. In fact, the throne and the various officials each possessed unique and frequently divergent interests and needs.

Conflicts of interest between the throne and the officials as well as among the officials themselves would have been of no consequence for the formation of Chinese imperial policy if the policy process were a simple, straightforward progression, guided and dominated by the throne, through the stages of planning, decision, command, and implementation. However, the throne could not simply consult personal advisors, make a decision, and — *ecce!* — produce policy that could then be put into effect by members of the bureaucracy.

The factor that raises the equation of policy formation to a higher and more complex order is that of *power*.[1] Power is

[1] Throughout this study, the term "power" signifies a relational or functional concept. That is, power is not viewed as an unchanging property or substance, independent of interpersonal relations. Power is defined rather as the capacity of one party, A, who is in possession or con-

1

never absolute — Lord Acton per contra — and policy that is desired by an emperor, dictator, president, or whatever, is nearly always modified, in one or more stages of the policy process, before the phase of implementation is completed. Power is invariably diffused within a polity, and a successful ruler, regardless of how preponderant his power may be, must constantly be sensitive to the interests of other power-holders. For instance, a subordinate in receipt of a command will attempt to foresee the consequences that the implementing of that command would have upon his own interests and the interests of his constituents (his own subordinates, family, friends, etc.). Customarily, the subordinate will judge that it is to his advantage to act in accordance with the command, for the ruler might otherwise deprive him of desirable values (wealth, prestige, position, etc.). But the command might be outside the subordinate's "area of acceptance." [2] That is, the subordinate might judge that his values would be threatened by implementation of the command, and he might therefore urge modifications in the command, act upon it with indifference, or even reject it. Because the ruler places a certain value upon the services of the subordinate, the subordinate's reaction may result in changes in the command. A power relationship is always, therefore, dynamic *and reciprocal*, involving a push-and-pull between power-holders.

Stupid rulers, or rulers driven to extremes, have sometimes

---

trol of some thing or quality, Q, that another party, B, values to the extent that A may, through the manipulation of Q, modify the acts of B. An illuminating distinction between the "substantive" and the "relational" concepts of power is made in Masao Maruyama, *Thought and Behaviour in Modern Japanese Politics*, ed. Ivan Morris (London, 1963), pp. 269–275.

"Authority," in contradistinction to "power," is the formal and legitimate right — but not necessarily the effective capacity — to modify the action of others.

[2] Herbert A. Simon, *Administrative Behavior: A Study of Decision-making Processes in Administrative Organization* (New York, 1949), pp. 133–134, discusses the concept of the area of acceptance.

attempted to realize their goals in utter disregard of the interests of other power-holders. Chinese history does not want for
examples of this phenomenon, but the use of such coercion is
never effective in the long run, and should never be employed
except as a *pis aller*. This fact of political life has been expressed by Charles E. Merriam in these words: "Power is not
strongest when it uses violence, but weakest. It is strongest
when it employs the instruments of substitution and counter
attraction, of allurement, of participation rather than of ex-
clusion, of education rather than annihilation. Rape is not an
evidence of irresistible power in politics or in sex." [3]

Because policy formulation involves the relationship of
forces whose influences do not always, indeed seldom do, correspond to the stratifications of formal authority, this study is
concerned but peripherally with the institutional framework of
the Chinese government.[4] To a much greater degree, this is a
study of power and of those holding power. It attempts, in
other words, to depict policy formation in the Chinese state,
not at the level of governmental ideals as discerned in the
Confucian classics and institutional structures, but at the more
commonplace level of political practice.

In the sections that follow, I shall introduce three power-
holders that exercised critical influence upon Chinese imperial

[3] Charles Edward Merriam, *Political Power: Its Composition and Inci-
dence* (New York and London, 1934), p. 180. Merriam's entire chapter
on "The Poverty of Power" (pp. 156–183) is suggestive on this point.
See also Simon, pp. 123–153; and Max Weber, "The Presuppositions and
Causes of Bureaucracy," *Reader in Bureaucracy*, ed. Robert King Merton,
et al. (Glencoe, Ill., 1960), p. 63. Richard E. Neustadt has applied this
concept brilliantly to American politics in his study, *Presidential Power:
The Politics of Leadership* (New York, 1964).

[4] Readers interested in the institutional aspect of Chinese policy formation should consult John K. Fairbank and Ssu-yü Teng, *Ch'ing Administration: Three Studies* (Cambridge, Mass., 1960), pp. 1–106; and
Pao Chao Hsieh, *The Government of China, 1644–1911* (Baltimore,
1925), chapter 4.

policy during the Sino-French controversy. These three were by no means the only political forces to impinge upon the policy process, but they do exemplify three principal types of political forces in the Chinese government. The first of these, the throne, is unique, and represents only itself. The second is Li Hung-chang, who represents high officials who derived their power largely from their administrative functions. And, finally, *ch'ing-i* (a term that will be defined below) typifies a political force within the Chinese governmental structure that is very roughly analogous to public opinion in the modern West.

The Throne. The term "throne," as used here, bears the dual connotation of (1) the ruler *qua* institution and (2) the ruler *qua* person. As an institution, the Chinese throne possessed authority that preponderated over any other single office or official in the empire. The institutional throne was, formally, autocratic and absolutist. An organizational chart of the imperial government would show all lines of command converging on the throne; moreover, there were legally no areas of Chinese life beyond its jurisdiction. A Chinese emperor might, with at least as much justification as Louis XIV of France, have declared: "L'état, c'est moi!"

The throne's authority had initially been founded, and to a degree perpetuated, with force. Since the early years of the Han dynasty (206 B.C.-A.D. 8), however, its authority had gradually been cloaked in a veil of legitimacy — that is, its rule had been made to appear right and proper — by acquiring the ideological support of Confucianism. Confucians proclaimed that the emperor was not merely a man of predominating might or talent; the emperor was, before everything else, the outstanding exemplar of virtue, by reason of which heaven had bestowed upon him a divine mandate to rule and care for all peoples.

4

This legitimizing myth of imperial virtue had little or no basis in fact — Chinese rulers have been no more, and probably less, virtuous than most of their subjects. This stark fact of reality was obscured, however, by elaborate ceremonies that removed the ruler-as-man from the eyes of fellow mortals. Few were permitted to view the imperial person except from a distance; those who did gain access to the throne dropped to their knees in the imperial presence. Even the highest ministers of state abjectly demeaned themselves before the throne: the emperor was the "son of heaven" (*t'ien-tzu*), while they were "servants" (*ch'en*) or "slaves" (*nu-ts'ai*).[1] In these several ways, through a philosophy of government and mystifying ritual, the authority of the institutional emperor was strengthened and safeguarded. And, since "authority in some degree confers effective power,"[2] the capacity of the personal emperor to participate in policy decisions was correspondingly enhanced.

Still, the institutional sources of the throne's political power can be, and I would suggest have been, overemphasized. There has recently been considerable discussion in sinological circles regarding an historical tendency toward increasing imperial despotism since the Sung and Ming dynasties.[3] Explanations of this phenomenon frequently revolve around, first, the changing

[1] On the importance of ceremony as a means of buttressing a ruler's power, see Robert Morrison MacIver, *The Web of Government* (New York, 1947), p. 46.

Joseph R. Levenson has suggested that the obscuring of the emperor from fellow mortals was not an *imperial* strategy designed to mask imperfect virtue, but a strategy of Confucian officials designed to limit the throne's pretensions to unlimited, godlike power. See Levenson, *Confucian China and Its Modern Fate* (Berkeley and Los Angeles, 1958–65), II, 90–99. The argument is not convincing.

[2] Samuel H. Beer, et al., *Patterns of Government: The Major Political Systems of Europe* (New York, 1962), p. 48.

[3] Examples are David S. Nivison, "Introduction," pp. 13–24, and Charles O. Hucker, "Confucianism and the Chinese Censorial System," pp. 182–208, both in David S. Nivison and Arthur F. Wright, eds., *Confucianism in Action* (Stanford, 1959).

socio-economic bases of political power in traditional China. Prior to the Sung dynasty (960–1279), it is explained, the power and pretensions of the throne were restrained by fabulously powerful and rich aristocratic families. This hereditary aristocracy possessed vast estates, often worked and defended by large numbers of tenants and armed retainers. During the Sung dynasty, these estates were gradually broken up and replaced by a more diffuse system of land tenure. Success in the examination system now became more important as an avenue to political influence than family background and influence. As a consequence, most officials possessed only modest economic bases of power. Officials became more dependent upon the throne, deriving wealth, power, and prestige primarily through the offices and good favor of the imperial ruler. Moreover, the number of potential officials had been enlarged by the new system; competition for office became sharp; and aspirants to official position were consequently reluctant to spoil their careers by displaying qualities of independence that might antagonize the ruler.

A second explanation of growing despotism in Chinese government is that Mongol rule during the Yüan dynasty (1271–1368) left an ineradicable stain upon the cultural and political life of China. Prior to the conquest by the Mongols, it is suggested, the emperors might still be touched by the officials' remonstrances and criticisms. However, the barbarian conquerors would brook no challenge, and reinforced their rule with methods that made terror a way of life. The Yüan dynasty was replaced, but its concepts and practices of government become a permanent part of the Chinese political system.

A third reputed cause of rising tyranny in China was the usurpation by the throne of the right to pronounce upon ideological interpretations of Confucianism. Particularly during the Ming dynasty, an ideological straitjacket was imposed upon the literati. The Chu Hsi interpretation of the classics became the sole standard by which official examinations were judged. Even the texts of Mencius were edited to remove passages that might conceivably give a literatus an intellectual basis from which to challenge the supreme authority of the throne.[4] In other words, interpretations of Confucianism were no longer the preserve of the Confucians, and in the process the Chinese emperor had become a law unto himself.

There is much to commend this theory. Much of the evidence is firmly grounded in fact; it also seems to bring order to an otherwise untidy mass of discrete historical episodes. Unfortunately, the effort to view Chinese intellectual and political history in terms of an inexorable growth of autocracy sometimes results in gross distortion. For example — and here I quote a scholar for whom I have immense respect — David S. Nivison has remarked that "the imperial triumph was consummated in the Ch'ing. The literati were taught (and apparently most of them believed) that running the state was the court's business, not theirs; that criticism of the monarch was inconceivable, so inconceivable that even feeling critical must be regarded as a moral failure on the part of the critic to 'identify his likes and dislikes with those of his prince.'"[5] This

[4] Hucker, "Confucianism," p. 199.

[5] Nivison, "Introduction," p. 16. Nivison elsewhere makes an important qualification to this statement when he correctly points out that officials' criticisms of the throne increased, during the latter half of the Ch'ing period, as the power of the throne faltered. See Nivison, "Ho-shen and His Accusers," in *Confucianism in Action*, p. 243. However, Nivison's qualification merely underlines the fact that, if officials did not criticize, it was a result of physical fear or political circumspection — not of a feeling that it was *immoral* to criticize. Frederick W. Mote, who argues that China experienced a period of "unlimited despotism," nevertheless supports my contention here that criticism of the throne never was considered morally reprehensible. Indeed, Mote states: "the servitors of an erring ruler *are required* to censure and guide him in a humble and respectful manner." (Frederick W. Mote, "Confucian Eremitism in the Yüan Period," in *The Confucian Persuasion*, ed. Arthur F. Wright [Stan-

statement is misleading, as the following chapters will, I trust, make evident.

Studies that depict the Chinese government as becoming increasingly despotic since the Sung dynasty distort historical reality, because they place insufficient stress upon a factor — human personality — that does not fit easily into a neat generalization. It is extremely significant, therefore, that Han Wu-ti (r. 140–87 B.C.) and Wu Tzu-t'ien (r. A.D. 684–705), whose malefactions certainly bear comparison with those of the worst Ming and Ch'ing rulers, appear not at the culmination of a trend toward growing despotism, but before the putative trend had even begun. The assertions that imperial rule in China was becoming progressively despotic may ultimately prove to be valid — though it ought to be recognized that, as of the present time, the problem requires further study. What is now perfectly clear, however, is that studies of the throne *qua* person (i.e., of the individual or individuals wielding imperial power) are even more important for an understanding of the political role of the throne at any point in time than are studies of institutional trends. It is probable that the officials never became spineless servitors of the emperors; it is certain that the officials never abandoned their standards of moral judgment to all-powerful occupants of the throne.

Throughout the greater part of the period covered by this study, the authority to rule was possessed by, and hence the "throne" was, Hsiao-ch'in, the Empress Dowager Tz'u-hsi. The reigning emperor, Kuang-hsü, was but a youth (twelve years old in 1883), and the powers of government had therefore been bestowed upon Tz'u-hsi, who was the boy's aunt (a coregent, Tz'u-an, died in 1881). Little need be remarked about the career of this woman, who was one of the most remarkable

---

ford, 1960], p. 230. Italics added.) See also Mote's perceptive article, "The Growth of Chinese Despotism: A Critique of Wittfogel's Theory of Oriental Despotism as Applied to China," in *Oriens Extremus*, 8.1:1–41 (Aug. 1961).

individuals to emerge from the annals of all Chinese history. Much has been written about her elsewhere,[6] and it will suffice for the purposes here merely to venture a guess regarding the goals toward which she used the authority and power vested in her. In many respects, Tz'u-hsi's goals were exceedingly commonplace: she was eminently human in her love of money, valuation of friendship (e.g., of the eunuch Li Lien-ying), and in her desire to preserve the heritage left her by her ancestors. Nevertheless, on the basis of her long public career, one conclusion is inescapable: these non-political goals were usually subordinate in her value system to political, or power-associated, goals. Consider, for example, her courageous but unscrupulous seizure of political authority in the Tsai-yüan Conspiracy (1861); or the alleged corruption of her own son, the T'ung-chih Emperor, in order to weaken his political aspirations. Indeed, her entire career gives unrelieved evidence of her determination to consolidate and extend her own power. While this determination characterized most emperors, it appeared in an almost unique degree in Tz'u-hsi. This is a fact of the utmost significance in comprehending this rare woman and in judging her actions during the Sino-French controversy.

The Officials. Despite the throne's monopoly of governmental authority, the officials were not devoid of power in their relations with the throne, for they were the administrators of the empire, and the self-proclaimed guardians and judges of Confucian morality. In consequence, they were able to influence the primary sources of imperial power: the administrative effectiveness and ideological legitimation of the throne. In other

[6] Unfortunately, there is no work about Tz'u-hsi in any language that can be recommended without reservation. In English, the best among a poor lot are probably J. O. P. Bland and E. Backhouse, *China under the Empress Dowager: Being the Life and Times of Tz'u Hsi* (Philadelphia, 1910); Harry Hussey, *Venerable Ancestor, The Life and Times of Tz'u Hsi* (Garden City, New York, 1949); and Princess Der Ling, *Old Buddha* (New York, 1928).

words, although the officials had initially derived their social and political positions from the throne, the throne in turn had become dependent upon the officials for the maintenance of its power.

Not all officials derived power, nor exercised that power in the policy process, in the same fashion. High-ranking officials, with large administrative responsibilities, seldom relied upon ideological sanctions in their attempts to influence decision-making. Low- and middle-ranking officials, on the other hand, whose minor administrative roles provided them with little if any power, made themselves an ineluctable factor in the throne's power calculus by acting as the conscience of the Confucian state.

Power Derived from an Administrative Role: Li Hung-chang. Even the most diligent of Chinese rulers was isolated from the routine administration of his government. The sheer quantity of business that was transacted in the vast empire insured that a ruler could attain close familiarity with only the most exceptional matters of administration. Furthermore, a ruler was immured in the court, physically remote from the governing process at the level of implementation. He was dependent, therefore, upon advisors and informants, each with particular interests and prejudices, who might or might not portray accurately affairs of administration outside the court.

High officials, on the contrary, were immersed in the details of administration; they also controlled sizable subgroups of the bureaucracy. They thereby amassed stores of invaluable information, acquired the loyal support of other officials dependent upon them, or gained control of military forces. As a consequence, the officials acquired leverage that could be exercised in the policy-making process. Illustration is provided by the case of Li Hung-chang. Actually, Li was atypical of the high administrative officials; his position was too high, his power too great, and his indifference to arguments based on Confucian morality too stark. Yet so significant was his role during the Sino-French controversy, and so instructive his example of an official whose political power was derived largely from his administrative value to the throne, that it is convenient to discuss Li in some detail here.

Li Hung-chang's rise to prominence began during the Taiping Rebellion, and, partially through the patronage of Tseng Kuo-fan, he had by 1865 risen to the office of governor-general. When in 1870 he was named to the governor-generalship of the capital province of Chihli, he had, at the age of forty-seven, risen to the pinnacle of provincial officialdom, and obtained the base that henceforth made him the most redoubtable provincial official in China.[1]

Li's political preeminence was a consequence primarily of his command of a military force and his participation in the conduct of diplomatic relations. He had formed in North China one of the most formidable armies in the empire. This force was of unique importance among the military units of China, for it was charged to defend the approaches to the capital city of Peking, an area that was generally considered to be more vital even than whole provinces in the south. It was a prime policy concern, therefore, that the defenses in the north always be prepared to resist an enemy march on Peking.[2] The Empress

[1] Arthur W. Hummel, ed., *Eminent Chinese of the Ch'ing Period, 1644–1912* (Washington, 1943), I, 464–466; Stanley Spector, *Li Hung-chang and the Huai Army: A Study in Nineteenth-Century Chinese Regionalism* (Seattle, 1964), *passim*.

[2] Pao-t'ing, for example, wrote: "We cannot lose Korea . . . though it be a foreign country, even if we lose Yunnan and Kweichow." "If it is lost, the entrance to the Gulf of Chihli will be utterly lost also." (CFCS, 3:6b, dcmt. 59, Pao-t'ing memorial, June 28, 1882 [KH8/5/13].) Pao-t'ing considered the Gulf of Chihli to be the approach to Peking — and not to Manchuria, as might be expected of a Manchu like Pao-t'ing — as the context of his statement makes clear.

This sentiment was not confined to the Manchus. A Chinese wrote, typically, that: "The Gulf of Chihli is the door to the capital and is rela-

Dowager Tz'u-hsi shared this concern for the capital,[3] and she consequently relied heavily upon Li Hung-chang. Li was thus provided with a solid basis for political power.

In foreign affairs, Li acquired power largely because other officials eschewed such matters, conceiving correctly that intercourse with the foreigners was a thankless and maligned occupation. In 1861, the Tsungli Yamen had been established as an office of foreign affairs, and it was through this office that the foreign ministers resident in Peking expected to make their representations to the Chinese government. The treatment accorded these ministers by the subordinate members of the Yamen — the relatively enlightened president of the Yamen, Prince Kung, was frequently absent — was seldom conducive to sympathetic and cordial relations. Whether it was their intention or not, they frequently caused the foreign representatives to despair of obtaining results at the Yamen, sensing temporization and even insults at every turn.[4]

---

tively more important than Yunnan or Kwangtung-Kwangsi." (CFCS, 15:3b, dcmt. 512, Teng Ch'eng-hsiu memorial, May 8, 1884 [KH10/4/14].)

[3] CFCS, 11:25b, dcmt. 351, decree to Li Hung-chang, Mar. 3, 1884 (KH10/2/6). Foreign writers have often averred that Tz'u-hsi's particular concern for the north stemmed from her fear that she would again be forced to flee from Peking as she had when the French and British attacked the capital in 1860. For example, Archibald R. Colquhoun wrote: "she resolved rather to yield everything than risk such an experience again." (*China in Transformation* [London and New York, 1912 rev. ed.], p. 75.) This sentiment may indeed have influenced the empress dowager. However, I have found no evidence to justify stressing it.

[4] Stanley Lane-Poole and F. V. Dickens, *The Life of Sir Harry Parkes* (London, 1894), II, 385–394; and E. V. G. Kiernan, *British Diplomacy in China, 1880 to 1885* (Cambridge, Eng., 1939), pp. 23–37 give entertaining, if perhaps supercilious, descriptions of the Yamen's methods of conducting business. That the ill-treatment accorded the foreigners may not have been wholly illusory is suggested in a communication from Prince Ch'un to the Grand Council: "When we meet with him [a foreigner], we can only arouse him with ridicule; we need not assume a serious demeanor in order to persuade him." I-huan (Prince Ch'un), "Ch'un Ch'in-wang I-huan chih Chün-chi-ch'u ch'ih-tu" (Letters from I-huan, the Prince Ch'un, to the Grand Council), CFCC, V, 43, dcmt. 9, 1884 (KH10/?/23).

Distraught by the tactics of the Yamen, the foreigners turned, with a sense of relief, to Li Hung-chang, who neither despised nor shunned foreign affairs. To the contrary, he made positive efforts to gather in his hands all foreign matters that would affect the area under his jurisdiction in North China.[5] The members of the Yamen, for their part, readily surrendered to Li problems regarding foreign matters that might prove embarrassing to them if settled in a manner acceptable to the foreigner.

Assessments of the relative influence of Li Hung-chang and the Tsungli Yamen in matters relating to foreign relations have varied widely. A British diplomat asserted in 1883 that "the Tsungli Yamen . . . is little more than a branch office of the Grand Secretary Li's Yamen at Tientsin."[6] On the other hand, Ssu-ming Meng has declared that "the Tsungli Yamen was [prior to April 1884] in reality, if not always in name, responsible for all policies and handling all matters concerning foreign affairs, and was sufficiently powerful to dictate its decisions to the provincial authorities."[7] My own view is that, at least during the period 1880–1885, Li Hung-chang was less influential in the policy-formation process than was the Yamen. Nevertheless, it cannot be denied that he had, as a result of his experience and interest, acquired a position where he was heavily relied upon by the central government in its conduct of foreign affairs. Li was, therefore, an important factor in the power equation that produced foreign policy.

Li Hung-chang merits particular attention here because he was the leading advocate during the controversy with France

[5] Ssu-ming Meng, *The Tsungli Yamen: Its Organization and Functions* (Cambridge, Mass., 1962), pp. 58–59.

[6] Kiernan, p. 31, citing communication from Grosvenor to Foreign Office, Mar. 17, 1883.

[7] Ssu-ming Meng, p. 53. This statement emphasizes the relative weakness of Li Hung-chang, but is not consonant with Meng's general thesis that the Yamen at no time dominated foreign affairs during its forty-year history. Cf. Meng, pp. 44–45.

of a policy of appeasement. Li insisted that he favored such a policy not because he feared war, as such, nor that he was unconcerned for the fate of Vietnam. "But I dare not be emotional," he averred, "and stake the existence of the entire empire on just one cast." [8] Most officials supported a militant policy against the French, and Li avowedly differed merely on the question of priorities. Trouble on the frontiers, he once remarked, is like an illness of the limbs, but the domestic enfeeblement of China is like a disease of the heart.[9] Li therefore proposed that China must accept an expedient peace whenever foreigners encroached upon the states on the periphery of the empire. The respite from war thus obtained could be used to "self-strengthen" China by training armies, building ships, and expanding trade. "How then can we not compete with all nations?" he inquired rhetorically.[10]

Li adduced an infinite variety of arguments against a war policy, and he was, in fact, prepared to pay almost any price to avoid war with France. One might, of course, accept at face value his argument that a war to preserve that "useless corner of land," as he referred to Tongking,[11] before China's self-strengthening movement had reached fruition, would have been inane and premature.

Another reason why Li opposed China's involvement in Vietnam may have been a consequence of events in Korea. Foreign powers, particularly Japan, attempted during the 1870's to "open" the Hermit Kingdom to trade and influence. In 1881, conduct of Korea's affairs was removed from the slow-moving,

[8] CFCS, 4:23b, dcmt. 120, Li memorial, June 16, 1883 (KH9/5/12). See also CFCS, 13:22b–23, dcmt. 438, Li to Tsungli Yamen, Apr. 20, 1884 (KH10/3/25).
[9] Yao Hsin-an, "Hai-fang yü sai-fang te cheng-lun" (The controversy over naval and internal frontier defenses), in Li Ting-i, et al., eds., *Chung-kuo chin-tai-shih lun-ts'ung* (Collection of essays on modern Chinese history; Taipei, 1956), 1st ser., V, 208.
[10] YNT, III, 1679, dcmt. 792, Li memorial, May 1, 1884 (KH10/4/7).
[11] CFCS, 6:20, dcmt. 194, Li memorial, Sept. 28, 1883 (KH9/8/28).

tradition-encumbered Board of Rites, and placed in Li's more vigorous hands. During 1881 and 1882, he supervised the conclusion of that country's first treaties with governments of the West. In 1882, also, a bloody riot occurred in Seoul. Li seized this as an opportunity to increase Chinese influence in the peninsula, and to exclude that of the Japanese. These activities demanded a full measure of Li's skill and energy. Moreover, as official guardian of North China, he feared above all else that Korea would fall to a foreign power. There were, therefore, cogent reasons why Li Hung-chang viewed events in Vietnam with less interest and less apprehension than he did events in Korea.

On the other hand, one suspects that Li was personally interested in avoiding wars on the distant frontiers of the empire. He had, for instance, in 1876 opposed Tso Tsung-t'ang's military expedition in Sinkiang because he was jealous of the funds thus diverted from his own enterprises in North China.[12] During the Sino-French hostilities too, despite all reasons and threats, he resisted efforts to transfer military forces from his command — even when, without reinforcements, the forces in Tongking, Taiwan and at Foochow were threatened with annihilation. Stanley Spector has commented that "Li well understood that his power in the north rested primarily upon his military strength. . . . He therefore had no idea of relinquishing control of his personal army."[13] I am convinced that one reason Li opposed war with France was that this would adversely affect his military base in the north, and would in consequence undermine his political power. And to maintain that power was, I believe, one of his prime ambitions. His

---

[12] Yao Hsin-an, p. 207.

[13] Spector, p. 142. Some of Li's fellow officials also noted his use of the Huai Army for his personal advantage. CFCS, 8:43b–44, dcmt. 278, addendum #1, Ch'in Chung-chien memorial, Dec. 21, 1883 (KH9/11/22).

value orientation, then, was similar to that of the Empress Dowager Tz'u-hsi.[14]

However, to attribute traitorous,[15] or even totally selfish, motives to Li does injustice to the complexity of human emotions. It seems, and this must be admitted to be sheer conjecture, that Li, who possessed a sizable streak of vainglory, believed the Chinese policy of self-strengthening depended largely upon his personal efforts in the north. A war would have deferred completion of his enterprises. And Japan might have been encouraged by Chinese preoccupations in Vietnam to make a thrust at Korea — with dreadful consequences to the defense of Peking and North China. In other words, what was good for Li Hung-chang was good for the empire — and he did not conceive that a war with France was good for Li Hung-chang.

Power Derived from an Ideological Role: Ch'ing-i. In traditional China, Confucian morality occupied a supreme place in government and society, for it served as the ultimate criterion of men's actions. He who could claim to speak as the interpreter and judge of Confucian morality might, therefore, become a potent force in human affairs. One of the curiosities of the Chinese state is that, despite the preeminent role of Confucianism in government, judgments upon Confucian morality never became a monopoly of any single office or group among the scholar-officials, as did law in the juridical courts of the West. This source of political power was consequently

[14] Ku Hung-ming, a contemporary of Li, noted that Li "devoted his attention exclusively to matters of immediate, practical advantage." In contrast, Ku observed that Chang Chih-tung revered China's moral heritage. See Kung-chuan Hsiao, "Weng T'ung-ho and the Reform Movement of 1898," *Tsing Hua Journal of Chinese Studies*, new ser., 1.2:153 (Apr. 1957).

[15] As do Fan Wen-lan, *Chung-kuo chin-tai-shih* (Modern Chinese history; Peking, 1961), p. 224; and Hu Sheng, *Imperialism and Chinese Politics* (Peking, 1955), p. 100.

diffused among Confucians of both high and low estate. Those who used this political power most effectively to influence policy during the Sino-French controversy formed an aggregation that has hitherto received little attention from students of Chinese government: *ch'ing-i.*

Literally, *ch'ing-i* might be rendered as "pure discussion," though a looser translation, such as "literati opinion," is doubtless more meaningful to a Western ear. Strong objections may be raised to such translations, however, and no attempt will be made in this study to use other than the transliteration of the Chinese term.[1]

There are two aspects of *ch'ing-i* during the nineteenth century that deserve to be differentiated. In its first aspect, *ch'ing-i* denoted the expressions of opinion by low- and middle-ranking officials[2] (or by literati without official rank) who intended thereby to preserve or improve the moral integrity of the Confucian state and society. Frequently, indeed usually, these expressions were formulated as criticisms of established

[1] "Pure discussion" is an unsatisfactory translation, because an explanation as elaborate as that for the Chinese term is required. "Literati opinion" and "public opinion," which have also been suggested as terms to signify *ch'ing-i,* are misleading, for *ch'ing-i* suggests righteousness, a connotation that the English terms lack. (This is true also of the Chinese term *kung-lun,* which was frequently interchangeable with *ch'ing-i.*) Furthermore, *ch'ing-i* was used exclusively by a Confucian-educated elite, and was dissimilar from opinions expressed by the "public." Note that Immanuel C. Y. Hsü has translated *ch'ing-i* as "public opinion," but he did so "for the sake of simplicity." (*China's Entrance into the Family of Nations: The Diplomatic Phase, 1858–1880* [Cambridge, Mass., 1960], p. 200.) A perusal of Akira Iriye, "Public Opinion in Late Ch'ing China" (mimeographed, Harvard, 1965, 37 pp.) will clarify the contrast between *ch'ing-i* and public opinion.

[2] Low- and middle-ranking officials are defined here as those below the third rank. Thus, grand councilors, grand secretaries, presidents and vice-presidents of the six boards, governors-general and governors of provinces, and similar officials who held offices at the policy-forming level, could not, strictly speaking, be *ch'ing-i.* Some of the distinctions between these three strata within officialdom are described in Ping-ti Ho, *The Ladder of Success in Imperial China: Aspects of Social Mobility, 1368–1911* (New York and London, 1962), pp. 24–26.

17

or proposed governmental policies, or as attacks on public persons whose conduct was construed to be unfilial, corrupt, or otherwise non-Confucian. Whatever form *ch'ing-i* statements were given, they were always — theoretically — prompted by lofty Confucian ideals and unblemished by considerations of private or partisan advantage.

In its second aspect, *ch'ing-i* appeared as a political tool with which low- or middle-ranking officials who were frequently more interested than they professed to be sought to advance their careers, to give vent to personal animosities, or otherwise to advance narrow and selfish interests. That *ch'ing-i* could serve such ends effectively in traditional China can hardly be doubted. Officials who attracted attention by their rigorous Confucianism were often promoted to higher posts. And charges that a political opponent had disregarded Confucian ritual, disrespected the emperor, or was a sycophant of the foreigners frequently sufficed to remove the object of attack from imperial favor.

The term *ch'ing-i* did not always refer merely to such statements, or the practice of making such statements. In conventional usage during the nineteenth century, the term was also used as a collective designation for the persons who expressed *ch'ing-i* types of opinion. That is, the term *ch'ing-i* might refer to the *expressor,* as well as to the *expression,* of such opinions. A caveat must be raised here, however, against presuming that the expressors of *ch'ing-i* — as a group — formed anything like a political party. True, they shared exaggerated pretensions to Confucian rectitude; the tone or spirit of their opinions was alike. But *ch'ing-i* formulated no common policies or programs, and their proposals and criticisms frequently diverged widely in details. There was no organization uniting them, and a score of divisive factors, such as regional affiliations or academic ties, precluded unanimity and cooperation among them. Neverthe-

18

less, *ch'ing-i* was a meaningful concept, for it constituted a powerful "current of thought," [3] however disparate the motives behind it, that served to maintain the primacy of Confucian values and of traditional practices.

Ch'ing-i sentiments might be broadcast by whatever means were available to the literati. Ordinary conversation, letters, poetry, and even ballads and decorative scrolls served as media of *ch'ing-i*.[4] Usually, however, *ch'ing-i* officials hoped to accomplish their ends in the most direct way possible: by submitting memorials to the throne. All upper-ranking and some middle-ranking officials were permitted to express their opinions on matters outside their official jurisdiction in memorials directly to the court.[5] Lesser officials wishing to advance similar opinions, but without the same privilege, could and did request higher officials to forward their opinions to the throne.

Contemporaries generally assumed that officials submitting the memorials of subordinates were in sympathy with the opinions expressed therein. Nevertheless, officials who did not agree to transmit memorials for lesser officials were exposing themselves to criticism. In 1884, a censor, Wu Hsün, charged that a chancellor of the Hanlin Academy, Ling-kuei, had repeatedly placed obstacles in the way of his subordinates in the Academy who wished him to transmit memorials for them. Ling-kuei either refused to receive these subordinates at his residence, or quibbled about the phraseology in the docu-

[3] The phrase is borrowed from Benjamin Schwartz, *In Search of Wealth and Power: Yen Fu and the West* (Cambridge, Mass., 1964), p. 15.

[4] Immanuel Hsü, p. 200.

[5] Generally, officials of the fourth rank or higher enjoyed this privilege. There were exceptions. Censors and diarists of the emperor's movements, among others, might also submit memorials directly to the court. See *Ch'in-ting Ta-Ch'ing hui-tien* (Collected statutes of the Ch'ing dynasty, Kuang-hsü reign; Taipei, 1963), 82:10b–11.

ments.[6] Ultimately Ling-kuei forwarded the memorials, but only after the subordinates had to resort to "embarrassing geniality." Wu Hsün recommended that Ling-kuei, for obstructing the flow of subordinates' opinions to the throne, be dismissed from office.[7]

Officially, a high-ranking mandarin like Ling-kuei was to "deliberate and decide" (*cho-ting*) before transmitting a subordinate's memorial — in other words, the subordinates' privilege of submitting memorials was not automatic, but was subject to the judgment of the superior.[8] In practice, however, high-ranking officials were exposed to pressures that induced them to transmit the memorials of their subordinates.

The privilege of submitting opinions to the throne by officials who were not responsible for the matter under discussion, whether they were of high or low rank, was called the *yen-lu* (literally, "pathway for words"). Occasionally, the *yen-lu* was "closed," which meant that the throne did not welcome

[6] The particular phrase to which Ling-kuei objected was: "the matter of the nation's survival is at a critical juncture." Ling-kuei asserted that "the emperor and empress dowager do not wish to hear this kind of talk." CFCS, 15:15b–16, dcmt. 528, May 10, 1884 (KH10/4/16).

[7] *Ibid.* Ling-kuei subsequently explained that he had not intended to obstruct the flow of opinions to the throne. He had judged, however, that the memorials contained "improper" and "violent" language, and he had refused to forward the documents until these phrases had been corrected. The throne expressed itself satisfied with Ling-kuei's explanation, and no punitive action was taken against him. *Shih-erh ch'ao tung-hua-lu* (Tung-hua documents of twelve reigns; Taipei, 1963), Kuang-hsü reign, III, 1675, May 5, 1884 (KH10/4/17).

[8] *Shih-erh ch'ao tung-hua-lu*, Hsien-feng reign, I, 177b, Mar. 20, 1853 (Hsien-feng 3/2/11). Evidence that this regulation, stipulating that the superior official must examine the subordinate's memorial for irregularities and untoward statements, was adhered to in practice is found in T'ang Chen, "Wei-yen" (Words of warning), in Chien Po-tsan, et al., eds., *Wu-hsü pien-fa* (The 1898 reform movement; Shanghai, 1957), I, 177.

Memorials of subordinate officials were submitted to the throne in the form of *fu-che* (supplementary memorials) to the higher officials' memorials. For an example, see CFCS, 15:23b–26, dcmt. 542, Ling-kuei transmitting the memorial of Chu I-hsin, et al., May 13, 1884 (KH10/4/19).

unsolicited advice. This had happened a number of times in the past,[9] though the *yen-lu* remained open during the greater part of the late nineteenth century. It was, however, as will be seen in Chapter VII, to be closed again in early 1885.[10]

To discover the origins of *ch'ing-i*, one must go back at least to the early period of the Latter Han dynasty (A.D. 25–220). At that time, men were theoretically selected for government on the basis of moral excellence, as defined by the Confucians. To determine moral fitness, the government actively encouraged discussion and criticism of the behavior and morality of the prospective office-holders. This "concrete criticism of persons" was called *ch'ing-i*.[11]

Toward the end of the Latter Han dynasty, *ch'ing-i* continued to be a prominent factor on the political scene. However, the discussion and criticism of persons was no longer encouraged as part of the official process of personnel selection; instead, *ch'ing-i* had become the weapon of a political opposition movement. The Latter Han dynasty, in its declining years, was characterized by extreme corruption and factionalism in government, and by outrageously profligate living by the rich. Government had become an exclusive instrument of

[9] For instance, during the Latter Han dynasty (Fan Yeh, *Hou Han shu* [History of the Latter Han dynasty; Shanghai, 1894], 104a:19b–20) and during the Cheng-te (1506–21) and Chia-ching (1522–66) reigns of the Ming dynasty (Chao I, *Nien-erh-shih cha-chi* [Studies from the twenty-two dynastic histories; Taipei, 1958], II, 507).

[10] See below, pp. 190–193.

[11] T'ang Chang-ju, *Wei Chin Nan-pei ch'ao shih lun-ts'ung* (Collected essays on the history of the Chin, Wei, and Northern and Southern dynasties; Peking, 1955), pp. 86 and 290. See also Yü Ying-shih, "Han Chin chih chi shih chih hsin tzu-chüeh yü hsin ssu-ch'ao" ("Self-awareness of the Literati and the New Intellectual Trend in China in the Second and Third Centuries"), *Hsin-ya hsüeh-pao* (New Asia journal), 4.1:58–60 (Aug. 1, 1959); and Ochi Shigeaki, "Shingi to kyōron" (*Ch'ing-i* and village opinion), *Tōyō gakuhō* (Journal of oriental studies), 48:1–48 (June 1965). A history of *ch'ing-i* from the Han through the Ming dynasty, replete with illustrative if sensationalist anecdotes, is in Lin Yu-tang, *A History of the Press and Public Opinion in China* (Chicago, 1936), pp. 28–73.

eunuchs and empresses' relatives. Confucian literati, by the thousands, found themselves deprived of power and privilege; many were sunk in abject poverty. Reacting against their condition and against those who wrought it, they "incessantly criticized . . . the wrongs of the government and deplored the misdeeds of their adversaries, raising their premonitory voices in innumerable remonstrances, memorials and petitions." [12] Just as in later years, these forms of protest were supplemented by placards and epigrams which, spread throughout the empire, further blackened the name of their political opponents.[13] This was *ch'ing-i* in its initial appearance as the instrument of a literati opposition movement and of self-appointed guardians of Confucian values.

Ch'ing-i reappeared frequently during subsequent centuries. During the Southern Sung dynasty, for example, *ch'ing-i* vehemently attacked the immoral, non-Confucian behavior of officials who sought to appease the aggressors from the north.[14] And the famous Tung-lin movement during the late Ming dynasty is a classic example of *ch'ing-i* opposition to immorality in government.[15]

While *ch'ing-i* appeared most prominently as a political

[12] Étienne Balázs, "La Crise Sociale et la Philosophie à la fin des Han," *T'oung Pao*, 34:87–88 (1949). This article has been translated into English in Etienne Balazs, *Chinese Civilization and Bureaucracy*, ed. Arthur F. Wright, tr. H. M. Wright (New Haven and London, 1964), pp. 187–225.

[13] Balázs, "La Crise Sociale," pp. 87–88.

[14] Huang Hsien-fan, *Sung-tai t'ai-hsüeh-sheng chiu-kuo yün-tung* (National salvation movement of students of the imperial academy during the Sung dynasty; Shanghai, 1936), pp. 73–78. See also Hao Yen-p'ing, "T'ung-Kuang hsin-cheng-chung te so-wei 'ch'ing-i' " (The so-called 'ch'ing-i' during the reforms of the T'ung-chih and Kuang-hsü reigns; Bachelor's thesis, Taiwan National University, 1958), p. 5; Immanuel Hsü, pp. 200–201.

[15] Charles O. Hucker, "The Tung-lin Movement of the Late Ming Period," in John K. Fairbank, ed., *Chinese Thought and Institutions* (Chicago, 1957), pp. 132–162; Heinrich Busch, "The Tung-lin Academy and Its Political and Philosophical Significance," *Monumenta Serica*, 14: 14 and *passim* (1949–55).

force, it served also as a guardian of social orthodoxy. During the Ming dynasty, for example, a government regulation, that literati might not take examinations while they were in mourning, was relaxed. However, none dared take advantage of the new freedom, because "the youth held *ch'ing-i* in awe." [16]

Even in the twentieth century, the banner of *ch'ing-i* has been unfurled. Liang Ch'i-ch'ao and K'ang Yu-wei carried their attack against imperial autocracy from 1899 to 1901 in their principal organ, the *Ch'ing-i Pao* (Journal). Again, in 1947 and 1948, the Kuomintang monopoly of the Nationalist Government was assailed in a monthy publication called simply the *Ch'ing-i*.[17] Thus, for nearly two thousand years, *ch'ing-i* was (and perhaps still is) a means used by those who would preserve social and political morality in the Chinese world.

Throughout the period of the T'ung-chih Restoration, that is, during the 1860's, *ch'ing-i* was muted. The ravages of internal rebellion, and the humiliation of defeat by the foreign powers, had caused Chinese officials to acquiesce in the efforts of government leaders to effect reconstruction and limited westernization.[18] The Tientsin Massacre in 1870 ended this period of political tranquillity. In a paroxysm of anti-foreign and anti-Christian rage, a Chinese mob slaughtered a number of French and Chinese Christians, and set fire to several buildings belonging to foreigners. The atmosphere throughout the country became charged with hysteria, and *ch'ing-i* spokesmen demanded a policy of war against the French.

[16] LJC, 40:27, May 5, 1883 (KH9/4/25).
[17] The *Journal* was edited by Liang in Yokohama. See John K. Fairbank and Kwang-ching Liu, *Modern China: A Bibliographical Guide to Chinese Works, 1898–1937* (Cambridge, Mass., 1950), p. 138; Ko Kung-chen, *Chung-kuo pao-hsüeh-shih* (History of Chinese journalism; Peking, 1955), pp. 124 and 132.
The *Ch'ing-i* was published by Chang Fang and edited by Hu T'ieh in Shanghai and Nanking. I have seen only the issues of volume 2, covering the year 1948, that are in the Harvard-Yenching Library.
[18] Mary Clabaugh Wright, *The Last Stand of Chinese Conservatism: The T'ung-Chih Restoration, 1862–1874* (Stanford, 1957), p. 7.

The aged Tseng Kuo-fan, on orders from the throne, undertook an investigation of the tragic incident. In his report, Tseng observed that "Ordinarily, I have known how to uphold the truth and have been awed by *ch'ing-i*," [19] but he went on to recommend that Peking conciliate the French in an effort to avoid hostilities.

To officials who participated in *ch'ing-i*, Tseng's report represented a servile surrender to the foreigners, and they so calumniated him for this, one of the last tasks in a long career, that Tseng was moved to "bitter cries and gushing tears." [20] Finally, the throne bowed before *ch'ing-i* and recalled Tseng from his management of the case.

After the Tientsin Massacre, and during the greater part of the 1870's, *ch'ing-i* criticisms were directed mainly against the modernization efforts of "self-strengthening" reformers. Attacks on Western-inspired innovations (such as railroads, the T'ung-wen Kuan or College of Languages, and the dispatch of diplomatic missions to foreign countries), or attacks on the leaders of the modernization movement, created a political atmosphere — analogous in some respects, I would suggest, to the McCarthy era in the United States — that seriously impeded the reform movement.[21]

The plight of Kuo Sung-tao during this decade illustrates the capacity of *ch'ing-i* to smother free expression and spoil the career of a progressive official. During the Margary Affair (1875–76), Kuo submitted a memorial that was interpreted by anti-Western officials as an attempt to ingratiate himself with the British.[22] As a result, a fellow official observed, Kuo "was

[19] Tseng Kuo-fan, "Tsou-i" (Memorials), *Tseng Wen-cheng Kung ch'üan-chi* (The complete works of Tseng Kuo-fan; Changsha, 1876), 35:40.

[20] Immanuel Hsü, p. 203.

[21] *Ibid.*, pp. 203–206; Hao Yen-p'ing, "A Study of the Ch'ing-liu Tang: The 'Disinterested' Scholar-Official Group (1875–1884)," *Papers on China*, 16:*passim* (Harvard, East Asian Research Center, 1962).

[22] Immanuel Hsü, p. 182.

greatly despised by *ch'ing-i*," [23] a phrase that illuminates contemporary usage of the term *ch'ing-i*, though it fails to suggest the awful wrath of the *ch'ing-i* attack on Kuo.[24]

Later, while Kuo was serving as China's first minister to Britain, his diary of his mission in Europe was printed by the Tsungli Yamen. Unaware that the diary was to be published, Kuo had indited an entry that vaguely praised the European nations. *Ch'ing-i* vitriol was again poured upon Kuo, and ultimately the printed edition of the diary was destroyed.[25] When he returned from Europe, Kuo was so intimidated that he dared not go to Peking, and went directly to his home province, resigning all thought of an official post.

During the last year or two of the seventies, *ch'ing-i* was less antagonistic to Western-type innovations within China than to the encroachments of the foreign powers on the dependencies of the empire. Prior to about 1878, Chinese officials had been generally indifferent to, or had acquiesced in, these acts of aggression. But the unrelenting and increasing threat of the Europeans and Japanese caused many officials to conclude that the conciliatory policies of the government were self-defeating. A spirit of bellicosity gradually arose that made articulators of *ch'ing-i*, for the next half decade, virtually identical with the so-called "war party," the chief difference being that, strictly speaking, the war party denoted high-ranking, pro-war officials, such as Prince Ch'un, Tso Tsung-t'ang and Tseng Chi-tse, as well as lesser officials.

The first strong manifestation of this new spirit appeared when the Japanese prevented the Ryukyuans from sending a tribute mission to Peking in 1879.[26] The same year, *ch'ing-i*

[23] Hao, "T'ung-Kuang 'ch'ing-i,'" p. 3, citing LJC.
[24] Immanuel Hsü, pp. 182–183.
[25] *Ibid.*, pp. 188–189.
[26] T. C. Lin, "Li Hung-chang: His Korea Policies, 1870–1885," *Chinese Social and Political Science Review*, 19.2:218 (July 1935); Thomas William Ayers, "Chang Chih-tung and Chinese Educational Change," Ph.D. thesis (Harvard, 1959), p. 107.

attained new heights of vituperation during the controversy with Russia over Ili. In the latter crisis, particularly, pro-war opinion was implacable. Victory over Russia — for such the Chinese considered the Ili settlement — made a profound impression throughout the empire; to many officials, the incident proved that China could effectively employ force, or the threat of force, to resist foreign encroachments. The Ili affair was thus a heartening experience for most Chinese officials — a fact that helps to explain the prevalence of pro-war sentiment during the Sino-French controversy.[27] And this penchant for war, incidentally, placed *ch'ing-i* in direct opposition to the appeasement policies favored by Li Hung-chang.

An extreme manifestation of *ch'ing-i* during the decade 1875–84, and one that deserves special attention, was a coterie of officials in Peking known as the Ch'ing-liu.[28] The few scholars who have approached the problem of the membership in this group have not fully agreed. There is, however, a consensus that Chang Chih-tung, Chang P'ei-lun, Ch'en Pao-ch'en, Huang T'i-fang, Pao-t'ing, Teng Ch'eng-hsiu, and Wu Ta-ch'eng constituted a nucleus around which a number of other officials — how many is not clear — assembled to form a group that was referred to as the Ch'ing-liu.[29] Historical materials are vague

[27] Chu Djang, "War and Diplomacy over Ili," *Chinese Social and Political Science Review*, 20.3:379–382 (Oct. 1936); Ayers, p. 119.

[28] Ch'ing-liu may be rendered literally as "pure group." Hao Yen-p'ing refers to them as the "disinterested scholar-official group" ("A Study," p. 40), while Ayers (p. 89) translates the term as the "purification clique."

Note that "liu" in the phrase Ch'ing-liu means not stream or current, but, as Immanuel Hsü has pointed out, a "circle, group, coterie etc." (letter to the author, July 17, 1962). Some writers refer to the group as the Ch'ing-liu Tang, which Hao translates as "pure current party" ("A Study," p. 40). This phrase is, however, a redundancy, because "liu" and "tang" are here similar in meaning. Writers during the 1880's avoided the redundancy, for, to my knowledge, they never spoke of "Ch'ing-liu Tang."

[29] *Ch'ing-shih* (History of the Ch'ing dynasty; Taipei, 1961), VI, 4906, 4937, 4939. Hao Yen-p'ing would limit the membership of the group

regarding the members of the group, suggesting that the term Ch'ing-liu was a highly vague designation even to contemporaries of the group. It is safe to assume, however, that Ch'ing-liu referred to this nucleus of seven officials and an indefinite number of their associates, who together, by their mordant criticisms and unceasing flow of policy suggestions, attained for themselves a certain distinctness in Peking politics.

Aside from their exaggerated expressions of *ch'ing-i*, the members of the Ch'ing-liu shared several common characteristics. The seven leading Ch'ing-liu officials were relatively young (their average age in 1880 was forty years) and, with the exception of Teng Ch'eng-hsiu who was a *chü-jen* and a censor, all had passed the metropolitan examination and were, or had been, members of the Hanlin Academy. On the other hand, only three of these seven came from the same province (Chihli), which suggests that the group was not founded, primarily, on a regional basis.[30]

It is, in fact, necessary to differentiate the Ch'ing-liu from a regional faction with which it has frequently been confused,

---

to nine, adding Li Hung-tsao and Liu En-p'u to those named above ("A Study," p. 41). Ayers (p. 93) makes no mention of Liu En-p'u and denies that Li Hung-tsao was a member. He adds, however, the names of Hsü Chih-hsiang and Sheng-yü (pp. 89–90) — though Hao specifically denies Sheng-yü's membership. Li Hung-tsao was considered a leader of the Ch'ing-liu, although he was not a member of that group (Hummel, I, 472; Ayers, p. 93). Ku Hung-ming, a contemporary of the movement and personal acquaintance of many of the participants, has also pointed to Ch'en Ch'i-t'ai as a "well-known" member (*The Story of a Chinese Oxford Movement* [Shanghai, 1912], pp. 19–20). And Sun I-yen referred to himself as Ch'ing-liu — although Li Tz'u-ming noted that, ironically, Sun smoked opium and neglected his official duties (LJC, 33:90b, Mar. 26, 1880 [KH6/2/16]).

The term Ch'ing-liu was not, as has been suggested elsewhere, a pejorative designation. Chang P'ei-lun, for example, like Sun I-yen, referred to his own activities as being "Ch'ing-liu." ("Chien-yü chi" [The collected writings of Chang P'ei-lun], CFCC, IV, 374).

[30] Hao Yen-p'ing, by using a different list of members, found that five of the nine were from Chihli, which indicates a slightly stronger regional tint ("A Study," p. 42). Ayers, on the other hand, concluded that the Ch'ing-liu was not bound by regional ties (pp. 89–90).

the Northern Party. Identifiable members of the Northern Party included Chang Chih-tung, Chang P'ei-lun, Pao-t'ing, Liu En-p'u, Sheng-yü, Li Jo-nung, and Li Hung-tsao.[31] Li Tz'u-ming, who hated this "blood brotherhood" (*ssu-tang*) of northerners with all the ardor of his southern blood, charged that they recommended each other for promotion; they protected each other from deserved punishments; they censured other officials as a means of revenge; and they sought high office by interfering in the affairs of the court.[32]

Of the Northern Party, Chang Chih-tung, Chang P'ei-lun, and Pao-t'ing clearly were also members of the Ch'ing-liu. This overlapping of the two groups contributed to the considerable misunderstanding concerning the Ch'ing-liu. What did differentiate the two groups — and here the line to be drawn is extremely thin — was that the Ch'ing-liu were, professedly, disinterested critics of the government, whereas the Northern Party was a typical regional faction acting to protect and advance mutual interests.

Adding to the difficulty of characterizing the Ch'ing-liu "Party" is the fact that, even among the leading members, Ch'ing-liu partisans did not form a tightly-knit, intimate group. Pao-t'ing and Ch'en Pao-ch'en, for example, were related only indirectly through the person of Chang Chih-tung.[33] And Teng Ch'eng-hsiu, a Ch'ing-liu member, but a southerner, was reportedly "profoundly aware of the perfidy of the two Changs [Chang Chih-tung and Chang P'ei-lun] and enumerated their deceits. Although he was recommended for office by little Chang [Chang P'ei-lun] and is closely allied with him, he also

[31] Sources suggesting this list of members are LJC, 38:5, June 23, 1882 (KH8/5/8); LJC, 42:93b, Sept. 1, 1884 (KH10/7/12); Hummel, I, 472.

[32] These northerners were one of Li Tz'u-ming's favorite passions, and he referred often to them in his diary. To cite three of the more interesting entries: LJC, 38:5, June 23, 1882 (KH8/5/8); 42:48, June 14, 1884 (KH10/5/21); 43:3b, Sept. 15, 1884 (KH10/7/26).

[33] Hao, "A Study," p. 42; p. 60, n. 13.

says this group is deceitful and cannot be completely trusted." [34]

The Ch'ing-liu was thus a relatively amorphous group. Its members were distinguished by the acrimony they imparted to *ch'ing-i*. They outdid other *ch'ing-i* officials in the causticity and frequency of their impeachments of fellow officials. And, in foreign affairs, their bellicose utterances set the tone for less articulate officials. Ch'ing-liu members were spokesmen of *ch'ing-i*, but spokesmen who frequently served as the bell-wether of *ch'ing-i* and gave that sentiment its most acrid expression.

[34] LJC, 42:48, June 14, 1884 (KH10/5/21).

II

FRANCE IN VIETNAM AND CHINA'S
INITIAL RESPONSES

Viewed from the Chinese side, the Sino-French controversy consisted of three main phases. The first, from 1880 to March 1883, was a period when the Chinese sensed little urgency regarding French activities in Vietnam; during the second phase, from March 1883 to August 1884, the Chinese recognized the critical state of affairs and resisted the French covertly in Vietnam; the third phase, from August 1884 to April 1885, was a period of open warfare in Vietnam and Taiwan.

The Chinese, even as late as the 1870's, had not realized the essential incompatibility between their traditional view of interstate relations, in which China was a universal empire rightfully superior to other states, and the Western concept of a *staatensystem*, in which all sovereign states are legally equal. A Sino-French "controversy" therefore took form only after the Chinese began to sense that French activities in Vietnam constituted a challenge to Chinese interests and pretensions there.

Because Vietnam had not become a source of poignant concern, imperial policy was formulated within conventional and routine channels. That is, those who formulated policy were not subjected to the advice and criticism of non-institutionalized forces such as *ch'ing-i*, and the throne seldom assumed an active role in policy formation. The policy process during this period was relatively decentralized and leisurely. The Tsungli Yamen and provincial officials, for example, enjoyed broad areas within which they might exercise their own initiative. And Peking frequently solicited the opinions of officials in the most remote provinces before making a decision, a practice that, given the state of communications in the 1880's, required two to four months.

As a sense of crisis increased, the throne assumed a more active part in policy formation. Policy discussions were progressively confined to the principal officials in Peking, because the pressure of time did not permit the luxury of communicating with provincial officials. And literati opinion became an influential force in the policy process.

Early French Interests in Vietnam. Since the reign of Louis XIV in the seventeenth century, Frenchmen had aspired to establish an empire in Southeast Asia. Their efforts had met with repeated, and sometimes farcical, rebuffs and failures. In Vietnam, for example, the reigning Nguyen dynasty (1802–1945) was rabidly anti-foreign and anti-Christian, and the French, beset by political difficulties at home, had been unable to sustain their efforts to overcome the dogged Vietnamese resistance. France's commercial interests in East Asia also remained negligible, and it failed to acquire a base of operations such as Hong Kong, which had proved so useful to British imperialist endeavors. Even at the times when Paris determined to pursue an active policy in Asia, its inability to provide adequate military forces resulted, time and time again, in dismal debacles. French prestige in the East had become badly tarnished. The Frenchman, who saw the Union Jack unfurled in ever-increasing brilliance throughout Asia, well knew the taste of gall.

Lacking merchants to serve as the vanguard of its imperial

expansion, Paris had become the self-styled protector of Catholic missions throughout the East. Frequently, France had not borne even this responsibility with distinction. But the accession of Louis Napoleon, an ardent proponent of the resuscitation of national prestige, inaugurated a period in which it was determined to achieve new glories through imperialist adventures. Napoleon's chief instrument was the pretext of protecting the missions.[1]

Initially, the French emperor sought to realize his desires by collaborating in a joint expedition with England against China. French forces shared in the victories of the resulting Arrow War (1856–60). France, however, was like a tail wagging at the rear of the indomitable British lion, and Napoleon desperately needed a victory independent of Britain if he were to challenge that nation's dominance in the East. As a consequence, Bonapartist policy came to focus on Vietnam. The traditional French interests in the area, the considerable Catholic activity there, and the palpable enfeeblement of the Nguyen dynasty conjoined to make Vietnam an obvious object of Napoleon's plans.

Vietnamese resistance proved to be more effective than the French had anticipated. Two expensive and only qualifiedly successful military campaigns, first in 1858–59 and again in 1861–62, resulted in the cession to France of three of Vietnam's provinces in Cochin China. However, continuing popular resistance to French rule in these provinces, and Napoleon's new penchant for aggrandizement in Mexico, caused the French ruler to curtail expenditures for undertakings in the East. The French adventure might have terminated early in the 1860's had the navy not felt that the name of the nation and

[1] John F. Cady, *The Roots of French Imperialism in Eastern Asia* (Ithaca, 1954), *passim;* A. A. Dorland, "A Preliminary Study of the Role of the French Protectorate of Roman Catholic Missions in Sino-French Diplomatic Relations," Master's thesis (Cornell, 1951), *passim.*

of the service had been denigrated by the Vietnamese fiasco. The navy, therefore, on its own initiative embarked on a policy intended to vindicate French honor. Despite strong anti-imperialist influences emanating from the Foreign Ministry, the coterie of like-minded, determined naval officers found an opportunity in 1874 to meet in battle some forces of a militarily weak Vietnam. The result was that a new Franco-Vietnamese treaty was negotiated in March of that year, in which Paris recognized "the sovereignty of the King of Annam [Vietnam] and his complete independence of all foreign powers." In return for the "protection" that France pledged, the government of Vietnam agreed to conform its foreign policy to that of France.[2]

This French attempt to establish the clear and legal independence of Vietnam was a result neither of a sense of benignity toward the Vietnamese nor of apathy regarding their own interests in the peninsular kingdom. To the contrary, as a French diplomat subsequently asserted, this treaty "was designed precisely to efface the last vestiges" of Chinese claims to sovereignty over Vietnam.[3]

In 1875, the French communicated the contents of the treaty to the Chinese office of foreign affairs, the Tsungli Yamen. In a reply, Prince Kung, speaking for the Yamen, demurred only indirectly to the establishment of a French protectorate over Vietnam and to the restriction of Vietnam's conduct of its own foreign relations. Vietnam had, Prince Kung asserted, long been a Chinese tributary and Chinese interests there were further sanctified by the close commercial relations obtaining between the two states. His reply concluded with the promise that China would investigate the matter, follow-

[2] The text of the treaty may be found in HR, II, 257–261.
[3] HR, II, 306, Patenotre to Waddington, Feb. 23, 1880. St. Hilaire expressed a similar view in a dispatch to Bourée on Nov. 26, 1880. (HR, II, 315.)

ing which further discussions on the subject could be conducted between France and China.[4]

During the ensuing five years, the Chinese did not again advert to the Franco-Vietnamese treaty of 1874. Furthermore, the French translation of Prince Kung's reply read that Vietnam "has been a tributary of China" (*a été tributaire de la Chine*), and on the Quai d'Orsay the use of the past perfect tense was understood to mean that the Sino-Vietnamese tributary tie was a thing of the past.[5] It appeared, therefore, that Peking had acquiesced in the treaty of 1874, and Vietnam was now legally independent but under a French protectorate.

Chinese Claims to Sovereignty over Vietnam. The political ties between Vietnam and China were first wrought during the early years of the Han dynasty. From the reign of Han Wu-ti until the unsettled period of the Five Dynasties (907–960), a span of one thousand years, northern Vietnam was an integral part of the Chinese empire — except for brief periods when this frequently restive province, encouraged at times of Chinese weakness, rebelled against the domination of its northern master. This political relationship was weakened considerably in the tenth century. Vietnamese rebels then expelled their Chinese conquerors, and established an independent state. Henceforward, Vietnam remained independent, with the exception of twenty years (1407–27) during the early years of the Ming dynasty when a Chinese administration was again

[4] Texts of the initial French communication and of the Tsungli Yamen reply are in HR, II, 279–283. The Chinese text of the latter document is in YNT, I, 11–12, dcmt. 6, June 15, 1875 (KH1/5/12). France also requested trade with Yunnan, but Prince Kung rejected this proposal unequivocally.

[5] This was patently an error of translation, for the Chinese text clearly indicated that China considered Vietnam still to be a tributary of the empire. Charles Boswell Norman asserted that this was a mistake that "entirely altered the whole gist of China's claim, and which it is hard to believe was unintentional." (*Tonkin; or France in the Far East* [London, 1884], pp. 182–183.)

established. During this extended period of independence, Vietnam was effectively autonomous. Yet it maintained with China, albeit not uninterruptedly, a relationship that provided the Chinese with pretensions to Vietnamese sovereignty, and ultimately brought the empire into a clash with France. This relationship was the tributary system.

A number of scholars have written about the tributary relationship, and the institutional outlines of the system are now clear.[1] Yet it is still difficult for a Westerner to comprehend a concept of interstate relations so alien to his own. To appreciate the concerns of Chinese literati during the Sino-French controversy, and to comprehend the sources of Chinese misunderstandings with the French, it will be necessary to determine how the Chinese themselves viewed the relations of the empire with the tributary states.

Chinese officials traditionally held two concepts of the tributary relationship that were not wholly harmonious: they stressed at one and the same time, but in ratios that varied from individual to individual, the *moral* and the *pragmatic* aspects of the system. On the one hand, Chinese viewed the tributary states through a veil of Confucian moralizations and myth. "Barbarians" — that is, the non-Chinese tribes and states — were thought to have been drawn to China by the peerless virtue of the emperor and the superior culture of his domain. They came, humbly, requesting the privilege of submitting to, and paying homage to, the Son of Heaven. This myth received

[1] The tributary system remains one of the relatively unexplored areas of Chinese history. Most suggestive of the existing works relating to the subject are John K. Fairbank and Ssu-yü Teng, *Ch'ing Administration,* pp. 107–218; John K. Fairbank, *Trade and Diplomacy on the China Coast* (Cambridge, Mass., 1953), pp. 23–38; T. C. Lin, "Manchurian Trade and Tribute in the Ming Dynasty: A Study of Chinese Theories and Methods of Control over Border Peoples," *Nankai Social and Economic Quarterly,* 4.4:855–892 (Jan. 1937); She I-tse, *Chung-kuo t'u-ssu chih-tu* (China's system of tribal chieftains; place of publication unknown, 1944); Herold Wiens, *China's March toward the Tropics* (Hamden, Conn., 1954), pp. 201–240.

official expression in a work compiled in the Ming dynasty: "The kings of former times cultivated their own refinement and virtue in order to subdue persons at a distance, whereupon the barbarians (of the east and north) came to Court to have audience." [2] Here was Confucian dogma applied to interstate relations: the belief that virtue was the moving force in human affairs. Here was substantiation of the belief that other peoples willingly submitted to, and were by right subordinate to, the Chinese universal empire.

Despite China's manifest right to rule over the barbarians, it was — again, in theory — a matter of utter indifference to the Chinese whether the barbarians chose to submit to the Son of Heaven. Coercion in human affairs was not the way of a true ruler. Thus, even as early as the Han dynasty, it was asserted that in Sino-barbarian relations: "Those who come will not be rejected, and those who leave will not be pursued." [3]

In fact, however, there was no indifference on the part of Chinese regarding the relationship of non-Chinese with the empire. Tribal tributaries that revolted against Chinese overlordship might be suppressed with force.[4] And imperial armies were even sent, on occasion, into tributary kingdoms to chasten insubordinate rulers.[5] Generally, however, the Chinese employed methods of inducements and rewards to retain the adherence of barbarians to the tributary system. It is true that the tributary rulers were required to submit gifts, or tribute, to the Son of Heaven. But these were, by regulation, not to be of excessive value, and on balance the Chinese probably suffered a loss in the exchange of gifts with the barbarians. "The Court," a Chinese scholar has asserted, "did not covet

[2] Fairbank and Teng, p. 113.
[3] Immanuel Hsü, p. 9.
[4] She I-tse, p. 33; Wiens, pp. 218–219.
[5] See, for example, *Ch'ing-shih*, VII, 5756; Le Than-Khoi, *Le Viet-Nam: Histoire et Civilisation* (Paris, 1955), pp. 306–309.

their [the barbarians'] wealth, and each time bestowed on them munificent rewards." "Was it perhaps with the intention of inducing many [barbarians] to come?" [6]

Moreover, the Chinese government permitted the barbarians to trade with the empire under highly advantageous conditions, scrupulously supervising the conditions of the market to guarantee that the barbarians had no cause for complaint.[7] The Chinese therefore were at pains to make the tributary system palatable to the non-Chinese — particularly to barbarians who were deemed to be vital to the security of the empire. "Tribute was," as two students of the system have observed, " a *substitute* for more forceful domination." [8]

In other words, the moral basis of the tributary system was less apparent in practice than in theory, and the Chinese frequently held a hardheaded, pragmatic view of the tributaries. The wealth of China had, from the earliest times, drawn non-Chinese peoples to the frontiers. Peaceable barbarians had sought trade; others sought plunder. These, not the virtue of the emperor, were the attractions. To control the access of these peoples to the empire, the Chinese periodically attempted to conquer the neighboring non-Chinese and to control them directly. This had been the Chinese policy in Vietnam for ten centuries after Han Wu-ti's conquest of the northern portion of the Indochinese Peninsula. However, difficult terrain, slow communications, and popular resistance, together with Chinese officials' ignorance of the barbarians' customs and languages, often made direct administration impracticable.[9] So, *faute de mieux,* the tributary system was employed.

[6] She I-tse, pp. 26, 29. See also the remarks of T. F. Tsiang, quoted in Fairbank and Teng, p. 112; and Wiens, p. 218.

[7] T. C. Lin, "Manchurian Trade and Tribute," p. 858.

[8] Fairbank and Teng, p. 130, n. 34 (italics in original). See also Wiens, pp. 218–219.

[9] *Ch'ing-shih,* VII, 5576–77, and Huang Fen-sheng, *Pien-chiang cheng-chiao chih yen-chiu* (Researches on administration and education in the

It is doubtful that, in Chinese eyes, the tributary system ever lost the essentially defensive function that had brought it into existence. This function was frequently obscured by moralistic pronunciamentos. Yet during the nineteenth century Chinese literati were poignantly aware of the strategic value of the tributary states as buffers against the encroachment of the Europeans. The following statement during the Sino-French controversy exemplifies this view:

> The border provinces are China's gates; the tributary states (*wai-fan*) are China's walls. We build the walls to protect the gates, and protect the gates to secure the house. If the walls fall, the gates are endangered; if the gates are endangered, the house is shaken.[10]

Indeed, so concerned were some officials for the defense of the empire that they utterly abandoned pretenses that China was a universal empire of which the tributaries were an integral part. Liu K'un-i, for instance, remarked in 1881 when the Japanese were making claims upon the Ryukyu Islands: "Though the Ryukyus are nominally our tributary, they are not essential to China's defense, and are not therefore worth our wasting effort to preserve." [11] Another official conveyed the

---

frontier areas; Shanghai, 1947), pp. 93–96. Huang is followed closely by Wiens, pp. 214–215. The close similarity of Chinese relations with foreign tributary states and with tributary tribes requires much further study. For pregnant remarks in this respect, see T. C. Lin, "Manchurian Trade and Tribute," pp. 877, 879; Wiens, pp. 217–218 and 225–226; and Huang Fen-sheng, p. 99.

[10] Liu Ch'ang-yu, "Liu Wu-shen Kung i-shu" (The collected writings of Liu Ch'ang-yu), CFCC, I, 87, Nov. 18, 1881 (KH7/9/17). Tseng Chi-tse neatly described the defensive function of the tributaries: "China's tributaries are not confined to one area. There is Korea in the east, the various areas beyond Tibet on the west, and Vietnam on the south. These several countries are China's screen." YNT, II, 1001, dcmt. 493, Tseng to Tsungli Yamen, Aug. 20, 1883 (KH9/7/18).

[11] Liu K'un-i, *Liu K'un-i i-chi* (The collected writings of Liu K'un-i; Peking, 1959), IV, 1932, Liu to Li Jo-nung, Apr. 27, 1881 (KH7/3/29). See also CFCS, 4:9, dcmt. 107, Ch'en Ch'i-t'ai memorial, May 17, 1883 (KH9/4/11).

same idea in 1884 regarding Vietnam: "In the present conflict, the protection of a tributary is a small matter; the firming
up of the defenses of the empire is a big matter." [12]

Implicit in these quotations is the suggestion that Chinese
were becoming nationalistic in their attitude toward interstate
relations. If the Chinese viewed their tributaries *merely* as
defensive outposts against other nations with which China was
in competition, there would have remained no place for the
traditionally ethnocentric and moralistic view of China as
master of *t'ien-hsia* (all under heaven). And if this keystone
were removed from the Chinese *weltanschauung*, the entire
ideological structure of the Chinese officials might have collapsed.

In contrast to the view that the tributaries were important
primarily for their defensive function, however, one finds that
officials' writings of the period are liberally sprinkled with assertions, for example, that China must uphold "the virtue of
caring for the weak" (*tzu-hsiao chih jen*) — that is, that the
empire was morally responsible for protecting the small states
that had rendered obeisance to the Chinese emperor. Tseng
Chi-tse also rejected the view that China fought for Vietnam
only because it was concerned for the defense of the Chinese
frontier. "Vietnam belongs to China," Tseng continued, and
therefore "China *is duty-bound* to protect Vietnam's entire
territory." [13] These professions of "the virtue of caring for the
weak" were for the most part sincere, exemplifying the
literati's ineradicable penchant for viewing all human relationships in moral terms. My own view is, nevertheless, that the
Chinese generally subordinated moral to pragmatic considerations when they contemplated the tributaries. It is doubtful,

[12] CFCS, 14:23a–b, dcmt. 496, Lung Chan-lin memorial, May 4, 1884
(KH10/4/10).
[13] "Tseng Chi-tse yü Fa wai-pu wang-lai chao-hui" (Communications
between Tseng Chi-tse and the French Foreign Ministry), CFCC, V, 80,
Tseng to French Foreign Ministry, Oct. 15, 1883. Italics added.

however, that more than a few of these officials would have admitted that a distinction could legitimately be made between these aspects of the system — for them it was both! It would therefore be rash and premature to conclude that Chinese officials had generally, during the 1880's, substituted a nationalistic for a culturalistic outlook upon the place of China in the world.

The majority of Frenchmen in the 1870's and early 1880's were blithely unmindful of the importance that the Chinese attached to a strategically significant tributary, and were complacent that Chinese pretensions to sovereignty over Vietnam had no validity. They recognized that "since 1407, that is to say since the occupation by the Ming, China has never intervened in the internal affairs of the kingdom: the succession to the throne, the administration, and the promulgation of laws have been accomplished without China having been consulted." [14]

The French knew also that the Chinese government had issued no protests when portions of Cochin China had fallen to French control in 1862; they knew that even more recently the Chinese had acquiesced in the treaty of 1874 which had asserted that Vietnam was "independent of all foreign powers." [15] To many Frenchmen, therefore, the relationship between China and Vietnam could be viewed as "merely Platonic . . . a tradition without practical importance." [16] Despite the prevalence of this view in France, an astute French governor of Cochin China observed in 1876 that France had "the greatest interest in not provoking a strict definition of Chinese rights in Annam [Vietnam]." [17]

[14] HR, II, 335.
[15] HR, II, 268.
[16] HR, II, 341.
[17] Brian Llewellyn Evans, "The Attitudes and Policies of Great Britain and China toward French Expansion in Cochin China, Cambodia, Annam and Tongking, 1858–83," Ph.D. thesis (University of London, 1961), p. 401.

It is now clear, and this is a fact of signal importance for an understanding of the Chinese concept of the tributary tie, that Prince Kung and his colleagues in the Chinese government had not sensed in 1875 that the Franco-Vietnamese treaty had nullified Vietnam's dependency relationship with the empire. The Chinese could not at this time conceive that a Western legal instrument could sever a relationship such as existed between China and Vietnam. During the reign of the Ch'ing dynasty, Vietnam had been one of the three or four states most faithful in presenting tribute to the court in Peking.[18] And on several occasions imperial arms had been sent to Vietnamese territory, at the request of the Vietnamese emperor, to suppress local bandits. To Chinese of the nineteenth century, these facts, together with the long historical relationship and cultural and racial ties, were sufficient proof of China's ineffaceable suzerainty in Vietnam.

That the Chinese had not comprehended in the mid-1870's that the tributary relationship had no status in Western international law may seem incredible.[19] This was over thirty years since China had first concluded treaties with the Western powers, and the first complete translation of a work on international law had been completed in 1864.[20] Yet, between 1874 and 1876, the Chinese not only once, but three times, saw Western-style treaties that recognized the independence of tributary states.[21] On each occasion, the Chinese misinter-

[18] Fairbank and Teng, p. 198. The vitality of the tributary relation is indicated by the fact that Vietnam had dispatched missions to Peking as recently as 1869 and 1871 (*ibid.*, p. 197) and 1873 (HR, II, 287).
[19] Even Mary C. Wright has asserted that "By 1867 the Tsungli-yamen knew . . . that the tributary tie was a logical impossibility in the modern world." ("The Adaptability of Ch'ing Diplomacy: The Case of Korea," *Journal of Asian Studies*, 17.3:381 [May 1958].)
[20] Immanuel Hsü, p. 128.
[21] The Kanghwa Treaty of 1876 between Japan and Korea, for example, declared that "Chosen [Korea], being an independent state [*tzu-chu*], enjoys the same sovereign rights as does Japan." (The full text of the English translation of the treaty is in John M. Maki, *Selected Docu-*

preted the significance if not the wording of the document, for their concept of interstate relations was fundamentally different from that of Europeans. The European view was that either one state was wholly a dependency of another state or that the two states were equal, neither being legally subordinate to the other. The Chinese interpretation did not allow such clear distinctions. According to the theory of the Chinese universal state, a tributary could be independent in both its domestic and foreign affairs, and still retain its traditional dependency tie with the empire.[22] The Chinese viewed the legal instruments of the West and the traditional practices of the Chinese universal state as operating in mutually exclusive spheres. There could therefore be no incompatibility between

---

ments, Far Eastern International Relations, 1688-1951 [Seattle, 1957], dcmt. 69, pp. 102-104.)

The phrase quoted here, in its Chinese version, is admittedly ambiguous. Peking conceivably understood *tzu-chu* to mean "self-ruling," which, if the case, would explain their failure to protest the treaty. (See M. Frederick Nelson, *Korea and the Old Orders in Eastern Asia* [Baton Rouge, 1945], p. 131, n. 63, n. 64; and T. C. Lin, "Li Hung-chang," p. 217.) I believe it more probable, however, that Peking did understand *tzu-chu* to mean "independent" or "sovereign." Seven years after the Treaty of Kanghwa, for example, Li Hung-chang fully understood that to call a former imperial dependency *tzu-chu* was to assert that the dependency tie was broken. (See ISHK, CFCC, IV, 57, Li-Tricou conversation, July 1, 1883 [KH9/5/27].) Moreover, T. F. Tsiang has observed with regard to the Kanghwa Treaty that the Chinese did not perceive that a legal instrument, recognizing the independence of a tributary, altered the traditional lord-vassal relationship so long as it remained assured of the loyalty of the tributary. (Tsiang, "Sino-Japanese Diplomatic Relations, 1870-1894," *Chinese Social and Political Science Review*, 17.1:53 [Apr. 1933].)

Hyman Kublin has arrived at a conclusion similar to that of Tsiang. Kublin contended that, while the Ryukyus continued to dispatch tribute missions to Peking, the Chinese did not apprehend that the diplomatic recognition of the Ryukyu people as Japanese subjects in 1874 had changed the relationship of that kingdom with China. (Hyman Kublin, "The Attitude of China during the Liu-ch'iu Controversy, 1871-1881," *Pacific Historical Review*, 18:228-229 [May 1949].)

[22] The conflicting Chinese and French versions of sovereignty were contrasted explicitly in a conversation between Tseng Chi-tse and Jules Ferry in 1883. (YNT, II, 1003-04, dcmt. 493, Tseng to Tsungli Yamen, Aug. 20, 1883 [KH9/7/18].)

them even though Western legal authorities might insist there existed an irresolvable contradiction.

The unique and, to a Western eye, essentially ambiguous character of the tributary tie may be illustrated by approaching the problem from yet another angle. The concept of fixed and precise boundaries between the empire and a tributary state was not alien to the Chinese mind. These boundaries, however, were not considered to mark a division of territorial sovereignties, but rather were thought to demark divisions of administrative jurisdiction. The following incident during the reign of the Yung-cheng Emperor (1723–35) offers graphic demonstration of this fact.[23]

In 1725, an area forty *li* (thirteen miles) in depth along the Vietnam-Yunnan border was in dispute. A Chinese provincial official proposed that a river at the southern edge of the contested territory be established as the boundary. The Vietnamese emperor vehemently protested this solution, whereupon the Chinese emperor replied: "We exercise universal authority over the whole world (*huan-ch'ü*). In all the present subject states, there is no territory that is not Ours. Why must you quibble over this mere forty *li* of land?" The decree continued by giving the Vietnamese emperor a sound scolding for his insubordinate behavior, adding that "the delineation of the frontiers and the determination of the borders ought to be the first tasks of government." After this tongue-lashing, the Vietnamese ruler reportedly expressed his abject repentance — whereupon Yung-cheng graciously bestowed the full forty *li* of contested territory on Vietnam in perpetuity.

As late as 1875, the Tsungli Yamen remarked that "although the aborigines of Yunnan live outside T'ieh-pi Pass [and thus in Burma], their territory [in Burma] still belongs to China." [24] Thus, despite the rather clear demarcation that

[23] The incident is related in *Ch'ing-shih*, VIII, 5754.
[24] WCSL, 1:15b, Tsungli Yamen memorial, May 2, 1874 (KH1/3/27). I am indebted to Brian Evans for bringing this passage to my attention.

might mark off the lands of a tributary from the empire, the Chinese did not consider that state boundaries circumscribed Chinese sovereignty. This quality of the tributary relationship between states may be analogous to the Chinese concept of land ownership: the emperor of China owned, so to speak, the subsoil rights to the area of the tributary, while the tributary ruler owned the topsoil, or use, rights. Or, at the risk of a semantic quarrel, it might be suggested that the relationship was a feudal one: that the Chinese lord bestowed on his vassal a fief, which, administered by the vassal, nevertheless ultimately remained the possession of the lord.

The *Book of Poetry* (*Shih Ching*) contains the following poem:

> Everywhere under vast Heaven
> There is no land that is not the king's.
> To the borders of those lands
> There are none who are not the king's servants.[25]

This must surely have been one of the most durable political doctrines in history. It originated some time between the tenth and seventh centuries B.C., and it persisted during the Sino-French controversy. During the last twenty years or so of the Ch'ing dynasty, when this venerable concept was dashed upon the realities of the modern world, a trauma was created in the Chinese mind, the extent of which has still to be measured.

Decline and Revival of French Activity in Vietnam. Had the Chinese held any misgivings in 1875 about the developments in Vietnam, events of the next few years would surely have eased their qualms. Significantly, the Vietnamese were also unaware that their treaty with France in 1874 implied nullifi-

[25] Derk Bodde, "Feudalism in China," ed. Rushton Coulborn, *Feudalism in History* (Copr. Princeton University Press, 1956), p. 58. There is a question whether this poem meant that the king held definite rights of property in other lands, or merely claimed political sovereignty in those lands (*ibid.*), but this does not affect our discussion.

cation of the tributary relationship with China, and in 1877 they sent their mission, on schedule as it were, to Peking.[1] Two years later, Tu-Duc, the Vietnamese emperor, addressed himself not to his French "protector" but to the Chinese, requesting aid in suppressing a bandit force (under Li Yang-ts'ai) that had been ravaging the Sino-Vietnamese border areas. The Chinese responded, in clear violation of the 1874 treaty, by sending government troops into Vietnam. This was done directly "under the eyes of our [the French] garrisons."[2] To the Chinese, it appeared that the Franco-Vietnamese treaty of 1874 had not changed the status of Vietnam.

The truth of the matter is that the French government had become temporarily indifferent to the prospect of empire-building in Vietnam. Anti-imperialist sentiment had waxed strong during the seventies, and France was preoccupied with domestic reconstruction after the recent debacle in the war against Germany. This, together with the factional bickering that pervaded Republican politics, temporarily diverted attention from such names as Saigon and Tongking.[3]

Gradually, however, the period of French colonial inactivity was drawing to a close. The retirement of the president of the Third Republic, Marie de MacMahon, in 1879 was followed by the rise of expansionist-minded republicans to positions of influence. An energetic civil servant, Charles le Myre de Vilers, was nominated to the post of governor of Cochin China in May 1879, and in the following year a vigorous proponent of colonialism, Jules Ferry, became premier.[4] These changes in personnel were quickly followed by concrete manifestations of a new policy. During 1880, French garrisons in the major cities

[1] HR, II, 287. An alternative explanation might be that the Vietnamese dispatched the tribute mission hoping that this would weaken French claims in Vietnam.
[2] HR, II, 295, Raindre to Patenotre, Nov. 1879.
[3] Cady, p. 289.
[4] Cady, pp. 290–294; HR, II, 291; Evans, pp. 421–423.

in southern Vietnam were reinforced; at the same time, French expeditions probed deeply into the Vietnamese interior, exploring mining possibilities and surveying the waterways.[5]

Finally, in July 1881, the French Chamber voted to finance an armed expedition into Tongking. Ostensibly the purpose of this undertaking was to establish order in the area, but there was an implicit agreement within the councils of the Foreign Ministry and the Ministry of Marine that the real aim of the expedition was to annex the entire territory of northern Vietnam.[6]

Two months later (September), Paris dispatched instructions to the French governor of Cochin China, le Myre de Vilers, to "restore the prestige of French authority diminished by our hesitations and our weaknesses."[7] At the same time, the French authorities revealed a degree of restraint, for de Vilers was cautioned "above all to forbear from rushing into the adventures of a military conquest."[8]

This cautionary advice posed a conundrum for the punctilious, bureaucratic-minded de Vilers, because the extension of French activities had aroused a determined resistance from an unlikely body of Vietnamese defenders called the Black Flags. Located in an area of northern Tongking along the Red River (between Lao-Kay in the north, just below Yunnan, and Hung-Hoa farther south), the Black Flags had cut off French trade along the Red River, and placed the lives of Frenchmen traveling in Tongking in perpetual peril.[9]

---

[5] Huang Ta-shou, *Chung-kuo chin-tai-shih* (Modern Chinese history; Taipei, 1954), II, 32–33.

[6] Shao Hsün-cheng, *Chung Fa Yüeh-nan kuan-hsi shih-mo* (Relations between China, France, and Vietnam; Peiping, 1935), p. 61; Norman, pp. 181, 190.

[7] Evans, p. 440.

[8] *Ibid.*

[9] CFCS, 2:9b-10, dcmt. 38, Chang Shu-sheng memorial, Feb. 14, 1882 (KH7/12/26); Liu Ch'ang-yu, "Liu Wu-shen Kung i-shu," CFCC, I, 94 and 96, Liu memorial, Feb. 16, 1882 (KH7/12/28).

Liu Yung-fu, the commander of the Black Flags, is one of the most colorful figures to decorate the annals of this period. Liu had been born into a Hakka family in the province of Kwangsi in 1837. Beset by poverty and emboldened by the social discontent of his neighbors, Liu had, at the age of twenty-one *sui,* joined an army of the Triad Society that had allied with the anti-dynastic forces during the Taiping Rebellion. It is now possible, if Liu's own words may be trusted, to sympathize with his motives for joining the rebellion. He had, he later asserted, taken arms against the dynasty because

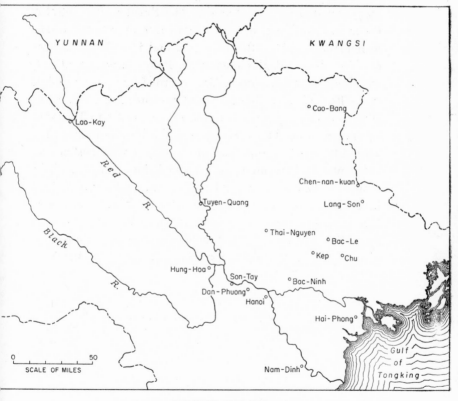

TONGKING 1884-1885

"It would have been shameful if I did nothing to benefit the people; besides, I could not continue night and day eating thin rice gruel to soothe my hunger." [10]

In the eyes of the Chinese government, however, Liu had become an outlaw. When the rebel effort disintegrated, he was forced to flee with some two hundred loyal followers, and in 1865 sought refuge across the Chinese border in Vietnam. There, in an area impoverished and insalubrious, he found himself in an intense competition for survival with other bandit groups not dissimilar from his own. Chance put him in opposition to the Miao tribesmen, whom the Vietnamese government viewed as the chief threat to its control of the area. Liu's band, which had grown to over two thousand in number, fought with distinction, and in 1869, at the age of thirty-three *sui*, this outlaw chieftain received legitimate status when the Vietnamese king awarded him official rank in recognition of his assistance. Henceforward, Liu collaborated with Vietnamese officers in restoring some order to Tongking. At the same time, he succeeded in establishing an independent administration that supported itself largely with customs assessments on mercantile traffic through his domain, and, by some reports, on the smuggling of opium and war matériel.[11] Indeed, so complete was his rule and his independence of Hué that a Chinese official reported that, after ten years of Black Flag domination, the people along the northern reaches of the Red River "know only Liu, and know not the Vietnamese king." [12]

[10] Huang Hai-an, *Liu Yung-fu li-shih ts'ao* (Draft history of Liu Yung-fu), ed. Lo Hsiang-lin (Taipei, 1957), p. 31.

[11] "Les Pavillons-Noirs" (unsigned), *Annales de L'Extreme Orient et de L'Afrique*, 6:31 (1883–84); YNT, III, 1372, dcmt. 649, Ts'en Yü-ying to Tsungli Yamen, Nov. 23, 1883 (KH9/10/24). It is interesting that Chinese officials never made reference to Liu's smuggling activities.

[12] CFCS, 3:23, dcmt. 75, addendum #1, Ts'en Yü-ying memorial, Nov. 21, 1882 (KH8/10/11). Except where otherwise indicated, this account of Liu Yung-fu is based on Huang Hai-an, *passim*.

The incapacity of the Vietnamese government to impose effective rule in Tongking provided ideal conditions for the realization of Liu Yung-fu's ambitions. The approach of French arms toward Tongking signaled disaster, however, and Liu resisted all French efforts to penetrate into the territory he considered to be his own. During the course of 1881, Liu had audaciously moved his forces south from their original habitat to the environs of Hanoi. There he had established cordial relations with Vietnamese governmental officials, and was soon cooperating with them in resisting the French.

Confronted by the Black Flag's challenge to French pretensions in Tongking, de Vilers was at a loss how to carry out his instructions to "restore the prestige of French authority" without recourse to military measures. In November 1881, he wrote to the French consul at Hanoi requesting advice on how he might "occupy Hanoi by surprise, and without having recourse to force." [13] The consul replied in early February 1882 proposing that the French contingent at Hanoi could parade, as they were wont to do, just outside the city walls. This unit could then, by a rapid movement to the left, burst through the city gate, cross the moat, "and our soldiers will be masters of the place without having fired a shot." [14]

This childish bit of duplicity was never put to a test, for de Vilers was becoming impatient. In late December 1881, he determined that "the fruit is ripe, the time has come to pick it," [15] and in mid-January 1882 had already issued to Commandant Henri Laurent Rivière of the French navy instructions to lead an expedition to Hanoi. There he was to reinforce the regular French garrison and expel the Black Flags from Tongking. [16]

[13] André Masson, *Hanoi pendant la périod héroique, 1873–1888* (Paris, 1929), p. 78.

[14] *Ibid.*

[15] Quoted in Evans, p. 444.

[16] HR, II, 345–347, de Vilers to Rivière, Jan. 17, 1882.

Rivière arrived at Hanoi on April 2 with somewhat over two hundred men. This was a small force. However, it alarmed the Vietnamese authorities, and, apprehending an attack, they began hurried preparations for the defense of the city. Fear fathered the fact. Rivière, assertedly afraid that the Vietnamese activities placed his command in jeopardy, bolstered his force to about six hundred men, and on April 25 he led the assault that marked the end of Vietnamese control in that city.[17]

Existing documents indicate that the occupation of Hanoi had not been ordered from Paris, nor even from Saigon, but was rather the escapade of a single naval officer acting in direct defiance of orders.

> You know, my dear Commandant, [read de Vilers' instructions to Rivière] the views of the government of the Republic, which wishes to avoid at all costs, four thousand leagues from France, a war of conquest that would involve the country in grave complications.
>
> It is politically, peacefully, and administratively that we must extend and consolidate our influence to Tongking and in Annam.[18]

In the face of growing Black Flag and Vietnamese defiance in Tongking, de Vilers' instructions were fatuous in the extreme, and a skeptical reader might wonder if they were not meant more for the historical record than as a guide for Rivière. However, Rivière himself subsequently wrote privately to a friend that "I went there like Fabius Cunctator, and I would not have crossed the Rubicon, like Caesar, if I had not been

---

[17] Masson, *Hanoi*, pp. 79–80; André Masson, ed., *Correspondance politique du Commandant Henri Rivière au Tonkin* (Paris and Hanoi, 1933), p. 61; Joseph Buttinger, *The Smaller Dragon: A Political History of Vietnam* (New York, 1958), p. 376; Hosea Ballou Morse, *The International Relations of the Chinese Empire* (London, 1918), II, 349–350; HR, II, 344–350; Georges Taboulet, *La Geste Française en Indochine* (Paris, 1955–56), II, 770.

[18] HR, II, 345–346, de Vilers to Rivière, Jan. 17, 1882.

absolutely forced." [19] It is probable, therefore, that the Hanoi expedition had been launched, unreasonably perhaps, with the hope that the "adventures of a military conquest" might be avoided. However, the general mood among the French was such that Rivière would not have tempered his actions with undue caution. Imperialist sentiments in France were approaching high tide in 1882. And, for his *fait accompli*, he was acclaimed a hero with hardly a voice raised in reproof.[20]

Chinese Reactions to the New French Advances. The activist policy of the French in Vietnam had scarcely been revived when the Chinese were alerted to the challenge. As early as August 1879, Chang Shu-sheng, the governor of Kwangsi, reported a rumor to Peking that the French were secretly transporting military equipment to Vietnam for the purpose of conquering key areas in Tongking.[1] And in January 1880, Tseng Chi-tse, Chinese minister to France, England, and later also to Russia, was instructed to inquire what French intentions in Vietnam were.[2] The French reply momentarily assuaged Chinese apprehensions. Nevertheless, the Tsungli Yamen received growing numbers of reports during 1880 that belied French professions.[3] In November 1880, therefore, the

[19] Masson, *Hanoi*, p. 79.

[20] Shao Hsün-cheng, pp. 66–67; Cho Huan-lai, *Les Origines du Conflit Franco-Chinois à propos du Tonkin jusqu'en 1883* (Paris, 1935), pp. 141–142; Albert Billot, *L'Affaire du Tonkin: histoire diplomatique de l'établissement de notre protectorat sur l'Annam et de notre conflit avec la Chine, 1882–1885* (Paris, 1888), p. 2; Taboulet, II, 770.

Not all Frenchmen were convinced by Rivière's account of the Vietnamese threat to his command at Hanoi. Henri Rochefort wrote that he considered it just one more invention by the promoters of the Tongking adventure to obtain popular ratification for an otherwise inexcusable action. (*Les Aventures de ma Vie* [Paris, 1898], IV, 313.)

[1] YNT, I, 124, dcmt. 74, Chang Shu-sheng to Tsungli Yamen, Aug. 24, 1879 (KH5/7/7).

[2] Demetrius C. Boulger, *The Life of Sir Halliday Macartney* (London, 1908), p. 358.

[3] For some of the earliest reports, see the press translations from the

Yamen again instructed Tseng to remonstrate with the Quai d'Orsay. The French foreign minister, Jules Barthélemy St. Hilaire, assured Tseng that French designs did not extend beyond Vietnam and were entirely pacific in intent. He allowed Tseng no room to doubt, however, that France intended to implement the treaty of 1874.[4]

St. Hilaire's declaration that the French were determined to implement the provisions of the treaty of 1874 still provoked no official response from Peking. But ominous reports from provincial officials regarding increased French activity in Vietnam continued to accumulate in the offices of the Tsungli Yamen during the summer and autumn of 1881. In July, Ho Ju-chang, minister to Japan, declared to the Yamen that "I hear that the French Foreign Ministry has declared to Tseng Chi-tse that it has no intention of seizing Vietnam. Yet, considering French actions, it seems there is cause for concern."[5] And several months later, the governor-general of Yunnan-Kweichow observed that the French were everywhere in Vietnam, building railroads, and spying on the Kwangtung borders. The situation was, he warned, "as precarious as piled eggs."[6]

By late 1881, the Tsungli Yamen recognized the necessity of framing some response to French encroachments, but it con-

---

T'ung-wen Kuan in YNT, I, 143, dcmt. 85, Feb. 14, 1880 (KH6/1/5); YNT, I, 144, dcmt. 86, Mar. 19, 1880 (KH6/2/9); and YNT, I, 145, dcmt. 88, Apr. 1, 1880 (KH6/2/22).

[4] This exchange between Tseng and St. Hilaire began in November 1880 when Tseng was in St. Petersberg in the midst of the Ili negotiations. Discussions continued when Tseng returned to Paris early the following year. (HR, II, 243, Tseng to St. Hilaire, Nov. 10, 1880; HR, II, 316–317, St. Hilaire to Tseng, Dec. 27, 1880; YNT, I, 149–152, dcmt. 92, Tseng to Tsungli Yamen, Mar. 18, 1881 [KH7/2/19].)

[5] YNT, I, 158, dcmt. 96, Ho to Tsungli Yamen, July 7, 1881 (KH7/6/12).

[6] Liu Ch'ang-yu, "Liu Wu-shen Kung i-shu," CFCC, I, 88–89, Nov. 8, 1881 (KH7/9/17). Other expressions of concern at this time are found in Liu K'un-i, IV, 1944–1945; and YNT, I, 158, dcmt. 97, Ting Jih-ch'ang to Tsungli Yamen, Aug. 6, 1881 (KH7/7/12).

fessed its inability to formulate a policy. Balefully it admitted that Vietnam was unable to stage a resistance, and "China also has very few means with which to deal with the French." [7] The machinery of Chinese policy-making therefore ground into motion when the Yamen in December 1881, and again in May 1882, solicited policy recommendations from seven high provincial officials and Tseng Chi-tse. [8]

Rapid communication was not a convenience extensively available to the Ch'ing government in the 1880's, however, and this practice of including remote officials in policy discussions made the process of decision-making extraordinarily cumbrous. For example, following the Yamen's December 1881 request for policy advice, a reply came from Nanking after only twenty-four days; but that from Kwangsi arrived after an interval of two months; from Yunnan after over three months; and Tseng Chi-tse's reply from Paris reached Peking five months and two days after the Yamen request. It is not surprising therefore that, as tension in Vietnam became greater, the throne relied increasingly upon officials closer to Peking for advice.

The Yamen had formulated no response to the French advances prior to Rivière's capture of Hanoi, for it conceived of the Vietnamese problem in terms that posed a dilemma: how could China maintain the defensive screen provided by Vietnam, while avoiding the responsibilities accruing to its status as suzerain of Vietnam? The Yamen's quandary is illustrated by the following excerpt from a memorial to the throne in mid-May 1882:

[7] CFCS, 2:2, dcmt. 31, addendum #1, Tsungli Yamen memorial, Dec. 6, 1881 (KH7/10/15).

[8] Because the Yamen was not organizationally superior to the governors and governors-general of the provinces, it was necessary for the Yamen to request in a memorial that the throne instruct these officials to give their advice. These officials would in turn send their replies to the throne.

If the French intend to occupy the whole of Vietnam, that state has no means to preserve itself. Regarding China's righteous concern for its dependencies, we should send troops to aid Vietnam, and use peaceful or warlike tactics as suits the situation. But, viewing the situation, the difficulty of settling on a satisfactory policy lies in the fact that *the strength of China is not yet adequate,* and Vietnam is weak and cannot sustain itself. Vietnam has long been divided into north and south. The southern part has already been lost, and the provinces of the northern part border on Yunnan, Kwangtung, and Kwangsi. If we wait until the French have entirely occupied the north before we inaugurate a plan of closing the passes for self-defense, then China's defenses will be drawn back and there will be no end to ensuing troubles. Nor will it be only France that rises up on all sides, nor only Vietnam which is placed in peril. This is not only a trouble that affects the borders, but one that affects the total situation.[9]

Despite the fears expressed in this document, Peking was wholly innocent of initiative. Indeed, the only defensive move thus far had been made by the governor of Kwangsi, Ch'ing-yü, who, acting on his own authority, dispatched a small body of troops into Tongking in August 1881 — the first positive action that a representative of the Chinese government had taken in anticipation of the French advance.[10] The throne subsequently lauded Ch'ing-yü for his "complete and satisfactory" defensive preparations.[11] However, these had been troop movements on a minuscule scale, and represented at best a tactical move. Prior to Rivière's capture of Hanoi, Peking had

[9] CFCS, 2:17, dcmt. 46, Tsungli Yamen memorial, May 12, 1882 (KH8/3/25). Italics added.

[10] CFCS, 2:7a-b, dcmt. 36, Ch'ing-yü memorial, Dec. 30, 1881 (KH7/11/10). Ch'ing-yü's forces actually reinforced imperial forces already in the Tongking provinces of Lang-Son and Cao-Bang, that had not been evacuated after the suppression of Li Yang-ts'ai in 1878. (CFCS, 2:9, dcmt. 38, Chang Shu-sheng memorial, Feb. 14, 1882 [KH7/12/26].)

[11] CFCS, 2:8b, dcmt. 37, decree to Ch'ing-yü, Feb. 1, 1882 (KH7/12/13). Ch'ing-yü informed the throne of this move only in response to the Yamen's request for advice in December 1881.

failed utterly to produce anything that could be dignified with the name "policy."

Rivière's assault stung the Chinese to action, and from this time China took the road that led directly to war. One can now only imagine the excitement that was prompted in Peking by news of the fall of Hanoi. During the previous two decades, the Chinese had become accustomed to the French occupation of Cochin China. But with the single exception of an earlier military adventure that had accomplished a temporary occupation of Hanoi (November 1873–March 1874), the military and political influence of France in northern Vietnam had remained limited and insignificant. Now the French had again occupied this commercial center of the north, and placed their military in a controlling position at the mouth of a direct, navigable water route to the Yunnan border.

Acting upon recommendations that had arrived from provincial officials, Peking quickly ordered the Cantonese "navy" to sail into Vietnamese waters. This force of some twenty vessels, only six of which remotely deserved the appellation "warships," had actually been assembled to combat pirates and smugglers in provincial waters. Peking recognized that this insignificant naval force would be incapable of resisting the French on the open sea. It was hoped, however, that exploratory cruises near the Vietnamese coast might "manifest the might" of the empire.[12]

Two weeks later, on June 17, 1882, again in response to a memorial from a provincial official, troops from Yunnan province were ordered to cross the border into Tongking.[13] There

[12] CFCS, 2:27b–28, dcmt. 52, decree to Chang Shu-sheng, May 30, 1882 (KH8/4/14); CFCS, 2:21b–22, dcmt. 49, Chang Shu-sheng memorial, Apr. 28, 1882 (KH8/3/11); Tseng Kuo-ch'üan, "Tseng Chung-hsiang Kung ch'üan-chi" (The complete writings of Tseng Kuo-ch'üan), CFCC, IV, 272, Tseng memorial, Sept. 27, 1882 (KH8/8/16).

[13] CFCS, 3:4a-b, dcmt. 55, decree to Liu Ch'ang-yu, June 17, 1882 (KH8/5/2).

they were to coordinate defensive measures with the Kwangsi forces that had been infiltrating the borders since August 1881.

It is noteworthy that at no time did the memorialists inquire into the legal aspects of exporting troops to Tongking. Not until the following year did the Vietnamese request assistance from China,[14] and from the Western point of view, therefore, this would clearly constitute a violation of international law. This technicality did not deter Peking, for, according to the traditional concept of the empire-tributary relationship, there were no physical boundaries beyond which imperial control could not theoretically be exercised.[15] Moreover, it was already a long-established tradition that the emperor might chastise unruly tribes in a tributary state as a means of preserving order there. The Chinese did not, therefore, anticipate that the dispatch of troops into Tongking might have international legal implications. As one official declared, "formerly, Kwangtung armies frequently were stationed beyond the frontier, so it seems [that the dispatch of troops there now] will not suddenly give cause for war." [16]

In the meantime, the Chinese government protested furiously to Paris against French aggression in Tongking. Tseng Chi-tse asserted, again and again, that (1) Vietnam was a Chinese dependency, and (2) China had never recognized, and could never recognize, the 1874 treaty between France and Vietnam. At one point, in fact, Tseng pressed these claims with such vigor that Paris notified the Chinese government,

[14] CFCS, 3:366-37b, dcmt. 88, May 30, 1883 (KH9/4/24).

[15] Nelson, pp. 102–103.

[16] CFCS, 2:5b, dcmt. 34, Liu K'un-i memorial, Dec. 22, 1881 (KH7/11/2). Foreigners accustomed to clearly delineated formulae of states' sovereignties were mystified by Chinese intervention in the affairs of another state. In a situation similar to the Vietnamese affair, China intervened in Seoul after the attempted revolution of the Taewongun in 1882. The cloudy relationship that united China to the ostensibly independent, but still dependent, Korea left Western observers puzzled. (Nelson, pp. 102–103.)

through its representative in Peking, that if Tseng did not change his insolent attitude he would no longer be welcome in Paris.[17]

The French, for their part, were as resolute as Tseng in their insistence that China had no legal basis for intervention in what they declared to be a matter solely between France and Vietnam. From their point of view, the treaty of 1874 had given legal expression to Vietnam's independence from all foreign powers. There existed, then, antipodal contentions that were based upon incompatible views of interstate relations. Cho Huan-lai summed up the nature of this conflict very neatly when he wrote that China believed its sovereignty over Vietnam was attested "by an incontestable series of historical facts," while the French position "had been stipulated not less formally by the clauses of a solemn treaty." [18]

By October 1882, France despaired of negotiating a solution to this difference stemming from irreconcilable principles. It would, instead, first consolidate its protectorate in Vietnam by coercing Tu-Duc to conclude a new treaty. This accomplished, France would again talk with the Chinese — and imperturbably listen to the howls of protest.[19]

The Bourée Negotiations. French plans to consolidate their position in Vietnam without further discussions with the Chinese were fated to go awry. The French minister to China, Frédéric Albert Bourée, was a man most independent of spirit and undiplomatic of mien, and the relatively slow communications between Paris and North China allowed him a broad area for the exercise of personal initiative.[1]

[17] Shao Hsün-cheng, p. 67.
[18] Cho Huan-lai, p. 147.
[19] Shao Hsün-cheng, p. 70; Evans, p. 457.
[1] Telegraph now connected Shanghai with Paris, but lengthy correspondence was still sent by ship through the Suez Canal, a route that required approximately six weeks.

Bourée viewed the Chinese response to the developments in Vietnam with mounting apprehension, and he repeatedly inquired of the Tsungli Yamen whether or not there was any truth to reports of Chinese war preparations that had been printed in the Shanghai newspapers. The Yamen insisted that such reports were unfounded rumors. On October 17, 1882, however, Bourée informed the Yamen that he had received indisputable evidence from Saigon that Chinese imperial forces had advanced into Vietnamese territory and had occupied a third of the territory of Tongking.[2] The Yamen admitted (though it subsequently denied) the presence of Chinese troops in Tongking, but added that their mission was solely to suppress bandits that were ravaging the area. There were no plans to advance these forces farther into Tongking, the Yamen declared, but neither would it be possible to recall them to the Chinese frontier.[3] This is where matters stood in early November 1882.

By this time, Bourée had determined that he would spend the winter in Shanghai, thinking that he would be in a better position to observe and influence events there than in Peking, which would soon be icebound.[4] Before his departure, he made another call upon the Tsungli Yamen, where it was suggested that the dispute over Vietnam might be resolved by creating a buffer zone in northern Tongking, which would be placed under a Chinese protectorate. No agreement was concluded during the visit, but the Yamen members thought that Bourée gave evidence of a new French willingness to seek a peaceful settlement of the controversy. Because Bourée would be passing through Tientsin enroute to Shanghai, the Yamen

[2] YNT, I, 500, dcmt. 241, Bourée to Tsungli Yamen, Oct. 17, 1882 (KH8/9/6).

[3] CFCS, 3:24–25, dcmt. 76, Tsungli Yamen memorial, Jan. 18, 1883 (KH8/12/10).

[4] Evans, p. 459.

informed Li Hung-chang of the conversation, and suggested to Li that he pursue the subject with Bourée there.[5]

Bourée arrived at Tientsin on November 13,[6] but he and Li did not meet for nearly two weeks. During the interim Bourée studied the extent of Chinese military preparations, and what he discovered increased his perturbation. Chinese forces, hardened by experience in Korea, and well-equipped with modern artillery, had been sent to Tongking; arsenals in Tientsin and elsewhere in the empire were producing large quantities of arms and ammunition. Most appalling was the report that Chinese forces had advanced all the way to the vicinity of Hanoi. Bourée believed that war had become virtually inevitable, and he was therefore in a state of high agitation when he finally met with Li Hung-chang on November 26. On the basis of an extended conversation with the governor-general, Bourée drafted a convention consisting of three articles that were to serve as the basis of later and more definitive negotiations.[7] These appeared acceptable to Li, and on November 28 he forwarded the convention to the Tsungli Yamen for approval.

The Bourée convention is noteworthy because, pressured

[5] CFCS, 3:24–25, dcmt. 76, Tsungli Yamen memorial, Jan. 18, 1883 (KH8/12/10); Shao Hsün-cheng, p. 71. Ssu-ming Meng (p. 54) was mistaken when he asserted that Li acted "under detailed instructions from the Tsungli Yamen" in his discussion with Bourée. I have used the same evidence cited by Meng (CFCS, dcmt. 76), which indicates that the Yamen merely sent to Li documents that would be pertinent to his forthcoming talks with Bourée. His instructions were in no sense "detailed." It is true, however, that Li could not independently make final decisions. That function was reserved for Peking.

[6] Evans, p. 460.

[7] Bourée later asserted that Li, much more than he, was the author of the articles. (HR, II, 371–372.) Li declared that Bourée wrote a draft of the articles, and that, on November 27, 1882, Li's assistant and translator, Ma Chien-chung, met with Bourée and "seven or eight" changes were made before the draft was acceptable. (ISHK, CFCC, IV, 32, Nov. 28, 1882 [KH8/10/18].)

by the imminence of war, Bourée and Li cut through the theoretical smog that had settled over the Sino-French discussions for almost three years. In the first of the three articles, it was agreed that Chinese troops would be withdrawn from their advanced positions within Tongking, in return for which the French would declare to the Tsungli Yamen that they had no intention of undertaking the conquest of Vietnam nor of diminishing Vietnamese sovereignty. The second article provided that France would be permitted to establish marketing facilities at Lao-Kay, a town on the upper reaches of the Red River, just south of Yunnan Province. There, also, China was to erect a customs house, and trade was to be conducted in accordance with regulations obtaining in the open ports on the coast. The final clause stipulated that a buffer zone would be constituted in the area between the Red River on the south, and the Chinese border on the north. The northern portion of this zone would be placed under a Chinese protectorate, while France would assume the same responsibilities in the southern sector.[8]

Each of these clauses was a practical solution to differences that had been drawing the two countries toward war. Questions of principle had been set aside. No mention had been made in the agreement either of the French protectorate over the greater part of Vietnam, or of Vietnam's tributary relation to China (although Li Hung-chang declared privately to the Yamen that Vietnam's dependency upon the empire, while "not stated, is implied").[9]

The succeeding month was a trial of patience for the French negotiator. Bourée anticipated that the Yamen would reply immediately, but there was no answer forthcoming. Days elapsed. Bourée made daily inquiries of Li's secretary to learn

[8] The Chinese text of the agreement is in CFCS, 3:25a-b, dcmt. 76, addendum #1. See also HR, II, 361–362.

[9] ISHK, CFCC, IV, 31, Nov. 28, 1882 (KH8/10/18).

if any word had yet been received from the Yamen.[10] He attributed the delay partially to the frigid weather that made communication with the capital slower than in more clement weather. However, he also noted that the first article of the agreement — pertaining to withdrawal of the imperial troops — was encountering "a stubborn resistance," [11] and that mounted couriers were going "at full speed from one town to the other in order to convey explanations, overcome the resistance of one or the other, and refute the objections deriving from fanaticism or from fear." [12]

Five days later, on December 2, Li informed Bourée that the Yamen still insisted that information regarding Chinese troops in the neighborhood of Hanoi was untrue. The troops would certainly not have assumed advanced positions without direct orders from the throne, declared the Yamen, and "there has not been a decree to this effect." [13] The lines were thus drawn: Bourée demanded the withdrawal of forces, the existence of which the Yamen stoutly denied. Between these contentions, there would seem to have been no reconciliation. However, the Yamen proposed a solution that pleased everyone: each army would withdraw "several miles" (*jo-kan li*) from their *present* positions.[14] Bourée was thus appeased, and the embarrassing probability that Peking did not know precisely where the Chinese troops in Tongking were was not admitted.

The Tsungli Yamen had not yet pronounced itself formally, however, and Bourée continued to be, as Li noted, "pro-

[10] *Ibid.*, p. 33, Dec. 5, 1882 (KH8/10/25).

[11] *Documents diplomatiques. Affaires du Tonkin, Première Partie, 1874–Décembre 1882* (Paris, 1883), p. 318, dcmt. 140, Bourée to Duclerc, Dec. 5, 1882.

[12] *Documents diplomatiques. Affaires du Tonkin, Deuxième Partie, Décembre 1882–1883* (Paris, 1883), p. 32, dcmt. 158, Bourée to Duclerc, Dec. 20, 1882.

[13] *Ibid.*, p. 39, dcmt. 158, annex II, Li-Bourée conversation, Dec. 2, 1882.

[14] ISHK, CFCC, IV, 32–33, Dec. 5, 1882 (KH8/10/25).

digiously agitated." [15] Finally, on December 5, Li informed the French negotiator that the Yamen believed a settlement was now possible. The Yamen proposed that the two nations initiate preparations for definitive negotiations on the basis of the three articles.[16]

At this point, neither government had committed itself to anything definite except that the armies were to withdraw from positions that had remained unspecified, and that preparations would be commenced for the subsequent talks. Bourée nevertheless left Tientsin for the warmer climes of Shanghai on December 9 thinking that now "the danger [of war] is averted." [17] And, despite some initial misgivings,[18] he soon became confident that the Tsungli Yamen would honor the agreement he had concluded with Li.

He was astonished, therefore, that the Yamen on December 13 drew up a number of new proposals that were "absolutely incompatible" with the previous arrangement. The most interesting of the Yamen's new proposals were that a repre-

---

[15] *Ibid.*, p. 33.

[16] *Documents diplomatiques. Affaires du Tonkin, Deuxième Partie*, p. 50, dcmt. 158, annex VII, Ma Chien-chung to Bourée, Dec. 5, 1882.

[17] *Documents diplomatiques. Affaires du Tonkin, Première Partie*, p. 318, dcmt. 140, Dec. 5, 1882; ISHK, CFCC, IV, 35, Dec. 15, 1882 (KH8/11/6).

[18] Bourée and the Tsungli Yamen were each distrustful of the other. Li had to use his greatest powers of persuasion before the Yamen would believe that, after the imperial forces withdrew, the French would not simply advance their troops into the area thus evacuated. (ISHK, CFCC, IV, 35–36, Dec. 15, 1882 [KH8/11/6].) Bourée, similarly, had not been satisfied that the Chinese evacuation of "several miles" would be accomplished, despite the Yamen's formal pronouncement, until he obtained a personal, written guarantee of that evacuation from Li Hung-chang. (ISHK, CFCC, IV, 33, Dec. 5, 1882 [KH8/10/25]; *Documents diplomatiques. Affaires du Tonkin, Deuxième Partie*, p. 44, dcmt. 158, annex IV, Bourée to Li, Dec. 3, 1882.) There had been, therefore, some further discussion regarding the terms of the agreement after Bourée reached Shanghai, where Li was represented by Ma Chien-chung. Several minor alterations were consequently made in the original agreement. (*Documents diplomatiques. Affaires du Tonkin, Deuxième Partie*, p. 52, dcmt. 160, Bourée to Duclerc, Dec. 27, 1882.)

sentative of Vietnam must participate in the forthcoming Sino-French negotiations, and that an agreement would not be considered definitive until it had received the sanction of the court at Hué.[19] Bourée had once rejected this proposal while he was still in Peking;[20] furthermore, the Tsungli Yamen had been, and presumably still was, indifferent to Hué's reaction to any agreement that might be made. It must be assumed, therefore, that the Yamen members had misgivings about the settlement as proposed in the three articles, and that they hoped in this manner to avert the loss of Vietnam to French control.

Bourée was at first nonplused by the new development, and he thought that his efforts of the previous two months had been in vain. At Ma Chien-chung's suggestion, however, he protested against the new conditions to Li Hung-chang, and, with that personage's intervention, the Yamen altered the objectionable terms to Bourée's satisfaction.[21] On December 29, 1882, again feeling assured that the recalcitrants in Peking would not wreck his work, he dispatched a telegram to the Quai d'Orsay relating the general features of the convention.[22]

Bourée's confidence was again misplaced. Thus far, the Chinese government had been represented only by the Tsungli Yamen and by Li Hung-chang. The center of authority, the throne, had not yet offered an opinion on the convention nor had it even been formally notified of the negotiations. In fact, Li Hung-chang waited until Paris declared its adherence to the principles of the settlement, on January 9, 1883, before he

[19] *Documents diplomatiques. Affaires du Tonkin, Deuxième Partie,* p. 59, dcmt. 162, Bourée to Duclerc, Jan. 8, 1883; YNT, I, 559, Tsungli Yamen to Bourée, Dec. 13, 1882 (KH8/11/4).

[20] Evans, p. 459.

[21] *Documents diplomatiques. Affaires du Tonkin, Deuxième Partie,* p. 60, dcmt. 162, Bourée to Duclerc, Jan. 8, 1883; ISHK, CFCC, IV, 37, Dec. 26, 1882 (KH8/11/17).

[22] HR, II, 361, Bourée to Foreign Ministry, Dec. 29, 1882.

suggested that the Yamen submit the proposed settlement for imperial consideration.[23] It is impossible to determine what was transpiring in the Tsungli Yamen at this time. In any case, the Yamen waited until January 18, nine days after receiving Li's suggestion, before memorializing the throne about the Bourée pourparlers and requesting that various high provincial officials memorialize their views regarding the proposed settlement.[24]

In view of the provincial officials' replies, it is exceedingly doubtful that the throne would have sanctioned the Li-Bourée agreement. Some objected that the proposed buffer zone was too narrow; others protested that the settlement would necessitate the removal of Liu Yung-fu's Black Flags from Tongking, thereby eliminating one of the principal obstacles to French encroachments. And a majority of the memorialists were reluctant to open the interior provinces of the empire to trade with a Western power.[25] There were calmer voices, like that of Tseng Chi-tse, who conceded (grudgingly, it is true) that "considering our present strength, it seems we can only manage it in this way."[26]

Whether or not the throne would have sanctioned the Bourée convention is now a strictly academic question, for French politics were too unstable to permit negotiations to be protracted as long as those between Li and Bourée. As a consequence, in March 1883 their diplomatic edifice came

[23] ISHK, CFCC, IV, 38, Li to Tsungli Yamen, Jan. 9, 1883 (KH8/12/1).

[24] CFCS, 3:24–25b, dcmt. 76, Tsungli Yamen memorial, Jan. 18, 1883 (KH8/12/10). A decree of the same date authorized the Yamen request. (YNT, I, 590, dcmt. 288, decree, Jan. 18, 1883 [KH8/12/10].)

[25] CFCS, 3:27–28, dcmt. 79, Ts'en Yü-ying memorial, Feb. 16, 1883 (KH9/1/9); CFCS, 3:29–30b, dcmt. 82, Ni Wen-wei memorial, Feb. 23, 1883 (KH9/1/16); Shao Hsün-cheng, p. 73.

[26] YNT, II, 615, dcmt. 302, Tseng to Tsungli Yamen, Feb. 9, 1883 (KH9/1/2). Tseng's uncle, Tseng Kuo-ch'üan, also urged division of the Vietnamese protectorate and granting of trade in order to avoid hostilities. (YNT, II, 728, dcmt. 347, Tseng Kuo-ch'üan to Tsungli Yamen, Apr. 4, 1883 [KH9/2/27].)

crashing down. The previous month, the ministry of Premier Charles de Freycinet had fallen, and was replaced by the second ministry of Jules Ferry — who was to be awarded the epithet of "le tonkinois" in recognition of his efforts to establish a French colony in Vietnam. Several days later, on March 5, Bourée was notified that the results of his negotiations had been disavowed by the new government, and that his term as minister was at an end.[27]

This denouement left Bourée surprised and piqued. It was true, as he recognized, that his government had determined to exclude the Chinese from further discussions regarding Vietnam until it could confront Peking with a *fait accompli*. Yet he had averted a war, and furthermore had obtained for France all the concrete concessions that it had desired, with the exception of the narrow, impoverished area that would have been placed under a Chinese protectorate. Moreover, the Freycinet ministry had also judged the terms of the agreement too favorable to be refused. Why, then, had the Ferry ministry decided to scrap the agreement?

By March 1883, Paris discerned new aspects of Bourée's accomplishment that had not initially been revealed to it. The Freycinet ministry had approved Bourée's agreement with Li on the basis of his telegram of December 29, which stated only that Yunnan would be opened to French commerce and that the Chinese would recognize the French protectorate over Vietnam with the exception of the zone along the Chinese border.[28] It was only in the period from January 23 to February 19, 1883 that Bourée's detailed explications, "coup sur coup," arrived at the Quai d'Orsay. And to the vexation of

[27] HR, II, 364.

[28] *Documents diplomatiques. Affaires du Tonkin, Deuxième Partie*, p. 1, dcmt. 145, Bourée to Duclerc, Dec. 29, 1882. Evans, pp. 462–464, and Billot, pp. 22–24, contain important insights to the struggle within the Freycinet ministry regarding Bourée's agreement. When Charles Duclerc was dismissed as the foreign minister at the end of January, Bourée lost his chief supporter.

the new ministry, these explications made it clear that Bourée's telegram had concealed as much as it had revealed. Bourée had in fact conceded to the Chinese that France would not attempt to conquer the whole of Tongking. Furthermore, and this was more crucial, he had agreed that French intervention would not alter the existing relationship between China and its tributary. In other words, Bourée had admitted China's right to intervene in Vietnamese affairs. This was, in the opinion of the Foreign Ministry, "the abandonment, without compensation, of our traditional policy." [29]

The flaws that Paris discerned in the Bourée agreement were not flaws when viewed through Bourée's eyes. It may be granted that there existed an inherent incompatibility between the French demands for complete and sole rights to the Vietnamese protectorate and the Chinese claims to Vietnamese sovereignty. However, an agreement that augured peace had been possible because, as Li observed to Bourée, they had approached their pourparlers "upon the terrain of things practical, and questions of principle were carefully set aside." [30] Until war was to inform the two governments with a more poignant desire for an end of the dispute, this was the only possible basis for a settlement of the Vietnamese problem. The new ministers in Paris had not taken this practical view of the situation. They had reasserted the old principles, and Bourée fell into disgrace as a result.

Consequences of the Collapse of the Negotiations. Until the collapse of the Li-Bourée pourparlers, few officials who were not directly involved in the policy process had expressed interest in the controversy over Vietnam. However, the French rejection of the Bourée convention and two subsequent incidents made Sino-French relations the foremost source of con-

[29] Billot, pp. 19–27.
[30] HR, II, 371, Bourée to Foreign Ministry, Mar. 30, 1883.

cern among literati and officials for the next two and one half years.

The sudden turn of events had put Bourée into a state of dudgeon that caused him to make a statement most unorthodox for a diplomat. Bourée had been permitted by his government to remain in China until his successor arrived. On March 30, he returned to Tientsin, and on the same day met with Li Hung-chang. In the ensuing conversation, Bourée averred that their agreement had been rejected by Paris because the French government was now at the mercy of financial speculators who held interests in the Société des Mines de Tonquin. When the Black Flags had obstructed the Société's efforts to exploit the resources of Tongking, the value of its stocks declined. The present development was, asserted Bourée, entirely due to these speculators who, having no concern for the friendly relations between China and France, had pressured the government to adopt a more forceful policy in Tongking in order to reestablish the value of their investments.[1]

Bourée then urged upon Li a definite course of action for China. China should reveal clearly its involvement in Vietnamese affairs by a demonstration of force and by ordering Tseng Chi-tse to register strenuous protests with the French government. Because the French people had no wish to become engaged in hostilities, peace would result. But if China continued its covert assistance to Vietnam and the Black

---

[1] The transcript of Li's conversation with Bourée is in YNT, II, 722–727, dcmt. 345, Chang Shu-sheng to Tsungli Yamen, Mar. 31, 1883 (KH9/2/23). See also YNT, II, 754, dcmt. 368, Lo Feng-lu to Tsungli Yamen, Apr. 21, 1883 (KH9/3/15). Bourée understandably did not disclose these declarations in his report to Paris of his conversation. (*Documents diplomatiques. Affaires du Tonkin, Deuxième Partie*, pp. 109–111, dcmt. 191, Mar. 30, 1883.) Bourée made similar charges elsewhere. (See Kiernan, p. 92.) Rochefort, IV, 313, was of the same opinion as Bourée, but T. F. Power, Jr., contends that "Economic factors . . . were hardly ever responsible for the initiation of French colonial policy." (*Jules Ferry and the Renaissance of French Imperialism* [Morningside Heights, New York, 1944], p. 197.)

Flags, the French citizenry would remain unaware of Chinese prerogatives in Vietnam, both governments would continue to reinforce their military establishments in the south, and war would be the final outcome.

The precise effect of the Bourée statement cannot, of course, be measured. It is noteworthy, however, that by coincidence or not the Chinese government did adopt a policy that followed closely the line of action proposed by the French diplomat. Tseng Chi-tse was instructed to remonstrate with the Ferry ministry, and Chinese troops were ordered to move to more advanced positions within Tongking. Furthermore, Bourée's assertion, that the French government was being manipulated by a small body of financiers and did not truly represent the will of the people, was to reappear in officials' memorials throughout the remainder of the controversy.

One other incident had a palpable effect upon Chinese attitudes. Shortly after Peking learned that Paris had rejected the settlement, it was also apprised of the French assault on and capture of Nam-Dinh, a key town on the river approaches to Hanoi. The French action had been taken because Vietnamese resistance units had been threatening French communications between Hanoi and the sea.[2] To the Chinese, however, it looked as though the French had engaged in the Bourée pourparlers only to cause the Chinese to relax their vigilance and to gain time to send reinforcements to Vietnam. That accomplished, they were now resuming the offensive.[3]

The net result, then, of the Li-Bourée talks had been to increase government resistance to the French encroachments, and to instill among the officials a profound distrust of all future French offers of peace negotiations. The rejection of the Bourée agreement seemed to offer conclusive evidence that

[2] HR, II, 374, Challemel-Lacour to Bourée, Apr. 11, 1883.
[3] YNT, II, 833, dcmt. 411, Ts'en Yü-ying to Tsungli Yamen, May 29, 1883 (KH9/4/23); Chang P'ei-lun, "Chien-yü chi," CFCC, IV, 348, Chang memorial, May 2, 1884 (KH10/4/8).

the French did not hold peaceful intentions, and were determined to conquer the whole of Vietnam. The Bourée episode was consequently a decisive turning point in Chinese attitudes. From then until 1885, the chorus of protests against French encroachments was loud and relentless.

III

THE TRICOU NEGOTIATIONS

Following the French rejection of the Bourée Convention, China was placed in a state of emergency. During the spring, 1883, imperial armies were transferred to the south; arsenals near Tientsin were operating long hours overtime, working even on holidays. To a German in the employ of the Chinese army, it appeared that "war was now an inevitable fact." [1] Even Li Hung-chang, who during the Sino-French controversy generally wished to avoid hostilities in Vietnam, shared this fear, and urged full military preparedness in Tongking. "The spring waters of the Red River have now risen," he warned, "and the French forces will probably grasp the opportunity to advance deeply" into the interior.[2]

The sense of crisis that now pervaded the Chinese government thrust policy formation into the public domain. Literati opinion quickly coalesced and became an awesome political force. The political power of the throne and of Li Hung-chang were now also placed in the balance for the first time since the Vietnamese affair erupted. The events of May and June 1883 provide our first opportunity to observe how these three

---

[1] Reports by Bourée, written on May 16, 17, and 18. (HR, II, 375–377.) Bourée conceivably overestimated the gravity of the situation. (See HR, II, 381; Billot, p. 43.) It is indubitable, however, that China was now actively making preparations for war.

[2] ISHK, CFCC, IV, 42, Li to Tsungli Yamen, Mar. 8, 1883 (KH9/1/29).

forces — *ch'ing-i,* the throne, and Li Hung-chang — interacted in the "making" of Chinese foreign policy.

Preparations for War. For a month after learning of Peking's disavowal of Bourée's agreement, the Chinese government maintained a strict silence on the diplomatic level. Not until April 2, 1883 did it instruct Tseng Chi-tse to inquire why Bourée had been recalled and if there was any foundation for reports that the French had been reinforcing the troops in Vietnam.[1] Paris replied again that it held no aggressive designs against the Chinese empire, and that it was intent only to "consolidate the situation authorized by our treaty of 1874."[2] Such asseverations did not placate the Chinese. Reports of re-newed French aggression and of fresh enemy reinforcements continued to arrive in Peking, and the full import of the French challenge to imperial pretensions in Vietnam seems now to have been realized. "The urgency of preparations at this time," wrote the Tsungli Yamen on April 14, "cannot be compared with that during the previous, uncritical situation."[3]

Before the Bourée episode, the Tsungli Yamen had refrained from offering policy recommendations and merely initiated the policy discussions by the provincial officials. The pressure of events now impelled the Yamen to shoulder a degree of responsibility, and it finally proposed a course of action to the throne.[4] Acting upon the Yamen's memorial, the throne immediately ordered the Yunnan and Kwangsi armies that had already occupied positions in Tongking to advance still farther. At the same time, the ships of the Cantonese navy, which had sailed as far south as Hainan, were instructed to commence their incursions upon the seas near Vietnam. These maneuvers

[1] HR, II, 373, Peking to Tseng, Apr. 2, 1883.
[2] HR, II, 374, Foreign Ministry to Bourée, Apr. 11, 1883.
[3] CFCS, 3:37b, dcmt. 89, Tsungli Yamen memorial, Apr. 14, 1883 (KH9/3/8).
[4] *Ibid.,* pp. 37b–38.

71

were in large part bluff, for the commanders were instructed that they should not start hostilities.[5]

An edict of May 1 provides further evidence that Peking was diverting the policy-formation process from routine channels. Available documents contain no relevant memorials antecedent to the May 1 edict; it must therefore be presumed that the throne, or its advisors in the Grand Council, were now taking an unaccustomed initiative, and were imparting a more positive direction to imperial policy.

> We hear [read the edict] that the French in Vietnam are now even more on the rampage. Vietnam is in an enfeebled condition, encroachments upon it are without end, and it can hardly preserve itself. That state is one of our dependencies, and we cannot but protect it. Also, the territory of Yunnan, Kwangtung and Kwangsi border on it, and if the screens of defense are drawn back, how can we bear to speak of the future troubles.[6]

The edict then ordered that a high official, one "prestigious and with a thorough comprehension of the situation," one who would "restore the prestige of the military," was needed to command the armies of Yunnan, Kwangtung, and Kwangsi. That official was Li Hung-chang, who was ordered to proceed "with haste" to Kwangtung. "Do not avoid warfare; this is a clear lesson of antiquity," he was reminded.[7] The throne had finally determined to take forceful countermeasures against French encroachments.

In Paris at this same time, one would have obtained the impression of a similar determination on the part of the French

---

[5] CFCS, 3:38b, dcmt. 90, decree, Apr. 14, 1883 (KH9/3/8). That the throne's policy at this time was bluff, and nothing more, is substantiated in PLHK, CFCC, IV, 7, Li Hung-chang to Chang Chih-tung, June 9, 1883 (KH9/5/5).

[6] CFCS, 3:40, dcmt. 94, decree to Li, May 1, 1883 (KH9/3/25).

[7] Ibid., p. 40b.

to settle the Vietnamese issue through a contest of arms. On April 26, the French government requested a large credit designed to enable the army to consolidate French hegemony in Tongking. The credit was approved by the Chamber during the next month by a vote of 351 to 48; a vote indicating that there was considerable support, at the moment, for the enterprise in Vietnam.[8]

French popular sentiment was given a fillip by an incident that occurred in Tongking. Captain Rivière, who had become a national hero after his occupation of Hanoi, was felled in a skirmish with the Black Flags on May 19, 1883. And, to make matters worse, it was reported in Paris that Rivière had been vilely beheaded.[9] The French public let out a cry for revenge. By mid-May 1883, both nations had taken long strides in the direction of war.

Li Hung-chang Avoids the Southern Command. Some officials in both camps were, however, dragging their feet. The Quai d'Orsay still hoped to attain its aims in Vietnam without provoking a war with the Chinese empire, and was solicitous that Peking realize that the rejection of the Bourée agreement "does not imply any hostile intentions." [1]

In China, Li Hung-chang, whose presence in Tongking was expected to transform the fighting quality of the imperial armies, was as anxious as the Quai d'Orsay to avoid a fight. After receiving the decree of May 1 ordering him to assume command of the military in the south, Li indited a memorial in which he desperately advanced reasons against his recent appointment. Tongking is impoverished, he argued, and the

[8] HR, II, 379; Buttinger, p. 377.
[9] HR, II, 379.
[1] HR, II, 364, Foreign Ministry to Bourée, Mar. 5, 1883. See also pp. 374 and 394.

French will not be willing to brave the dangers of malaria and the difficulties of terrain to take such a worthless piece of territory. As soon as the French depart from the water routes, they are virtually helpless. Our present forces in the south are hence adequate to maintain the land defenses. Our navy is weak, we cannot prevent French occupation of areas where the French navy can maneuver. Besides, the French do not intend to occupy the whole of Vietnam, but seek only to force Vietnam to conclude a new treaty with France; China should not interfere, because Vietnam failed to ask China's permission to sign the 1874 treaty.

Li added practical obstacles to those of principle and those of principle to the practical as he squirmed to shed the new command. A unified command of the forces of Yunnan, Kwangtung, and Kwangsi is not feasible, he continued, due to the difficulties of liaison. My *Huai* armies, composed of men from the north, will be struck down by attacks of fever if stationed in the south. And if my troops go to the south, the French will attack in the north. Should I go to the south without my troops, my own reputation and that of the nation will suffer as a consequence.[2]

These are but a portion of the difficulties Li foresaw. The vaunted warrior was in a most unmartial frame of mind.

Li Hung-chang's basic opposition to policies that might lead to war with France has already been noted. His attitude as expressed in this memorial is further explicable if we realize that nomination to the post in the south actually constituted a direct threat to his political prosperity. If he were, in effect, rusticated to the south, he would be removed from his regional base and effectively deprived of the diplomatic and military means of exerting political leverage on Peking. Furthermore, he was probably convinced, as he repeatedly asserted in his communications to the capital, that China could not defeat

[2] CFCS, 4:3–4b, dcmt. 102, May 7, 1883 (KH9/4/1).

74

France in a prolonged conflict. If he were to command the imperial forces, defeat could mean the end of his career, exile, or even death. A British diplomat remarked at the time, and I think accurately, that Li "regarded the appointment as a plot of his enemies to ruin him." [3] This was, therefore, a critical point in Li's career, and his manifold objections to the imperial decree reflect the importance of the moment.

Li Hung-chang in mid-May 1883 had already departed for Kwangtung. Still, the throne could not disregard the objections of a subordinate as powerful as the governor-general of Chihli. In consequence, Li was instructed to proceed no farther than Shanghai — the throne justifying the new instructions with the feeble assertion that circumstances had changed, and that a reassessment of the situation need be made.[4] The compromise apparently saved the "faces" of both the throne and Li Hung-chang.

This incident offers the first example during the Sino-French controversy of the delicate power balance that characterized the relationship between these two forces in the government. In this instance, the throne had stopped short of aggrieving the capable and useful Li. The Li-Tricou negotiations that ensued reveal, however, that there was another side to the coin and that the throne was not always so solicitous of the governor-general's concerns.

[3] Kiernan, p. 93. In a private letter to Chang Chih-tung at this time, Li expressed other reasons why he had avoided the appointment: "I am incomparably weak and tired. I have repeatedly encountered misfortunes. My will and interest have declined so that I am of no aid to the administration of a militant nation. Recently, I returned [to my home in Anhwei] and planned to continue my leave there as a pretext to conceal my incapacity and redeem my errors. And then, because of the Vietnamese difficulties, I repeatedly received orders from the court pressing me to assume my duties. I could not rightly refuse." (PLHK, CFCC, IV, 6, June 9, 1883 [KH9/5/5].) I doubt that much weight need be given to this demeaning statement. It sounds like an inept and ritualistic attempt by Li to win the sympathy of Chang, and thereby, perhaps, decrease the opposition of the Ch'ing-liu.

[4] CFCS, 4:4b–5, dcmt. 103, decree, May 13, 1883 (KH9/4/7).

The Tricou Negotiations. Li arrived at Shanghai on May 28,[1] and there an opportunity appeared that was more to his liking than fighting a war. On June 6, 1883 Arthur Tricou, French minister to Japan and now *Envoyé extraordinaire* in China until Bourée's successor arrived, debarked at Shanghai. Li Hungchang met him the same day, and the two began substantive discussions two days later.

In coming to China, Tricou carried instructions "not only to determine, without prejudice, the actual state of affairs, but to facilitate a rapprochement between the two countries." As a means to accomplish the latter purpose, Tricou was to establish in practice the conditions that had been granted France by the 1874 treaty with Vietnam. At the same time, he was to obtain a clear statement from the Chinese whether they intended, overtly or covertly, to assist the Vietnamese in resisting French efforts in that country.[2]

In his second meeting with Li, on June 8, Tricou expounded the demands of his government. Li's response to the French demands was — as Tricou reported to Paris — entirely favorable. Tricou obtained the impression that China would henceforth refrain from intervening in Vietnamese affairs, and that it would no longer protest the establishment of a French protectorate over that country. Only on the question of Chinese sovereignty in Vietnam had Li registered any objections. Tricou was satisfied, nevertheless, that even the initial repugnance the Chinese felt toward this point could soon be overcome.[3]

Li Hung-chang's report to the Tsungli Yamen conveyed an entirely different picture of the same conversation. Indeed, Li made himself sound like one of the staunchest opponents of

[1] YNT, II, 871, dcmt. 430, Li memorial, June 7, 1883 (KH9/5/3).

[2] HR, II, 394, Foreign Ministry to Tricou, May 15, 1883.

[3] *Documents diplomatiques. Affaires du Tonkin, Deuxième Partie,* p. 177, dcmt. 236, Tricou to Challemel-Lacour, June 22, 1883; and p. 133, dcmt. 209, same to same, June 8, 1883.

French encroachments. Not only did he assert that he had informed Tricou that China would not recognize the 1874 treaty, but that China was also bound by a sense of justice to assist Vietnam in securing a fair settlement. Li did acknowledge, however, that he told Tricou that China had no intention of aiding the Vietnamese resistance movement against France. In short, Li asserted to the Tsungli Yamen that he had rejected all but one of Tricou's demands. Li summed up his own reactions to this meeting by declaring that "whether Tricou is at Shanghai or proceeds to Peking, it will certainly be difficult to bring him to terms." [4]

Li and Tricou did not meet again until a stormy confrontation on June 17. Li now asserted that, because Vietnam was a Chinese dependency, the empire could not be disinterested in developments in that country. Furthermore, Li informed Tricou — truthfully, as we now know — that he could only refer points of controversy to Peking, because he did not possess plenipotentiary powers. The Frenchman insisted that Li had earlier affirmed that he had full powers to negotiate; Li insisted that Tricou was mistaken. Tricou thought that Li was shamming. He believed that Li now "opposes us with a systematic resistance, and even affects the most arrogant attitude"; he flew into a towering rage at the governor-general's equivocations, and the meeting thereupon broke up.[5] Tricou literally could not believe his ears — or, more probably, he wanted a documentary record of Li's statements — and he requested that Li declare in writing that he did not possess the necessary powers to treat and that China would not recognize the treaty of 1874. Li complied, repeating his previous verbal declarations.[6]

[4] ISHK, CFCC, IV, 48–49, Li-Tricou conversation, June 8, 1883 (KH9/5/4); *ibid.*, p. 45, Li to Tsungli Yamen, same date.

[5] ISHK, CFCC, IV, 50–51, Li-Tricou conversation, June 17, 1883 (KH9/5/13); *Documents diplomatiques. Affaires du Tonkin, Deuxième Partie*, p. 139, dcmt. 215, Tricou to Challemel-Lacour, June 18, 1883.

[6] *Documents diplomatiques. Affaires du Tonkin, Deuxième Partie*, pp.

The two negotiators did not meet again for almost two weeks. Li, despite his belief that the danger of war was imminent, had been piqued by what he termed the Frenchman's "overbearing and discourteous" manner, and he declared that French bluster precluded all possibility of an amicable settlement.[7] Tricou, curiously, remained hopeful. On June 30, and again on July 1, he approached Li, and so moderated his demands that he put aside all questions of principle, just as Bourée had done before him.[8] Despite Tricou's new attempts at conciliation, Li was adamantly unreceptive to the new proposals.

During their fifth and final conversation on July 1, Li Hung-chang informed Tricou that he had received a decree ordering him to return to Tientsin.[9] (Li did not mention to Tricou that the decree had been issued on June 7, almost a month previously and before they had commenced negotiations![10] Li needed a pretext to terminate the discussions with Tricou, however, and this served his purpose as well as any other.) Li remained in Shanghai another four days, and on July 2, 3, and 4, Tricou sought to resume the discussions. Li would now have none of it, and on July 5 he sailed for Tientsin without having met with the Frenchman again.[11]

179–181, dcmt. 236, annexes I & II, Tricou to Li and Li to Tricou, June 19, 1883; ISHK, CFCC, IV, 51–52, Li to Tricou, June 19, 1883 (KH9/5/15).

[7] TK, CFCC, IV, 133, Li to Tseng Chi-tse, June 27, 1883 (KH9/5/23); *ibid.*, p. 129, Li to Tsungli Yamen, June 17, 1883 (KH9/5/13).

[8] *Documents diplomatiques. Affaires du Tonkin, Deuxième Partie*, p. 151, dcmt. 224, Tricou to Challemel-Lacour, July 3, 1883; ISHK, CFCC, IV, 55, Li-Tricou conversation, June 30, 1883 (KH9/5/26), and pp. 57–59, Li-Tricou conversation, July 1, 1883 (KH9/5/27).

[9] ISHK, CFCC, IV, 59, Li to Tsungli Yamen, July 1, 1883 (KH9/5/27); CFCS, 4:21b, dcmt. 119, decree to Li, June 20, 1883 (KH9/5/16).

[10] YNT, II, 871, dcmt. 429, decree, June 7, 1883 (KH9/5/3).

[11] TK, CFCC, IV, 135, Li to Tsungli Yamen, July 4, 1883 (KH9/6/1); Shao Hsün-cheng, p. 81.

Causes of the Failure of the Tricou Negotiations. One of the knottiest problems in this study has been to determine what actually took place during the June talks between Arthur Tricou and Li Hung-chang. So disparate were the reports of the two negotiators regarding the proceedings of their second meeting on June 8 that the encounter at first appears as evidence for Pirandello's view of "truth" — that truth is relative to the perception of each person participating in an event. Probing more deeply into the events leads one to suspect, however, first, that Li had intentionally distorted his report to the Yamen of the June 8 conversation, and that the French version of the proceedings more closely represented the actual events; and, second, that Peking had by June 17 determined on a firm stand against the French, and that Li was but a diplomatic pawn constrained to act contrary to his own dictates.

According to an official French report, Li in the June 17 meeting had abruptly abandoned his conciliatory stance as a result of "influences that would be fruitless to determine at the present time." As a consequence, all subsequent discussions had been fruitless.[1] Later, in addressing the Chamber on the subject, the foreign minister, Paul Challemel-Lacour, asserted that "certain persons" had persuaded Peking that France had neither the will nor the means to sustain its efforts in Tongking. The French deputies were never provided further information. Albert Billot, who at the time had been serving as head of the political affairs section in the Foreign Ministry, could only conclude from his own researches that "It remains therefore an enigma."[2]

Chinese sources provide a key to the enigma. On June 15, just two days before the meeting in question, Li Hung-chang received from the Yamen a telegram that read:

[1] *Documents diplomatiques. Affaires du Tonkin, Exposé de la situation, Octobre 1883* (Paris, 1883), p. 17.
[2] Billot, p. 48.

On the 9th we again received a telegram from Tseng Chi-tse which read: "I have just had a long conversation with former French premier [William Henry] Waddington. He declared that the Vietnamese affair is being run according to the dictates of political parties without unanimous approval of the people. . . . I believe that French political parties are composed entirely of opportunists, so that if we permit them to attain their ends, they will continue to advance. But if we render them a setback, the parties' policies will change. . . . It seems that we cannot again be conciliatory." [3]

Tseng was convinced, therefore, that Li must, either through insolence to or avoidance of Tricou, prevent a solution of the crisis at this time. Tseng knew that Challemel-Lacour was scheduled to be interpellated by the Chamber on July 10. If Challemel-Lacour could give the deputies no evidence then that relations with China were improving, Tseng was convinced that there would be another change of ministries and a consequent improvement of China's prospects. [4]

Had Li Hung-chang been acting upon his own authority, Tseng's views would not have dissuaded him from concluding a settlement with Tricou. Indeed, on June 16 — one day after receiving Tseng's telegram and the day before the turbulent third meeting of the two diplomats — Li sent a memorial to the throne that pointedly warned against involvement in hostilities against the French. [5] But he was not a free agent. "I am not myself able to decide policies," he complained to an acquaintance on June 24, "but must wait for imperial orders

[3] TK, CFCC, IV, 129, received June 15, 1883 (KH9/5/11). The Tsungli Yamen received a fuller transcript of Tseng's conversation with Waddington on August 7. The latter transcript records only that Waddington stated that the French had gotten deeply into the Vietnamese mess as a result of the frequent cabinet changes. That is, Tseng's interpretation of Waddington's statement appears to have been unwarranted. (See YNT, II, 957, dcmt. 473, Aug. 7, 1883 [KH9/7/5].)

[4] TK, CFCC, IV, 135, Li Hung-chang to Tsungli Yamen, July 4, 1883 (KH9/6/1).

[5] CFCS, 4:22–23b, dcmt. 120, June 16, 1883 (KH9/5/12).

and act accordingly." [6] The basic reason that the Li-Tricou negotiations failed, therefore, was that Waddington's statement had convinced Tseng, and through him the throne and its advisors in Peking, that a peace settlement at this juncture was inopportune.

It remains necessary to explain Li Hung-chang's exceedingly curious behavior during the negotiations. Albert Billot was convinced that Li was merely playing a "diplomatic game" in order to determine French intentions. [7] I think, to the contrary, that Li was initially negotiating in deadly seriousness, but that his political position was so slippery that he resorted to duplicity.

Li, it seems certain, had indicated a willingness to make, if he had not actually made, the concessions that Tricou attributed to him. But he had not dared reveal the full extent of his concessions to Peking. The recall of Bourée had shaken many Chinese officials out of their apathy regarding French activity in Vietnam. *Ch'ing-i* had become virulent, and its sentiment was infectious. Li was therefore constrained to be cautious: "What is the Tsungli Yamen going to say," he is reported to have inquired of a French diplomat at this time, "if I submit this plan for its approval? I would be risking my neck. You know the fate that was prepared for Ch'ung-hou . . . ?" [8] The reality of Li's fears may be judged from a memorial by Chang P'ei-lun, who declared that "Should Li Hung-chang be lenient with the enemy [in the negotiations], and thus permit them to cause the emperor anxiety — this cannot be tolerated of a high official!" [9]

Li was acutely sensitive to this form of harassment from

[6] PLHK, CFCC, IV, 8, Li to Chang K'uei-chai, June 24, 1883 (KH9/5/20).

[7] Billot, p. 63.

[8] Billot, p. 63.

[9] CFCS, 4:29, dcmt. 121, addendum #1, June 21, 1883 (KH9/5/17). Other memorials in this genre during May and June 1883 are CFCS, dcmts. 107, 108, 111, 122, 129, 130, 132.

ch'ing-i and other pro-war officials. On June 24, he bewailed
that "I am plagued by the irresponsible talk of officials not
in positions of authority. . . . They discuss matters of policy,
and after matters of policy, they discuss men. Most engage
in bullying." [10] Indeed, so vociferous had pro-war sentiment
become that a foreign acquaintance commiserated with the
governor-general, stating: "The present Vietnamese affair is
like the Sino-Russian situation of last year. However, there are
now more who are desirous of fighting a war than before, and
those who previously joined forces with you to attain a peaceful settlement between China and Russia have now all retired
from office and do not discuss affairs. Thus, Your Excellency
encounters even greater difficulties in managing this affair." [11]

In this context of captious critics, Li could not permit himself to appear too ready to appease the French. At the same
time, however, he had much to gain from negotiating a settlement, and he was undoubtedly hopeful that the political air
in Peking would clear. Did he have like-minded colleagues
within the upper councils in Peking who might win Tz'u-hsi's
support for a *détente?* Or did he anticipate that the Tsungli
Yamen would accept the advice offered it by Robert Hart,
inspector general of the Chinese Maritime Customs Service? [12]
There is no way of knowing Li's inner thoughts at this time.
But it seems likely that he sought to keep the negotiations
alive by allowing Tricou hope that an agreement was possible,

[10] PLHK, CFCC, IV, 8, Li to Chang K'uei-chai, June 24, 1883
(KH9/5/20).

[11] ISHK, CFCC, IV, 46, Brandt to Li, May 28, 1883 (KH9/4/22).

[12] Li might have expected support particularly from Prince Kung and
Weng T'ung-ho in the Grand Council and Chou Chia-mei and Wu
T'ing-fen in the Tsungli Yamen. Twice during June, Hart presented the
Yamen with proposals for a settlement. The crux of these proposals was
that French hegemony in Vietnam south of the 16th parallel be recognized, that Hanoi and Hai-Phong be opened to foreign trade, but
that Vietnam's tributary status with the empire be preserved. (See YNT,
II, 874, dcmt. 434, June 11, 1883 [KH9/5/7]; and YNT, II, 897–900,
dcmt. 451, June 21, 1883 [KH9/5/17].)

while he, Li, simultaneously worked to gain the throne's support for such an agreement.

Li had been obliged, in the meeting of June 17, to abandon his conciliatory attitude, as a result of Tseng's interpretation of his conversation with Waddington. The Yamen, it is true, had not *commanded* Li to break off the talks; that the Yamen theoretically had no authority to do. It had only offered him information "to facilitate your considerations." [13] Nevertheless, in view of the relative influence of Li and the Yamen at this time, the telegrams were in effect commands, and Li judged that it would be prudent to comply. By July 1, Li doubtless realized that no change in attitude could be expected in Peking. The throne had recently reminded him of his instructions to return to Tientsin,[14] and he could not remain indefinitely in Shanghai contrary to imperial commands. Hence, despite Tricou's newly conciliatory proposals, he terminated the discussions, having advised the Frenchman to go to Peking and there negotiate directly with the Tsungli Yamen.[15]

Li's adventures in May and June 1883 point out a political truth: policy is more easily influenced negatively than positively. His success in avoiding the appointment in the south indicates that the throne valued him too highly not to conciliate him where his legitimate interests were directly threatened. An official who was valued less, which is to say one who was less powerful, would surely have had no alternative but to acquiesce in the nomination to the new post. But the throne needed his political talents and military skills; needed them more, that is, than it needed a skilled commander in Tongking. This was the fulcrum for Li's political leverage, and he succeeded,

[13] TK, CFCC, IV, 129, received June 14, 1883 (KH9/5/10).
[14] CFCS, 4:21b, dcmt. 119, decree to Li, June 20, 1883 (KH9/5/16).
[15] Li had actually been so discomfited by the negotiations in Shanghai that he repeatedly advised Tricou to carry the negotiations to Peking. (ISHK, CFCC, IV, 49, June 8, 1883 [KH9/5/4]; p. 50, June 17, 1883 [KH9/5/13]; p. 54, June 30, 1883 [KH9/5/26].)

therefore, in diverting imperial policy from the course that had been plotted in Peking.

Nevertheless, Li had not the power single-handedly to channel imperial policy into a new direction. His premonitory memorials had not been sufficiently compelling, nor his political position sufficiently strong, to dissuade the throne from following the advice of anti-appeasement partisans such as Tseng Chi-tse and *ch'ing-i*. China therefore moved inexorably toward war.

IV

INCREASING CHINESE BELLIGERENCE
AND THE FALL OF PRINCE KUNG

The French Autumn Offensive, 1883. The collapse of the Li-Tricou negotiations on July 1, 1883 caused a marked increase of military activity in the camps of the two antagonists. Relatively large concentrations of Chinese troops (between ten and twenty thousand men) were already encamped in Tongking, and "huge quantities" of weapons, as well as gunboats, had been purchased abroad and were being brought to China.[1] At the same time, the French were rapidly enlarging their own military establishment in Vietnam, their forces, not counting the native conscripts, numbering about nine thousand.[2] Neither government relished the prospect of a clash between these forces, but it was becoming increasingly evident that a pacific settlement of the quarrel was not possible. Indeed, Tseng Chi-tse's relations with the French authorities became so strained in late June that he absented himself from the Quai d'Orsay for nearly a month and a half.[3]

---

[1] TK, CFCC, IV, 131, Li to Tsungli Yamen, June 23, 1883 (KH9/5/19); Stanley Fowler Wright, *Hart and the Chinese Customs* (Belfast, 1950), p. 509.

[2] Shao Hsün-cheng, p. 107; HR, II, 382; ISHK, CFCC, IV, 55, Li-Tricou conversation, June 30, 1883 (KH9/5/26).

[3] Tseng explained his absence by stating that he wished to avoid the insults of Challemel-Lacour, with whom he was on the worst possible terms. (Tseng Chi-tse, "Tseng Hui-min Kung i-chi" [The collected writings of Tseng Chi-tse], CFCC, IV, 262, Tseng to Tsungli Yamen,

The French meanwhile were losing patience, and by August they had readied a military operation that they expected would put an end to the Vietnamese complications. They still hoped to avert hostilities, however, and on August 1, 1883, the foreign minister, Challemel-Lacour, presented to Tseng Chi-tse (who had now emerged from hiding) a final demand that China withdraw its troops from Vietnamese territory. The consequent exchange provides tragi-comic illustration of Peking's refusal at this time to consider a reconciliatory solution in Vietnam. To Challemel-Lacour's demand, Tseng replied equivocally that (1) there absolutely were no imperial troops in Tongking, (2) if any troops had entered Tongking, they had done so inadvertently, because the border was not clearly defined, and (3) he would ask Peking if there were troops in Tongking. On August 8, Tseng announced to Challemel-Lacour that a reply had arrived from the Tsungli Yamen. Unfortunately, he said, there were several portions of the Yamen telegram that were not clear, and that he had had again to ask elucidation from Peking. "However, I fear that the Yamen reply will not be immediate," Tseng added, "because China must first inquire into the situation there; then and only then can it be decided whether or not to withdraw troops. That area is remote, and places cannot be reached by telegraph. An investigation will unavoidably require many days." If it were learned that troops had indeed advanced beyond the Chinese frontier, Peking

---

July 20, 1883 [KH9/6/17].) The true explanation probably is that he was chagrined after having affirmed that Li Hung-chang had full powers to conclude a settlement with Tricou. (*Documents diplomatiques. Affaires du Tonkin, Deuxième Partie*, pp. 141–146, dcmt. 218, June 21, 1883.) Tseng subsequently protested that he had not done so (YNT, II, 1090–91, dcmt. 535, Tseng to Tsungli Yamen, Sept. 10, 1883 [KH9/8/10]), but the French allegation that Tseng had made such a statement greatly embarrassed Li in Shanghai. (See Li-Tricou conversations in ISHK, CFCC, IV, 53–56 and 56–59, June 30 and July 1, 1883 [KH9/5/26 and 27].)

would then have to consider whether or not to order a with-drawal.[4]

Challemel-Lacour was not noted for being long on patience. He became enraged and asserted that *the French knew* there were Chinese troops in Tongking. He said that the situation was dangerous "because it is intolerable!" and adjourned the meeting.[5] Further negotiations were clearly pointless and, in mid-August 1883, the French military struck.

On the assumption that Chinese aspirations rested largely on Liu Yung-fu, the French directed one body of troops to destroy the Black Flags. At the same time, the French meant to end all legalistic quibbling regarding the status of Vietnam by forcing the Vietnamese court to sign a new treaty. Toward the latter goal, they scored an immediate success. French forces, under the command of Admiral Amédé Courbet, at-tacked and quickly overwhelmed the defenses of Hué, and on August 25 a new treaty was concluded that reduced Vietnam, in unequivocal terms, to the position of a French protectorate.[6] The French fell short of their former goal, however. Their expedition encountered the Black Flags, who were now well equipped. A series of engagements in August culminated in

[4] YNT, III, 1254, dcmt. 598, Tseng memorial, no date. Peking did not directly acknowledge the fact (which the French had known all along) that Chinese troops were stationed in Tongking, until four months after the acrimonious encounter between Tseng and Challemel-Lacour. On December 9, the Tsungli Yamen informed the French repre-sentative in Peking, Semallé, that Chinese forces had actually been located in Tongking for more than ten years. If Tseng had earlier denied their presence, he had been mistaken, and, the Yamen added, had done so without informing Peking. This again was a brazen lie, for the Yamen had learned of Tseng's previous fib as early as October 1, 1883. (YNT, III, 1420–21, dcmt. 666, Tsungli Yamen to Semallé, Dec. 9, 1883 [KH9/11/10]. Cf. YNT, III, 1227–29, dcmt. 585, Tseng to Tsungli Yamen, Oct. 1, 1883 [KH9/9/1]; and YNT, III, 1254, dcmt. 598, Tseng to Tsungli Yamen, no date.)

[5] *Documents diplomatiques. Affaires du Tonkin, Deuxième Partie,* p. 182, dcmt. 237, Aug. 8, 1883.

[6] The French and Chinese texts of this treaty are in HR, II, 388–392, and CFCS, 6:32b–35, dcmt. 205, addendum #2, respectively.

a battle at Dan-Phuong, in the valley of the Red River midway
between Hanoi and Son-Tay, which lasted three days, September 1–3. Liu Yung-fu kept his attackers off balance by varying
his tactics, once fighting from securely entrenched defense
works and then laying skillful ambushes. The fighting was
bloody, and the French commander demanded reinforcements.
These were not immediately available, and the offensive
ground to a halt. Liu Yung-fu remained to harass the French.[7]

While their military was enjoying only partial success in
Vietnam, the French government encountered other discouraging developments in Europe. Prompted by the indifferent
achievements of their nation's arms, the French opposition
parties of both right and left denounced the Vietnamese adventure. Simultaneously, other European powers had adopted
a minatory posture toward France; consequently, France's own
borders seemed in peril. Now, as Billot observed, "It would
have been imprudent to precipitate a rupture with China and
to disregard a chance of a settlement, at the very moment when
we were threatened with grave complications on our frontiers." [8] Their failure to deliver a *coup de grace* to the resistance in Tongking compelled the French again to proffer negotiations and conciliatory terms to the Chinese.

Shortly after the autumn offensive had bogged down,
Challemel-Lacour made a new proposal that could conceivably
have been accepted by the Chinese. The main point of this
"September 15 Memorandum" called for the establishment of
a demilitarized buffer area south of the Chinese frontier, to be
administered by the Vietnamese. This scheme had actually
originated in the mind of Tseng Chi-tse, and been suggested to
the French by him the previous month.[9]

[7] Billot, pp. 104–105; YNT, III, 1291–92, dcmt. 612, Chang Shu-sheng
to Tsungli Yamen, Oct. 16, 1883 (KH9/9/16).
[8] Billot, p. 73.
[9] Billot, p. 91; HR, II, 411–412; YNT, II, 1005, dcmt. 493, Tseng to
Tsungli Yamen, Aug. 20, 1883 (KH9/7/18).

The autumn offensive had so provoked Chinese intransigence, however, that Tseng now flatly rejected the same buffer concept that he had originally suggested as a basis for a settlement. Instead, he insisted that China's rights as sovereign of the whole of Vietnam be respected. He further proposed a division of the Vietnamese protectorate — not a buffer zone — along a line far to the south of the Red River. This would effectually have eliminated the French from Tongking.[10]

The French, desirous of a peaceful settlement, recognized the necessity of giving China some territorial concessions to assure China the security of its frontiers. They felt, however, that Tseng's new conditions were incredible and inadmissible. By December 1883, they determined again to conclude the controversy with armed force.

Increased Chinese Bellicosity. Chinese militancy, meanwhile, had received fresh impetus from the French bombardment of Hué and the resultant conclusion of the new Franco-Vietnamese treaty. Until these events, the general sentiment among *ch'ing-i* officials had been that covert resistance would suffice to repulse French aggression. They had been content to urge that the Black Flags be supplied with money and arms, and that imperial troops be sent into Tongking under the pretext of subduing the bandits in the area. After the treaty of August 25, the throne was bombarded with memorials demanding that the government openly declare its resistance to the French.

To the Quai d'Orsay, this reaction of the Chinese was deeply disappointing, for it had anticipated that China would relinquish its claims in Vietnam after the new treaty had expressly declared the establishment of a French protectorate there. However, as Cho Huan-lai has observed: "as a result of

[10] "Tseng Chi-tse yü Fa wai-pu wang-lai chao-hui," CFCC, V, 80–81, Tseng to French Foreign Ministry, Oct. 15, 1883.

a deplorable lack of understanding of the respective states of mind of the protagonists, it always resulted that what happened was precisely the opposite of what was expected." [1]

The new stridency in *ch'ing-i* remonstrations was first apparent in a memorial from the paladin of the *ch'ing-i* officials, Chang P'ei-lun. Chang praised the court for its earnest efforts to establish frontier defenses. Nevertheless, he voiced the fear that some officials would compromise Chinese honor and security by withdrawing the imperial armies from Vietnam and then would negotiate a peace settlement — a typically fawning bow to the throne, and an ill-disguised attack on Li Hung-chang. Chang deplored the passive and half-hearted efforts that had hitherto characterized Chinese resistance. China had concentrated on defensive measures, and sent only pittances of aid to Liu Yung-fu. As a consequence, the French had suffered no major setbacks, and the Vietnamese had succumbed to French aggression, thinking that their attacker was powerful and that China was weak. The time had arrived, Chang insisted, when Chinese opposition to France and aid to the Black Flags must be rendered openly and resolutely. [2]

Other officials quickly followed the lead of Chang P'ei-lun. Ch'in Chung-chien, a junior metropolitan censor, dwelled upon a theme derived from the classical philosophers, asserting that when China clandestinely supported the Black Flags, "the name is not correct and our words are not in harmony." Should China send its troops into battle with the truth thus distorted, their morale would be low, and they would be defeated. [3] (This type of moral awareness, encountered frequently in *ch'ing-i* writings, was not conspicuous in the utterances of the

[1] Cho Huan-lai, p. 206.
[2] CFCS, 5:30b–31b, dcmt. 159, Chang P'ei-lun memorial, Sept. 3, 1883 (KH9/8/3).
[3] CFCS, 6:3b, dcmt. 180, Ch'in Chung-chien memorial, Sept. 19, 1883 (KH9/8/19). For Confucius' statement of this view, see H. G. Creel, *Chinese Thought from Confucius to Mao Tse-tung* (New York, 1960), p. 30.

responsible authorities. For instance, Tseng Chi-tse's blithe disregard for factual accuracy in his talks with Challemel-Lacour has already been noted.[4] Indeed, I doubt, despite the constant surveillance of moral behavior by *ch'ing-i*, that Confucianism in China resulted in much less duplicity in the conduct of state affairs than did Christianity in France.)

Attempts to maintain a cloak of secrecy over the resistance to the French would, in any case, have been absurd if *ch'ing-i* proposals had been adopted. As at no time prior to the conclusion of the Hué treaty, officials were pressing for an advance of the imperial forces and a recovery even of Hué from French control. Most of the memorialists believed that, unsupported, the Black Flags were incapable of this undertaking. They therefore urged that imperial armies make a full-scale, undisguised invasion of the whole of Tongking.[5]

Nor was it only the *ch'ing-i* officials who urged that Chinese resistance become overt. The governor and governor-general in Kwangtung, Ni Wen-wei and Chang Shu-sheng, for example, had been galvanized into a new awareness of the critical situation in the south. They believed that, in coordination with the "righteous" groups in Vietnam, it would be an easy matter for the Black Flags and the imperial troops to expel the French from Tongking.[6] The governor-general of Yunnan-Kweichow, Ts'en Yü-ying, also envisaged not only the recapture of Tongking but even of Saigon.[7]

A minority of the officials opposed this aggressive *démarche*. Weng T'ung-ho wrote in his diary that "Many claim our wishes

[4] See above, pp. 86–87 and n. 4.

[5] Examples of this argument may be found in: CFCS, 5:44, dcmt. 170, Ting Chen-to memorial, Sept. 12, 1883 (KH9/8/12); CFCS, 6:7, dcmt. 184, Ho Ch'ung-kuang memorial, Sept. 24, 1883 (KH9/8/24); CFCS, 6:25, dcmt. 198, Liao Shou-heng memorial, Oct. 1, 1883 (KH9/9/1).

[6] CFCS, 7:20b–22, dcmt. 230, Chang Shu-sheng memorial, Oct. 19, 1883 (KH9/9/19); CFCS, 7:23–24, dcmt. 232, Ni Wen-wei memorial, same date.

[7] CFCS, 8:8a-b, dcmt. 247, Ts'en Yü-ying memorial, Nov. 8, 1883 (KH9/10/9).

could be fulfilled by sending troops into Vietnam. Why don't these people appraise our own strength?"[8] The principal contention of this minority, of which Li Hung-chang was characteristically a spokesman, was that the French remained deceived by the Chinese pretext of suppressing bandits in Tongking. They feared, above all, that the French would increase their military commitment against the empire if Chinese forces openly assumed the offensive.[9]

Robert Hart's Appraisal of China's Situation. When only nineteen years of age, Robert Hart had arrived in China as a student interpreter in the British Consular Service. During the early period of his career, when he held various consular posts in South China, he had acquired a rich knowledge of China, the Chinese people, and the Chinese language. In 1863, at the ripe age of twenty-seven, he left the employ of the British government, and assumed the duties of inspector-general of the recently created Chinese Maritime Customs Service, a position that he was to retain for well over forty years. Hart was no ordinary bureaucrat. His interests extended far beyond the confines of his official responsibilities, and he held a lively interest in, indeed, an almost patronizing concern for, the welfare of the nation that was his home for the greater part of his life. His affable nature and keen insight into the affairs of the country had made him a valued and trusted consultant for the Chinese government, and the Tsungli Yamen frequently solicited and heeded his opinions on manifold problems related

[8] WJC, 22:39b, May 17, 1883, quoted with slight changes from Kung-chuan Hsiao, "Weng T'ung-ho and the Reform Movement of 1898," *Tsing Hua Journal of Chinese Studies,* new ser., 1.2:116–117 (Apr. 1957).
[9] CFCS, 6:20, dcmt. 194, Li memorial, Sept. 28, 1883 (KH9/8/28); CFCS, 7:9a-b, dcmt. 219, Lu Ch'uan-lin memorial, Oct. 13, 1883 (KH9/9/13).

to foreign affairs.[1] While Robert Hart was not, in the usual sense, a Chinese official, the advice he tendered the Yamen during a conversation in November 1883 is of interest here, because his opinions undoubtedly bore weight in Peking's policy considerations. In addition, they indicate how an extraordinarily well-informed Westerner in 1883 conceived China's prospects in a war with France. As such, they serve as an effective makeweight in our analyses of the officials' mercurial expressions.

During the conversation, Hart studiously expressed his sympathy with the Chinese ire against the French. Nevertheless, he admonished the Yamen members, "anger is not military strength." It therefore behooved the Chinese government to control its vexation and formulate its policy on the basis of an objective analysis of the situation. Scrupulously, the inspector-general outlined for the Yamen the facts as he perceived them. If the empire had a pact with Germany by which it could solicit that country's aid, France would have no chance of succeeding in its Vietnamese enterprise. But no such pact existed. The Chinese also anticipated British assistance in a war against France. Hart reminded the Chinese, however, that although seventy to eighty per cent of the foreign merchants in China were of British origin, these accounted for only five to six per cent of all British subjects engaged in overseas trade. There could not, therefore, be any confidence that Britain would be provoked into a war with the French, even to protect its mercantile interests in China. Hart ruled out the feasibility of employing private American adventurers, and in like manner deflated the Chinese hope that the French population would revolt against their government. Ultimately, concluded Hart, China stood alone.

Hart suggested that the present policy of the Chinese gov-

[1] Stanley Fowler Wright, *passim.*

ernment was based as much on a number of external and un-realistic "if" factors as on China's own capabilities. He acknowledged that China could still hold out hope for victory if France limited itself to the use of only ten or twenty thousand men. But he warned that France was capable of throwing some fifty to sixty thousand troops into a campaign against the empire. Hart therefore advised that "not to fight is the best policy."

Hart concluded by offering several policy recommendations. These reveal that his position was strikingly close to that of Li Hung-chang. China should, Hart proposed, withdraw its forces from Tongking and thereby avoid conflict with the French. Possibly, after the French had occupied Tongking, they would learn that the area possessed no great value for them. They might, therefore, voluntarily relinquish the area. For the present, China should exert its full and constant efforts to strengthen itself militarily. Then, even if France did not of its own volition withdraw from Tongking, China had already published its claim to Vietnamese sovereignty, and therefore retained a legal pretext to reopen the Vietnamese question at some time in the future. After several decades, with its armies strengthened, the empire could legitimately force a just solution to the problem. "In this way," Hart optimistically predicted, "China can enjoy domestic repose without concern for foreign difficulties." [2]

Viewed in retrospect, the inspector-general analyzed the situation with remarkable accuracy. The Chinese anticipation of aid from France's European rivals was to be proved baseless; and, while the French had only about twenty thousand troops in the theater, imperial arms were to register some notable successes. Whether a larger French contingent could have produced the more devastating consequences foretold by

[2] YNT, III, 1358, dcmt. 634, Nov. 11, 1883 (KH9/10/12).

Hart was never to be learned, for peace opportunely intervened. Only on one point did he definitely err. China's self-strengthening movement never attained the potency he forecast.

Government Responses to the Officials' Policy Demands. The causative relationship between expressions of unofficial opinion, like *ch'ing-i,* and policy decision is seldom clear or palpable. Chinese imperial policy became more aggressive simultaneously with the rising *ch'ing-i* outcry following the French offensive in the autumn of 1883. This is a fact; that the aggressive policy was a *result* of *ch'ing-i* necessarily remains inferential. It is a circumstantial fact, however, that Chinese policy planners were greatly harried by *ch'ing-i* militancy. Tseng Chi-tse, who was never a friend of the French, complained to some Europeans that the situation had gotten out of control. Even his less than moderate advice was, he averred, no longer sufficiently extreme to be of influence in Peking.[1]

In this context of volatile pro-war sentiment, fresh imperial troops were recruited and reinforcements were dispatched to the south. On October 20, the throne instructed the forces of Yunnan and Kwangsi to reassume strategic positions in Tongking that had been evacuated, without imperial authorization, after the Treaty of Hué had been concluded.[2] Two days later,

---

[1] HR, II, 417; Cho Huan-lai, p. 207. In a letter to a friend, Tseng also asserted that the Tsungli Yamen decision to apprise the French of the presence of Chinese troops within Tongking proved that office to be more bellicose than he. (Tseng Chi-tse, "Tseng Hui-min Kung i-chi," CFCC, IV, 264, Tseng to Shao Hsiao-ts'un, Feb. 19, 1884 [KH10/1/23].)

[2] CFCS, 7:5b, dcmt. 216, decree to Ts'en Yü-ying, et al., Oct. 20, 1883 (KH9/9/20). Upon receiving word that Vietnam had concluded the Hué treaty on August 25, the Yunnan commanders, Ts'en Yü-ying and T'ang Chiung, had, without the sanction of Peking, withdrawn their forces from Tongking — presumably on the assumption that the treaty

a decree ordered that the Black Flags be granted supplies. The throne also encouraged Liu Yung-fu to attempt the recapture of Hanoi, promising him and his men extraordinary rewards if they succeeded in this undertaking.[3]

The full measure of China's determination to maintain its traditional position in Vietnam seemed to be revealed when, on November 16, the Tsungli Yamen issued a formal declaration to the French and other foreign powers. The substance of this proclamation was that, if French troops advancing in Tongking should encounter imperial forces, it would be a *casus belli* for which France would have to bear full responsibility.[4] Nor was this declaration sheer bluster, apparently, for a week later a decree to the armies in Tongking proscribed withdrawal from their positions should the French attack them.[5]

The Fall of Son-Tay and Officialdom's Reactions. Chinese determination to block French advances into Tongking was soon put to a test. We have already noted Paris' decision to launch a new offensive. During the first week of December 1883, Chinese commanders in Tongking were reporting French patrols in the neighborhood of Bac-Ninh and Son-Tay. Only days later, Admiral Courbet landed several thousand men only twelve kilometers from Son-Tay. The defensive forces, composed largely of Black Flags but containing also elements of the Yunnan and Kwangsi armies, began to dig in, and on December 13 — apparently for the first time — the Chinese

---

settled the whole dispute. If these officials had then been ready to assent to a French *fait accompli*, Peking was now in no wise willing to do so.

[3] CFCS, 7:8b, dcmt. 218, decree to Ni Wen-wei, et al., Oct. 22, 1883 (KH9/9/22).

[4] HR, II, 413–414. Copies of this communication were also presented to other nations with representatives in China. The declaration is mentioned in YNT, III, 1420, dcmt. 666, Tsungli Yamen to Semallé, Dec. 9, 1883 (KH9/11/10).

[5] CFCS, 8:5b, dcmt. 245, decree to Hsü Yen-hsü, Nov. 23, 1883 (KH9/10/24).

lofted their own flags, and revealed their imperial insignia and uniforms.[1]

Courbet, undeterred, attacked the following day. The result, after two days of fighting, was a major victory for the French. It rendered "a terrible, if not mortal, blow" to the Black Flags; and the fall of Son-Tay, which commanded the approach to Tongking by way of the Red River, laid the basis for the subsequent French successes in northern Vietnam.[2] The full import of this blow did not escape the Chinese. Commanders wrote from the front describing the losses — reports that evoked from Weng T'ung-ho the bitter cry that "the Vietnamese affair has been reduced to a pulp." [3]

Peking's declaration of November 16, that a French attack on imperial armies would signal the start of war, had been straightforward and seemingly irrevocable. Yet the Chinese flag had been openly displayed at Son-Tay, and Courbet had nonetheless stormed the city's defenses. This was, according to Peking's declaration, a *casus belli.*

However, the decision-makers in Peking now hesitated. They had no wish to rush headlong into another war with a European power — and, indeed, only two weeks after the declaration of November 16 the throne had admonished an overly zealous commander that "China must not be the first to give cause for opening hostilities." [4] The determination that seemed to have been imparted to imperial policy by the November 16 declaration had, therefore, been spurious.

[1] CFCS, 10:5a-b, dcmt. 310, Hsü Yen-hsü memorial, Dec. 27, 1883 (KH9/11/28); CFCS, 10:18, dcmt. 319, T'ang Chiung memorial, same date.

[2] HR, II, 481 and 483.

[3] WJC, CFCC, II, 8, Dec. 24, 1883 (KH9/11/25). CFCS, 11:1a–b, dcmt. 329, Ts'en Yü-ying memorial, Jan. 12, 1884 (KH9/12/15), which, though of a later date than Weng's diary entry, fully describes the extent of the defeat. See also CFCS, 10:17b–8b, dcmt. 319, T'ang Chiung memorial, Dec. 27, 1883 (KH9/11/28).

[4] CFCS, 8:12, dcmt. 252, decree to P'eng Yü-lin, Nov. 29, 1883 (KH9/10/30).

The explanation for this marvelous ambiguity in imperial policy, I would suggest, is that the outraged *ch'ing-i* response to the Treaty of Hué in August had forced the throne to adopt a belligerent stance that it was not prepared to maintain in the face of a show of strength by the French. The throne was therefore caught in a squeeze between two forces, both of which sorely challenged the throne's power. Desirous of preserving its position in Tongking and simultaneously requiring the support of the Confucian bureaucracy, the throne would not sue for peace, neither would it declare war.

The French, for reasons of their own, did not follow up their victory with continued attacks. Courbet had thought to attack next Hung-Hoa on the Red River, but low waters on the river precluded support by supply and gun boats. He considered launching an assault on Bac-Ninh, but the Chinese had concentrated a strong force there, and he would need reinforcements before undertaking a campaign in that direction. He therefore contented himself by mopping up insurgents at his rear, most of whom were remnants of the Black Flags. In consequence, the French did not push their advantage after the victory at Son-Tay, and for the next three months there was little contact between the two adversaries.[5]

The ire of Chinese officials seemed to thrive on defeat. Chang Chih-tung presented two detailed memorials shortly after news of the Son-Tay defeat reached him at his post of governor of Shansi. He argued that, in war, initial defeats must be expected. Yet if China would put up a resolute resistance, even though it continued to incur defeats, the foreigners would perceive that China could not be regarded lightly. Daunted by Chinese willingness to fight, the foreigners would revoke plans for future aggression. Chang further warned that the present passivity of the French armies did not mean they had renounced further aggression. They hoped rather that, by

[5] Shao Hsün-cheng, p. 110; HR, II, 483.

remaining inactive, they would delude the Chinese into an enervating sense of security.[6]

One circuit censor admonished the throne in terms that evoke memories of Franklin D. Roosevelt's phrase, "The only thing we have to fear is fear itself." Put aside all hesitancy, he implored, and advance to the attack.[7] Another censor made light of French military abilities, and asserted that now was the time to grasp the opportunity to attack — to which opportunity he referred, just after the devastating defeat at Son-Tay, is left unclear. Chinese troops in cooperation with the Black Flags should take Hanoi. Having attained that initial goal, the recovery of the rest of Vietnam would be "as easy as splitting bamboo"—a vivid simile for those who had seen bamboo being split.[8]

All of these arguments for a stronger war effort now sounded trite and unconvincing by dint of their constant repetition. The true measure of the excitement created by the hostilities at Son-Tay is found in the fact that Li Hung-chang now momentarily urged a forceful policy. He asserted that a single defeat must not prevent the court from pressing its operations against the French. If resistance were maintained long enough, averred Li, French supplies would be depleted and their spirit dissipated. Li's memorial could well have come from the brush of a participant of *ch'ing-i*.[9]

There were, indeed, some military commanders who protested the aggressive policies that they were charged to implement. Both T'ang Chiung and Hsü Yen-hsü, commanders

[6] CFCS, 9:19–21 and 9:21–25, dcmts. 298 and 299, both dated Jan. 3, 1884 (KH9/12/6).
[7] CFCS, 11:8b, dcmt. 337, T'ien Kuo-chün memorial, Feb. 17, 1884 (KH10/1/21).
[8] CFCS, 12:1b, dcmt. 366, Feng Ying-shou memorial, Mar. 22, 1884 (KH10/2/25).
[9] CFCS, 9:1, dcmt. 287, Li memorial, Dec. 27, 1883 (KH9/11/28). See also Chang P'ei-lun, "Chien-yü chi," CFCC, IV, 374, Chang to Li Hung-chang, no date.

of the Yunnan and Kwangsi forces, respectively, urged for practical reasons a postponement of the order to advance their forces. They argued that Tongking was still too soaked from the monsoon rains for effective military action, and that Liu Yung-fu had not recovered from the fighting at Son-Tay.[10] This was throwing words to the winds. *Ch'ing-i* officials desired a defeat of the French, and details such as wet ground deterred them not at all.

Despite the militancy that characterized most memorials reaching the throne at this time, there was some concern expressed that the French might now launch an attack from the sea against the north and Peking, as the foreigners had done during the Opium and Arrow Wars.[11] Li Hung-chang had suggested this possibility earlier in the year when he had been named commander of the southern forces. Authors of *ch'ing-i* memorials were more sanguine about the prospect. Wu Ta-ch'eng, a military commander and member of the Ch'ing-liu, imagined that the French were fully preoccupied in the south. "How can they have any excess strength left to trouble other places? They can do no more than bluff us with empty talk [about attacking in the north]." [12] In general, bellicose officials viewed Tongking as the soft underbelly of the French. Consequently, whenever there was a warning of a French attack in the north, they proposed that, rather than divert forces for defense, the attack should be pressed where the adversary was most vulnerable.[13] This view was consistent with their premise that offense was the best defense.

[10] Shao Hsün-cheng, p. 106.

[11] CFCS, 11:14b, dcmt. 342, Ting memorial, Feb. 7, 1884 (KH10/1/11).

[12] CFCS, 11:17, dcmt. 343, Wu memorial, Feb. 23, 1884 (KH10/1/27).

[13] CFCS, 21:27b, dcmt. 963, addendum #2, Hsü Shu-ming memorial, Aug. 7, 1884 (KH10/6/17); CFCS, 21:31, dcmt. 970, Wu Hsün memorial, Aug. 8, 1884 (KH10/6/18); CFCS, 22:21, dcmt. 1039, Ch'ü Te-lin memorial, Aug. 12, 1884 (KH10/6/22).

The Defeat of Bac-Ninh and Tz'u-hsi's April Coup. Although
the imperial government did not opt for war after the battle
of Son-Tay, neither did it abandon its efforts to discomfit the
French in Tongking. In January 1884, Ts'en Yü-ying, governor-
general of Yunnan-Kweichow, was given permission to direct
the defense of his forces from headquarters inside Vietnamese
territory. At the same time, all armies were commanded to plan
an advance deeper into Vietnam.[1] Ties with Liu Yung-fu were
drawn even tighter. The organization of his forces was re-
vamped to correspond to that of the Chinese army. He was also
rewarded for his past merit, and promised renewed support.

The combined Chinese forces — including the three thousand men in the Black Flags — now numbered close to fifty
thousand. These were so situated that they formed a semi-
circle bounded by Hung-Hoa, Thai-Nguyen, and Bac-Ninh.
To oppose these Chinese forces, the French had a force of approximately sixteen thousand men in the French-occupied area
of Tongking.[2]

Despite the numerical inferiority of their forces, the French,
after three months of relative inactivity, determined in the
spring of 1884 to resume the offensive. For several months,
Courbet's patrols had been scouting Bac-Ninh, a military target
of prime importance for it commanded the eastern route
through Tongking to China.[3] On March 12 and 13, a French
force attacked Chinese positions on the outskirts of Bac-Ninh.

[1] YNT, III, 1402, dcmt. 654, decree, Nov. 28, 1883 (KH9/10/29);
YNT, III, 1475, dcmt. 696, decree, Dec. 29, 1883 (KH9/12/1).
[2] Huang Ta-shou, II, 50–51; HR, II, 484. Approximately one-fourth
of the French army was comprised of native recruits. (H. Nimier,
Histoire Chirurgicale de la Guerre au Tonkin et à Formose [*1883–1884–
1885*] [Paris, 1889], p. 31.) Jules Ferry wrote that there were 12,800
effectives from France serving in the Vietnamese theater in 1884. (Ferry,
Le Tonkin et la mère-patrie: témoignages et documents [Paris, 1890],
pp. 359–364.)
[3] CFCS, 10:5, dcmt. 310, Hsü Yen-hsü memorial, Dec. 27, 1883 (KH9/
11/28); CFCS, 5:44, dcmt. 170, Ting Chen-to memorial, Sept. 12, 1883
(KH9/8/12).

Liu Yung-fu repulsed a flank of the French assault. But the Chinese position became untenable, Bac-Ninh fell, and the French rolled back the imperial forces along the entire front from such other key points as Thai-Nguyen, Tuyen-Quang, and Hung-Hoa.[4]

As a result of this humiliating and crucial defeat, the Chinese forces had the edifying experience of witnessing two of their officers beheaded only two weeks after the battle.[5] Another officer committed suicide by swallowing opium to avoid the same fate. Hsü Yen-hsü, governor of Kwangsi and commander of the defeated troops at Bac-Ninh, was brought to Peking for trial, and later died in prison there.[6]

By far the biggest head to fall, and this time only figuratively, was that of I-hsin, the first Prince Kung. On April 3, 1884, Sheng-yü, a member of the imperial clan and of the Hanlin Academy, submitted to the throne an impeachment of Prince Kung and other members of the Grand Council. In this memorial, he charged that, while Hsü Yen-hsü and other military officers could not be absolved of responsibility for the dire state of affairs in Vietnam, the most grave guilt was attributable to Prince Kung and his fellow grand councilors.[7] After receiving Sheng-yü's memorial, the empress dowager on April 8 issued a decree clearing the Grand Council of its incumbents, and, in another decree, naming five replacements.[8]

[4] HR, II, 484; CFCS, 13:1–2b, dcmt. 400, Chang Shu-sheng memorial, Mar. 26, 1884 (KH10/2/29).

[5] YNT, III, 1654, dcmt. 773, decree, Apr. 12, 1884 (KH10/3/17).

[6] Ch'ing-shih, VII, 5028; Huang Ta-shou, II, 52.

[7] Sheng-yü's memorial is reproduced in Wu Hsiang-hsiang, Wan-Ch'ing kung-t'ing shih-chi (Records of the court during the latter part of the Ch'ing dynasty; Taipei, 1952), pp. 132–134.

[8] Ch'ing-shih-lu, 179:10–11b, decree, Apr. 8, 1884 (KH10/3/13), and 179:11b–12, decree, same date; HR, II, 424–425.

These dismissals met a degree of ineffectual opposition from some of the officials in the court — and from surprising sources. Two ch'ing-i officials contended that the experience and knowledge of Prince Kung should not be wasted; they were even more adamant in opposing the

The same day, four of the Tsungli Yamen's nine members fell to Tz'u-hsi's far-reaching axe.[9]

These April dismissals represented a veritable *coup d'état*, for they struck at the heart of the government, transforming the composition of the two principal policy-making organs under the throne. The subsequent appointments of Prince Li and Prince Ch'ing (to head the Grand Council and the Tsungli Yamen, respectively) were deemed inconsequential by contemporary observers. The fact that Prince Ch'un, the father of the emperor, was to participate in all major policy discussions[10] was, on the other hand, thought to be an event of primary significance. Prince Ch'un was regarded as a passionate advocate of a war policy; Prince Kung as one of the more moderate voices in the government.[11] It was therefore expected that China would now adopt a firm, antagonistic stance to the French encroachments on its southern dependency. As Albert Billot observed, regarding the nomination of Prince Ch'un, "this was the supreme effort of the war party at Peking. Other indications allowed no further doubt that the counsels of peace did not prevail." [12]

The "other indications" probably referred to the several appointments that now followed in quick succession. The Yamen,

---

nomination of Prince Ch'un, whose position as father of the emperor seemed to be incompatible with that of principal policy advisor. (CFCS, 13:13b–15b, dcmt. 428, Ch'ing Chung-chien memorial, Apr. 20, 1884 [KH10/3/25]; CFCS, 13:15b–16, dcmt. 429, Teng Ch'eng-hsiu memorial, Apr. 18, 1884 [KH10/3/23].) Sheng-yü, whose memorial had given the signal for the dismissals, also opposed Prince Ch'un's direct involvement in government. (*Translation of the Peking Gazette for 1884* [Shanghai, 1885], pp. 59–60, Apr. 27, 1884. See also *Ch'ing-shih*, V, 3501.)

[9] Ssu-ming Meng, p. 96.

[10] *Ch'ing-shih-lu*, 179:12, decree, Apr. 9, 1884 (KH10/3/14).

[11] HR, II, 423–424; Rutherford Alcock, "China and Its Foreign Relations," *Contemporary Review*, 38:1015 (Dec. 1880); M. J. Semallé, *Quatre ans à Pékin, aout 1880–aout 1884. Le Tonkin* (Paris, 1933), p. 213; Ssu-ming Meng, p. 54.

[12] Billot, p. 154.

which had been regarded as skilled in the art of compromise,[13] was reinforced by the addition of Chou Te-jun, a definite — indeed extreme — advocate of war.[14] It should be noted also that Chang P'ei-lun, regarded with good reason as "the most violent champion of resistance," [15] had not been touched by the dismissals from the Yamen. Similarly, the appointment at this same time of Chang Chih-tung to the governor-generalship of Kwangtung-Kwangsi buttressed the impression that the party of war was in the ascendancy.

In fact, however, Peking's policy of avoiding open hostilities with the French was not changed by this political upheaval. What, then, was the significance of the coup of April 1884?

A real and basic cause of the dismissals was the deep personal animosity that Tz'u-hsi bore toward her brother-in-law, Prince Kung. Following his rise to political eminence upon the conclusion of the Arrow War, Prince Kung had accrued enormous prestige and consolidated a broad basis of power.[16] The foreign powers looked upon him with favor, he was supported by moderates within the bureaucracy, and he enjoyed the goodwill and backing of the Empress Dowager Tz'u-an. His relations with Tz'u-hsi, however, had become increasingly abrasive. He was not an entirely pliable instrument in her hands, and she disliked him particularly because he opposed her efforts to repair her beloved Summer Palace. Ssu-ming Meng declares that he was the only man in the country she feared[17] — a fact that was probably at the base of her enmity for him. As long as Prince Kung remained in a position of in-

[13] CFCS, 6:14b, dcmt. 192, Liu En-p'u memorial, Sept. 26, 1883 (KH9/8/26).

[14] His earlier memorials clearly delineated his position. See, for instance, CFCS, 2:2b–3b, dcmt. 32, Dec. 19, 1881 (KH7/10/28); CFCS, 7:10–11b, dcmt. 220, Oct. 26, 1883 (KH9/9/26); CFCS, 4:5–8, dcmt. 104, May 13, 1883 (KH9/4/7).

[15] Semallé, p. 188.

[16] Ssu-ming Meng, pp. 50–51.

[17] Ibid., p. 51; Ch'ing-shih, VI, 4902.

fluence, her monopoly of power in Peking was incomplete. In 1865, she had actually removed him from all his offices only to have the pressure of court opinion force her to restore him to office and honor.[18]

Until 1881, Tz'u-hsi's control of the government was occasionally counterbalanced by that of her coregent. However, with the death of Tz'u-an in April of that year, Tz'u-hsi's authority was unchallenged, and Prince Kung's influence and power thereafter gradually dwindled. All Tz'u-hsi needed now was a suitable pretext to be rid of her well-hated in-law. Sheng-yü's memorial offered her that pretext.

Despite these matters of political and personal animus that led to the dismissal of Prince Kung, the coup of April also signified a decision on the part of the Old Buddha to enlist a group of advisors who would assist her in resolutely prosecuting the war against the French. Li Tz'u-ming's diary contains the following enlightening entry:

Tz'u-hsi anxiously and diligently seeks good rule — a hundred times more than a female Yao or Shun [archetypal rulers of the mythical period]. Since March [1884, after the Bac-Ninh defeat], she has single-mindedly advocated war. She summoned the members of the Grand Council to court and decreed to them: "the Hsien-feng Emperor regarded the war of 1860 [that culminated in the joint Anglo-French occupation of Peking] with great remorse, but He died with an ambition unfulfilled. Now we ought to wipe out the humiliation for the former emperor." However, all the officials [of the Grand Council] alike shirked their duties, and none could be tolerated in office. So she changed the members of the government.[19]

[18] Ssu-ming Meng, p. 51.

[19] LJC, 42:85b, Aug. 23, 1884 (KH10/7/3). Li's comments are supported by: CFCS, 17:8b, dcmt. 599, Shen Shang-i memorial, June 9, 1884 (KH10/5/16); CFCS, 13:15b, dcmt. 429, Teng Ch'eng-hsiu memorial, Apr. 18, 1884 (KH10/3/23); and LJC, 42: 86, quoted below, p. 106.

Indeed, the growing number of military setbacks and the unrelieved vacillation that characterized imperial foreign policy
would in any government have provided adequate grounds
for similar dismissals. With the replacement of Prince Kung
by Prince Ch'un as her leading advisor, Tz'u-hsi acquired a
minister who would abet, not impede, her conduct of a policy
of more determined resistance to the French. Tz'u-hsi's April
coup, then, did indicate a determination to shift to a more
aggressive policy.

The irony of the events of April is that they wrought no
significant change in imperial policy. The military situation in
Tongking continued to worsen, and a fresh opportunity for a
negotiated settlement of the controversy appeared. In these
circumstances, several of Tz'u-hsi's recent appointees to the
Grand Council and the Tsungli Yamen soon constituted a new
stronghold of opposition to a war policy.[20] The Old Buddha's
personal inclination was to press the fighting against the
French, but the dire premonitions of her councilors again dissuaded her. To one of the war advocates, she bemoaned:

> The words of you imperial advisors (*chien-kuan*) in the
> outer court often accord with my own ideas, but the officials
> in the Grand Council and the Tsungli Yamen do not agree.
> Initially I was dissatisfied with those who formerly headed
> the government, and so I replaced them. . . . Of those who
> now agree with me, there is only Prince Ch'un. Besides
> him, there is not one who is capable of conducting the war.
> Alas that it has come to this! [21]

But even Tz'u-hsi's favorite, Prince Ch'un, was incapable of
decision regarding resistance to the French. He too was disturbed by the cautionary advice of these new councilors, and
he wavered between the alternatives of war and peace.[22] In

[20] See below, p. 148.
[21] LJC, 42:86, Aug. 23, 1884 (KH10/7/3).
[22] LJC, 43:10, Sept. 26, 1884 (KH10/8/8); WJC, CFCC, II, 25, Sept.
4, 1883 (KH10/7/15), and p. 20, Aug. 1, 1884 (KH10/6/11).

any case, Prince Ch'un did not wield the powers of final decision. A perusal of his communications to the Grand Council during the Sino-French controversy leaves one with the deep impression that here was a minister not in control of the situation. At most, he was *primus inter pares* among the empress dowager's many advisors.[23]

Competing with Prince Ch'un for the ear of the imperial mistress were scores of other diverse-minded, but influential, officials (like Li Hung-chang, Yen Ching-ming, and Tso Tsung-t'ang, not to mention the spokesmen of *ch'ing-i*).[24] There were also the eunuchs. The influence upon policy of these often-vilified palace attendants has more often been the subject of hearsay than of knowledge. It is, for this reason, an illuminating fact that Prince Ch'un felt sharp concern that the eunuchs might present to the throne documents pertaining to foreign policy, and presumably provide counsel, before the grand councilors were able to do so.[25]

The influence of these several advisors upon Tz'u-hsi varied from person to person and from time to time. But she made the final decisions. The dismissal of Prince Kung did not, therefore, remove the cause of policy vacillation.[26]

[23] I-huan, "Ch'un Ch'in-wang I-huan chih Chün-chi-ch'u ch'ih-tu," CFCC, V, 39–71.
[24] Yen Ching-ming and Tso Tsung-t'ang are discussed below, pp. 149–150.
[25] I-huan, "Ch'un Ch'in-wang I-huan chih Chün-chi-ch'u ch'ih-tu," CFCC, V, 59, dcmt. 55, 1884 (KH10/?/?). Kung-chuan Hsiao has asserted that the chief eunuch Li Lien-ying "became widely known as the most powerful person at court . . . and a major influence on the empress-dowager." (Hsiao, "Weng," p. 138.)
[26] The most obvious demonstration of the empress dowager's indecision is to view Chinese policy as a whole during these years. However, Weng T'ung-ho's occasional comments about her lack of resolution should be noted: for example, WJC, CFCC, II, 8, Dec. 22, 1883 (KH9/11/23); p. 20, Aug. 1, 1884 (KH10/6/11); and p. 21, Aug. 10, 1884 (KH10/6/20). Also see below, pp. 210–217.

V

THE LI-FOURNIER NEGOTIATIONS

No other incident during the dispute with France revealed the influence of *ch'ing-i* on imperial policy more clearly than did the Li-Fournier negotiations. After Tz'u-hsi's coup of April 1884, the military situation so deteriorated that the Chinese government could no longer seriously consider assuming the offensive against the French. Indeed, it appeared that the French in Tongking would now sweep all before them. But then Captain Fournier of the French navy appeared proposing anew a conciliatory settlement of the controversy. The Chinese were incredulous, and *ch'ing-i* remarked acidly about the inscrutability of the barbarians' motives. Nevertheless, the throne had little choice but to accept the offer of renewed negotiations and again named Li Hung-chang as its representative. The results were disastrous, for Li was continually harried by his colleagues, and it was necessary for him to withhold from public view the least palatable of his concessions. With the failure of his negotiations, hostilities became overt.

Fournier's Terms for a Settlement. Captain François Ernest Fournier had been serving the French navy in East Asia since 1876, and during those years of service had become a highly respected acquaintance of Li Hung-chang. Indeed, in 1879, Li had proposed to Fournier that he leave the French navy to take command of the entire *Pei-yang* (Northern Chinese) navy, a post in which he would have had full powers of organization and appointment. Again, in the autumn of 1883, he had assisted Tricou during the negotiations of that period, and had again impressed the governor-general of Chihli with his comprehension of affairs and candor of statement.[1]

At the end of March 1884, shortly before the dismissal of Prince Kung, Fournier was commanding the *Volta*, a dispatch boat operating in southern Chinese waters. At this same time, Gustav Detring, the German commissioner of Chinese Maritime Customs who had spent several years at Tientsin as an intimate of Li Hung-chang, was passing through Hong Kong on his return to China from a year's leave in Europe. On invitation, Detring took passage on the *Volta* from Hong Kong to Canton, which was to be his next post in the Customs Service. During the voyage, Detring entered into a discussion of the Vietnamese difficulties with his host, Captain Fournier. In the course of this conversation, the two speculated upon terms that might serve as a basis for an equitable and peaceful solution to the controversy between their respective employers.[2]

This conversation was merely between private persons. But upon arrival in Canton, Detring informed Li in Tientsin of his talk with the French officer. To Li, it seemed that a door leading to an end of the dispute had been opened. On March 27, therefore, he requested the Tsungli Yamen to instruct Detring's superior in the Customs Service, Robert Hart, to order Detring

[1] CFCS, 13:22b, dcmt. 438, Li Hung-chang to Tsungli Yamen, Apr. 20, 1884 (KH10/3/25); A. Gervais, "Diplomatie chinoise: Li-Hung-Chang et le commandant Fournier," *Revue politique et littéraire*, 34.15:449 (Oct. 11, 1884); François Ernest Fournier, "La France et la Chine au traité de Tien-Tsin," *Revue des Deux Mondes*, 6.65:759–776 (Oct. 15, 1921).

[2] The relationship between Detring and Li had become very close during the former's long years as commissioner of Customs at Tientsin. Detring himself characterized this relationship, though Li would probably have objected, as that of a rudder to a ship — Li being the ship and Detring the rudder. (Stanley Fowler Wright, p. 511.)

to come to the north.[3] Hart was loath to accede to this request, and asserted that he did not wish to defer Detring's assumption of his new duties at Canton.[4] This may have been only an excuse to prevent Detring's involvement in the affair, for Hart was at this time by no means happy with his subordinate's diplomatic methods.[5] Nevertheless, Hart granted the desired permission, and Detring arrived in Tientsin three weeks later, on April 17, 1884, bearing a letter from Fournier setting forth the French conditions for an entente. Fournier was actually not empowered by Paris to negotiate until April 30. He had, however, been authorized by his immediate superior, Admiral Sébastien Lespès, to pursue discussions further, so that his views were acquiring an official character.[6]

Fournier's demands were simple and direct.[7] France meant to control the lower course of the Red River. In order to protect that area against further attacks from the Black Flags, it was essential that France be granted possession of the entire area of the river that had fallen into French hands after the triumph at Bac-Ninh — an area that was at some points within twenty kilometers of the Chinese border! China might retain the portion of Tongking to the north of that territory.

A second condition was that the southern Chinese provinces be opened to French trade. Yet another condition was that Tseng Chi-tse be dismissed from his post as minister to France. This was, in fact, a demand that must be fulfilled before the other conditions could be seriously discussed.[8] Tseng had made himself the *bête noire* of the French Foreign Ministry as a

[3] TK, CFCC, IV, 143, Li to Tsungli Yamen, Mar. 27, 1884 (KH10/3/1).

[4] YNT, III, 1646, dcmt. 763, Hart to Tsungli Yamen, Mar. 31, 1884 (KH10/3/5).

[5] Stanley Fowler Wright, pp. 516–517.

[6] HR, II, 432.

[7] The Chinese text of Fournier's letter to Li is in CFCS, 13:24–25b, dcmt. 438, addendum #2, Li to Tsungli Yamen, Apr. 20, 1884 (KH10/3/25).

[8] Fournier, pp. 777–780.

result of his intransigent demands, his incisive and inflammatory reports to the Tsungli Yamen on the political conditions of France, and, not least, his use of the European press to turn public sympathies away from France — a friendly press obtained, it was alleged, through the liberal distribution of largesse.[9] Fournier hoped to accomplish more than simply remove an irritating diplomat. If Li could fulfill this condition, it would prove that he possessed the powers to execute any agreement he might make, and also that Peking was willing to engage in serious pourparlers. With this formula, Fournier thought that he would avoid the ambiguities that had baffled Tricou.[10]

Finally, Fournier wrote that France intended to demand an indemnity from China, and to occupy an area of China's coast as a guarantee of the indemnity payments. He added that if China acted in a friendly manner the demand for an indemnity and guarantee might be dropped, but, if his conditions were not quickly accepted, France would attack — and the object of the attack would be China, not Vietnam!

The threat had its effect. On the day after Detring handed Fournier's letter to him, Li dispatched a telegram to the Tsungli Yamen. The situation was deteriorating, he cautioned, and requested that he be permitted to treat with Fournier.[11] Three days later, he again wrote to the Yamen, warning that the situation had become critical and that unless Tseng Chi-tse were dismissed Fournier would not negotiate. Li added — quite speciously, it might be added — that he and Tseng were great friends, and that he urged Tseng's dismissal with the greatest reluctance.[12]

---

[9] Billot, pp. 58 and 106; HR, II, 486; Fournier, p. 777.
[10] Fournier, p. 777.
[11] CFCS, 13:10, dcmt. 419, Li to Tsungli Yamen, Apr. 18, 1884 (KH10/3/23).
[12] CFCS, 13:23, dcmt. 438, Li to Tsungli Yamen, Apr. 20, 1884 (KH10/3/25).

Preparations for the Negotiations. The situation, from the Chinese point of view, had become critical. A French fleet, under the command of Admiral Lespès, had departed from Hong Kong moving northward along the China Coast. Ostensibly, it was bringing Fournier to meet with Li, but the Chinese knew that a refusal of the initial French conditions would cause Lespès' force to bare its cannon.[1]

The recent appointments to the Grand Council and the Tsungli Yamen had been made with the intention of implementing a policy of stiffened resistance, but the turn of events had suddenly made such a course of action peculiarly inopportune. With the French fleet daily progressing toward the north, the following counsel from Li Hung-chang on April 20 assumed particular cogency: "If we negotiate now, we can probably avoid payment of an indemnity, and a border settlement can be discussed; but if we wait until French troops have advanced farther, and French ships have occupied a place on the coast, I fear none of this can be negotiated."[2] Prince Ch'un and the grand councilors quickly concurred that Li should enter into pourparlers on the basis of Fournier's letter. The throne momentarily harbored misgivings, but it too relented. On April 22, it decreed that Li might engage in discussions with the French naval captain, admonishing Li, however, that the "national polity" (*kuo-t'i*) must not be damaged.[3] Peking simultaneously instructed the provincial officials to ready their defenses.[4]

Events moved slowly; Fournier was only dilatorily making his way toward Tientsin. But the passage of time did not ease the court's apprehensions. On April 25, a dispirited report on

[1] CFCS, 13:18, dcmt. 432, Li Hung-chang telegram, Apr. 21, 1884 (KH10/3/26).

[2] CFCS, 13:22b, dcmt. 438, Li to Tsungli Yamen, Apr. 20, 1884 (KH10/3/25).

[3] CFCS, 13:25b, dcmt. 439, Grand Council to Li, Apr. 22, 1884 (KH10/3/27); WJC, CFCC, II, 12, Apr. 22, 1884 (KH10/3/27).

[4] CFCS, 13:21b–22, dcmt. 436, decree, Apr. 21, 1884 (KH10/3/26).

the military situation in Tongking arrived from Ts'en Yü-ying. Ts'en reported that the city of Thai-Nguyen had fallen to the French in the wake of the Bac-Ninh disaster; he complained of serious shortages of food and matériel; and implied that the troops were badly demoralized. Ts'en was "unspeakably worried," and he warned that unless imperial forces were withdrawn from Tongking, they would in all likelihood be annihilated.[5] Then, as though China were not assailed by enough troubles, word was received on April 27 that the entire fleet of the dreaded Courbet was coming to join forces with Lespès. "This is hard to swallow!" was Weng T'ung-ho's reaction to this news[6] — a sentiment probably shared by the whole of officialdom.

In these circumstances, Peking acted promptly when Fournier requested tangible assurances of the empire's good faith. Upon the recommendation of the Tsungli Yamen, the throne on April 28 replaced Tseng as minister to France (although he retained his posts in London and St. Petersburg). Li Hung-chang hastily informed Fournier, and further adjured him to obtain a cessation of all French military activity.[7]

Li viewed the approaching negotiations with pessimism and diffidence. The situation had so deteriorated, he warned, that China must, "descrying a storm, furl its sails." [8] That is, the empire must now appease the French in order to gain peace. The purchased respite could be used to strengthen the empire's military capacity with the anticipation of redeeming the situation in the future.

Li recognized that such a proposal was anathema to the pro-war officials. On May 1, he memorialized:

[5] CFCS, 13:26b–27, dcmt. 444, Ts'en memorial, Mar. 26, 1884 (KH10/2/29), received Apr. 25, 1884 (KH10/4/1).
[6] WJC, CFCC, II, 12, Apr. 27, 1884 (KH10/4/3).
[7] CFCS, 13:37a–b, dcmt. 457, Tsungli Yamen memorial, Apr. 28, 1884 (KH10/4/4); CFCS, 13:38b, dcmt. 461, Li telegram, received Apr. 29, 1884 (KH10/4/5).
[8] CFCS, 14:2b, dcmt. 466, Li memorial, Apr. 28, 1884 (KH10/4/4).

in demarking the borders, some will aver that the areas obtained by China are too small; and there will be others who declare that China should refuse to open the Yunnan border to trade. The other items negotiated will not be few, and those who point out flaws will be many.

Since I have now been entrusted with this weighty mission, I must abide by this trust, and dare not shirk the responsibilities . . . through fear of criticism.[9]

Although he was prepared once again to undertake the onerous task of negotiating, Li desired assurances that he would have the backing of the throne after the storm of criticism broke. He therefore requested that the throne delineate precisely the limits beyond which he could not make concessions to Fournier.[10]

The throne was by now clearly desirous of an accord with the French.

We have sent troops to protect Vietnam [read a decree of April 30], but that country has no gratitude. The French also create difficulties, and to engage them in interminable conflict is not a perfect policy. Since the French have come at their own behest to negotiate, they show that they also wish to preserve the peace. So the best course of action may be to . . . guard the borders and give repose to the people.[11]

Despite its peaceable predilections, the throne shared Li Hung-chang's apprehensions regarding the officials' response to the projected negotiations. It therefore called for a court conference at noon, May 2.[12]

A court conference was a unique institution in which the throne instructed all high officials in the capital, from the grand councilors through the censors to the diarists of the emperor's movements, to repair at a prescribed time to the offices

[9] YNT, III, 1679, dcmt. 792, Li memorial, KH10/4/4, received by Tsungli Yamen, May 1, 1884 (KH10/4/7).
[10] Ibid.
[11] CFCS, 14:3b, dcmt. 467, decree, Apr. 30, 1884 (KH10/4/6).
[12] Ibid.

of the Grand Secretariat. There, they perused documents relevant to the particular crisis. Having informed themselves of all the facts, the officials memorialized their opinions and policy suggestions to the throne. Sometimes the papers to be read on such occasions could best be counted by volumes. One can now only contemplate with some amusement the pandemonium that ensued when the approximately two hundred staid venerables pushed and crowded into the offices of the Grand Secretariat, and there attempted, over the shoulders of their long-robed colleagues, to scan through the masses of documents that had flowed between the throne, the officials, and the foreign representatives.[13]

Court conferences were convoked irregularly, usually only during periods of extreme crisis. The throne chose such times to encourage the expression of officials' opinions because it was an effective means of fortifying the imperial position. In the first place, opening the *yen-lu* was good politics, for it appealed to the officials who liked to think that the ruler hearkened to their wisdom and experience. Secondly, a court conference served to identify the officials with imperial policy, weakening thereby the base of future policy criticisms.

Ssu-ming Meng has commented that "The throne never rejected the collective wisdom of this kind of a conference." [14] This statement, while factually correct, is nevertheless misleading, for it overlooks the fact that the throne called a court conference only when it was reasonably certain that the prevailing sentiment within the bureaucracy approximated its own views. But what if the throne miscalculated? Suppose that the conferees opposed the imperial wishes. A consensus of the officials would undoubtedly weigh heavily in the throne's final decision; as already noted, the Confucian bureaucracy wielded

[13] See CSTL, CFCC, VI, 74, Wu Hsün memorial, Oct. 31, 1884 (KH10/9/13) for a censorious description of a teeming gathering in the Grand Secretariat later in the year.
[14] Ssu-ming Meng, p. 47.

power that the throne could not disregard. But China had not yet been exposed to the peculiar notion that the opinions of each and every individual should be given equal weight. Indeed, the throne held in imperious disdain opinions that differed from its own. And, later in 1884, the throne sought a peace settlement only six weeks after a court conference had indicated overwhelming sentiment in favor of a war policy.[15] The "vote" of a court conference therefore in no way constituted a mandate that the throne was bound to follow.

The conference that was convoked in the Grand Secretariat on May 2 resulted in a spate of the officials' memorials unprecedented during the period of this study. Within a period of only five days, one hundred and ninety officials, in forty-seven separate memorials, poured out their fears regarding the Vietnamese situation. For the most part, the conferees supported the forthcoming negotiations, although they expressed misgivings. At Bac-Ninh, France had just conducted its most successful campaign of the hostilities. Even the Black Flags had been put into a near rout. The memorialists therefore viewed the French offer to negotiate with general incredulity, and they feared this was but one more of the French barbarians' insidious tricks. The prevalent sentiment was, consequently, that "we cannot bend before the French in compromise." [16]

A sizable minority of the memorialists, however, opposed negotiations in any form. Bargaining just after having incurred military defeats would, they were persuaded, inevitably necessitate granting concessions and would encourage the other foreign powers to emulate the French accomplishment. France, they declared, "has a fierce exterior, but within it is weak" (*wai-ch'iang chung-kan*) — an epithet similar to the "paper tiger" description applied to latter-day imperialists. Therefore,

---

[15] See below, pp. 183–188.

[16] CFCS, 14:16, dcmt. 491, Po-yen-na-mo-hu, et al. memorial, May 4, 1884 (KH10/4/10).

despite the recent Chinese defeats, they were convinced that the French military effort would collapse before a determined resistance.[17]

The Officials' Attack on Li Hung-chang. The butt of the memorialists' invectives, second only to the French, was he who was charged to conduct the negotiations. Since Li Hung-chang was the principal spokesman of the "appeasement" point of view during the negotiations with Fournier and throughout the controversy with the French, he was naturally the bugbear of the pro-war officials. They attacked him with a vengeance. He was likened to Ch'in Kuei, traditionally one of the most infamous appeasers in Chinese history. He was charged with toadying to the foreigner, and of having no sense of shame.[1] In his conduct of peace negotiations, if it was not that he was acting traitorously, it was that he was too easily duped by the French. "The wily plans of the French," wrote one official, "are known even by lads and servants. Only Li Hung-chang does not know." [2] "I fear," lamented another official, "that Li Hung-chang has been deluded by the French, and that the court has in turn been deluded by Li Hung-chang." [3]

Not always were his attackers so charitable as to suggest merely that he was "deluded" by the enemy. He was accused also of "cheating" and "disrespecting" the court.[4] One me-

[17] CFCS, 14:22b, dcmt. 495, Li Tuan-fen, et al. memorial, May 4, 1884 (KH10/4/10); CFCS, 14:34, dcmt. 506, Kuei-hsien memorial, same date; CFCS, 14:28b, dcmt. 500, Wu Hsün memorial, same date.

[1] CFCS, 14:28b, dcmt. 500, Wu Hsün memorial, May 4, 1884 (KH10/4/10); CFCS, 20:6b, dcmt. 809, Liu En-p'u memorial, July 24, 1884 (KH10/6/3); CFCS, 21:8, dcmt. 906, Shang-hsien memorial, Aug. 2, 1884 (KH10/6/12).

[2] CFCS, 18:24, dcmt. 692, Shang-hsien memorial, July 8, 1884 (KH10/jun 5/16).

[3] CFCS, 14:12, dcmt. 485, K'ung Hsien-chüeh, et al. memorial, May 4, 1884 (KH10/4/10).

[4] CFCS, 21:8, dcmt. 906, Shang-hsien memorial, Aug. 2, 1884 (KH10/6/12); CFCS, 14:28b, dcmt. 500, Wu Hsün memorial, May 4, 1884 (KH10/4/10).

morial, co-authored by nine officials, charged that Li was usurping the imperial authority so that it was within his power even to give away those tributaries that had been won by previous emperors of the dynasty[5] — an indictment that emperors of the eighteenth century had admonished their officials not to suggest even as a possibility.[6]

One of the chief allegations made against Li was that his efforts to create a modern, effective military force had failed. He had, they charged, spent untold sums of money on the project. Now, when there was need of such a force, he "fears difficulties and evades responsibilities" in order to conceal the failure of his self-strengthening efforts. In this way, the merit he earned fighting against the Taiping rebels he now "throws away like dirt" out of love for himself.[7]

Demands that Li Hung-chang be removed from office became almost routine; two particularly vindictive officials even requested that he be put to death.[8] So violent, indeed, did the attacks become that the throne finally admonished the officials to be more restrained in their criticisms. They had, an imperial decree read, "frequently given voice to slanderous criticisms and their discussions of affairs have not been free from prejudice." [9] It is a tribute to Li's pertinacity, even courage, that, in the face of this attack, he continued throughout most of the controversy to voice his views forthrightly. It is, at the same time, a mark of his influence with the throne that he was not dismissed from his high offices.

[5] CFCS, 17:8b, dcmt. 599, Shen Shang-i memorial, June 9, 1884 (KH10/5/16).

[6] Nivision, "Introduction," p. 21.

[7] CFCS, 14:28b, dcmt. 500, Wu Hsün memorial, May 4, 1884 (KH10/4/10); CFCS, 14:13b, dcmt. 486, Teng Ch'eng-hsiu, et al. memorial, same date; CFCS, 18:25, dcmt. 683, Hsi-chün memorial, June 8, 1884 (KH10/jun 5/16).

[8] LJC, 42:48b, July 14, 1884 (KH10/5/22); Chou Chia-mei, "Ch'i-pu-fu chai ch'üan-chi" (The complete writings of Chou Chia-mei), CFCC, IV, 542.

[9] Ch'ing-shih-lu, 200:1, Jan. 31, 1885 (KH10/12/16).

Negotiation of the Li-Fournier Convention. Despite the vitriolic attacks upon Li Hung-chang, and the multifarious fears expressed regarding French stratagems, the throne instructed Li to proceed with the negotiations. However, in accordance with the general sentiments of the memorialists, it admonished Li that the following principles were not to be compromised:

(1) The dependency relationship of Vietnam to China must be maintained.
(2) The French may not engage in commerce within Yunnan province.
(3) The Black Flags must not be extirpated.
(4) China must not pay an indemnity.[1]

Fournier arrived at Tientsin on May 5, and the following afternoon went to Li Hung-chang's offices, where the two immediately began discussions. Disagreements appeared immediately. Fournier was adamant that no clear statement of Vietnam's dependency relationship with China could be inserted in a Sino-French agreement. For the past three years, the two countries had debated this point; the French government would under no conditions condone such an admission now.[2] Fournier was willing, however, that a new Franco-Vietnamese treaty be negotiated to supersede those of 1874 and 1883, in which there would be no expressions specifically denying the tributary status of Vietnam or that could otherwise be construed as derogatory to the dignity of China. Li was less than happy with this solution of the question. Nonetheless, he explained to Peking — without justification, per-

[1] CFCS, 14:14, dcmt. 487, decree to Li Hung-chang, May 4, 1884 (KH10/4/10); H. B. Morse, II, 354. Morse erred in writing that no trade *with* Yunnan could be permitted. Cordier's interpretation that European trade *within* Yunnan would not be condoned is truer to the original. (HR, II, 444.)
[2] CFCS, 15:11b, dcmt. 522, addendum #1, Li-Fournier conversation, May 7, 1884 (KH10/4/13).

haps — that it satisfied the imperial condition that the traditional relationship with Vietnam be maintained.[3]

Fournier next demanded an indemnity, despite his earlier assertion that this would, in all likelihood, be avoidable. Fournier in fact never expected the governor-general to yield on this point, and many years later he admitted that he had raised the indemnity issue only to obtain from Li a reciprocal concession on the opening of Yunnan to commerce.[4] This strategy met with only partial success. Fournier had sought for France commercial privileges throughout the province of Yunnan. But Li Hung-chang tenaciously maintained that even the opening of an entrepôt and establishment of a consulate inside the Chinese frontier were impermissible. He could agree, however, to the sale of goods on the frontier.[5] Fournier felt constrained to accept this proposal, the details of which were to be worked out later in a commercial treaty. Li had effectively denied the French access to the interior of China, and it seems, therefore, that there is no basis for the allegation that Li did not, on this point, fulfill his none too precise instructions.[6]

On two other points, however, Li was sorely derelict. In the conversation of May 6, Fournier expressed the French intention to attack and subdue the Black Flags. They had, he declared, for years obstructed commerce, and only after their suppression could France reduce the size of its military in Vietnam.[7] Yet in Li's initial account of this conversation to the Yamen, he stated that Fournier had not broached the subject of Liu's forces. He further observed that the disposition of the Black Flags could be determined three months later when the defini-

[3] CFCS, 15:10, dcmt. 522, Li to Tsungli Yamen, May 7, 1884 (KH10/4/13).

[4] Fournier, p. 782.

[5] CFCS, 15:10, dcmt. 522, Li to Tsungli Yamen, May 7, 1884 (KH10/4/13). See n. 1 above, this section.

[6] As H. B. Morse (II, 354) charged.

[7] ISHK, CFCC, IV, 99, KH10/5/23; PLHK, CFCC, IV, 15, May 29, 1884 (KH10/5/5).

tive treaty was negotiated.[8] This was clearly not the purport of Fournier's statement, and Li's failure to inform Peking of French intentions regarding the Black Flags directly violated one of the four principles that the throne had established for his guidance.

The second — and ultimately the most crucial — matter for which Li must be held culpable was that regarding the withdrawal of imperial troops from Tongking. The preliminary convention that Li and Fournier now concluded stipulated that imperial troops were to retire immediately to the Chinese frontier (Article II).[9]

Li understood that this clause meant just what it said.[10] Yet he dared not exacerbate opposition to the agreement by informing Peking that Chinese troops were now to pull out of Tongking. He therefore informed the Yamen that there would be no violation of the agreement if imperial troops remained in their present locations. He attempted no justification of this curious interpretation of Article II other than to observe that the troops had already retreated to Lang-Son and Lao-Kay, cities in Tongking that were close to the Chinese frontier.[11]

[8] CFCS, 15:10, dcmt. 522, Li to Tsungli Yamen, May 7, 1884 (KH10/4/13).

[9] For the complete articles, see below, pp. 123–124.

[10] A perusal of the following documents can leave no doubts on this point: ISHK, CFCC, IV, 99, Li to Tsungli Yamen, June 16, 1884 (KH10/5/23); TK, CFCC, IV, 150, Li to Chang Shu-sheng, June 5, 1884 (KH10/5/12); TK, CFCC, IV, 155, Li to P'an Ting-hsin, July 7, 1884 (KH10/jun 5/15); and CFCS, 17:16b, dcmt. 603, P'an Ting-hsin telegram, June 16, 1884 (KH10/5/23). Shao Hsün-cheng (p. 127) has arrived at the same conclusion.

It might be suggested that the crux of the misunderstanding was in the translation of the agreement into Chinese, in which the temporal quality of the French phrase "à retirer immédiatement, sur ses frontières," was subdued by being translated as *chi hsing tiao-hui pien-chieh*. When Article V is read in conjunction with the rest of the convention, however, it becomes clear that the real trouble lay not in the indefiniteness of the character *chi*, but in the faulty wording of the original document.

[11] CFCS, 15:10b, dcmt. 522, Li to Tsungli Yamen, May 7, 1884 (KH10/4/13).

121

Li was pressured from two sides: on the one hand, there were the threats of the French; on the other, the assaults of political enemies. In his intense desire for peace, however, Li attempted to avoid both horns of the dilemma. He therefore appeased the French by granting most of the concessions demanded from him; and he forestalled the attacks of his domestic foes by withholding from Peking information regarding the least acceptable of these concessions, viz., those provisions relating to the Black Flags and the withdrawal of the imperial armies. This expedient succeeded in effecting a temporary reconciliation of the two countries, and it was now necessary merely to apply signatures to the document. The pourparlers had commenced with the understanding that Admiral Lespès would sign for the French. But with the draft of the convention completed, Li, for reasons that remain unclear, became exceedingly anxious to conclude the agreement, and he pressed Fournier to ask for the necessary powers to sign, rather than wait for the arrival of the admiral.[12] Fournier acquiesced, and since Jules Ferry found the agreement "good in all respects," plenipotentiary powers were quickly granted.[13] Peking, ignorant of course of Li's machinations, expressed itself similarly disposed. It did remark that the article concerning trade had not been drawn up with sufficient precision, but on May 10 it invested Li with full powers to sign for China.[14]

Once in possession of these powers, Li suddenly felt doubts about the convention that he and Fournier had agreed to sign on the following day. Exactly what his misgivings were is

[12] It could be speculated that Li's anxiety stemmed from fear that the war advocates in Peking might wreck his accomplishment. There are indications, however, that Li's fear of, or spite for, Sir Harry Parkes may have been a more immediate consideration. See HR, II, 433; and Fournier, pp. 784–785.

[13] HR, II, 433.

[14] CFCS, 15:17, dcmt. 531, decree to Li, May 10, 1884 (KH10/4/16); CFCS, 15:12b–13, dcmt. 523, decree, May 9, 1884 (KH10/4/15); CFCS, 15:5b, dcmt. 514, decree to Li, May 8, 1884 (KH10/4/14).

not known, but he proposed to Fournier that they renew their discussions with the intention of revising their recently completed draft. Apparently believing this to be but a delaying tactic, Fournier flatly rejected the proposal. If Li did not sign within three days, Fournier declared, he would leave Tientsin, and the French navy would immediately launch an attack along the coast.

Presented with this ultimatum, Li had no alternative. On May 11, he and Fournier affixed their signatures to the following preliminary accord:

ARTICLE I.

France undertakes to respect and protect against any aggressive measures whatsoever, and under all circumstances, the southern frontiers of China bordering on Tongking.

ARTICLE II.

The Celestial Empire, reassured of the formal guarantees of good-neighbourly feeling accorded to her by France as regards the integrity and safety of the southern frontiers of China, undertakes:

1. To *withdraw immediately to her frontiers the Chinese garrisons* of Tongking.

2. To respect, now and in the future, the treaties directly concluded, or to be concluded, between France and the Court of Hué.

ARTICLE III.

In recognition of the conciliatory attitude of the Government of the Celestial Empire, and as a tribute to the patriotic wisdom of his Excellency Li Hung-chang, the negotiator of this convention, *France will not ask for an indemnity from China.* In return for this, China undertakes to permit, over the whole extent of her southern frontiers bordering on Tongking, free traffic in goods between Vietnam and France on the one part and China on the other, to be regulated by a Commercial and Customs Convention, which shall be drawn up in the most conciliatory spirit on the part of the Chinese negotiators, and under the most advantageous conditions possible for French commerce.

ARTICLE IV.

The French Government undertake to make use of no expression calculated to affect prejudicially the prestige of the Celestial Empire in drafting the definitive treaty which they are about to conclude with Vietnam and which will annul former treaties relative to Tongking.

ARTICLE V.

As soon as the present convention shall have been signed, *the two Governments shall name their plenipotentiaries, who shall meet in three months' time to work out the details of a definitive treaty* on the bases established by the preceding articles.

In conformity with diplomatic usage, the French text shall be binding.[15]

The Li-Fournier Convention, as this document is commonly called, was received with general approval. Among the most joyous and complacent for the future of Sino-French relations was the soon-to-be-enraged Jules Ferry in Paris.[16] In Tientsin, lavish feasting accompanied the exchange of mutual congratulations among the participating diplomats. Fournier in particular viewed affairs with satisfaction, childishly viewing himself as a "mysterious plenipotentiary." [17] On May 18, he left Tientsin for Paris personally to present to his government the document that had so swiftly achieved an end of the controversy.

Peking was somewhat less pleased with the final document. The throne noted a number of points — the relationship of Vietnam with China, and the border and trade agreements — that would have to be clarified in the definitive treaty. The

[15] Harley Farnsworth MacNair, *Modern Chinese History: Selected Readings* (Shanghai, 1923), pp. 481–482. Italics added for emphasis, and with slight changes in orthography.

[16] HR, II, 436–441.

[17] HR, II, 441, Fournier to Naval Minister, May 12, 1884.

French, the throne added, are filled with "treacherous schemes," and the final treaty would have to be drafted with the utmost care to deprive the crafty barbarians of loopholes.[18] Nevertheless, none suspected in mid-May 1884 that Peking did not intend to honor the work of Li Hung-chang and François Ernest Fournier. That charge was not raised until after the Bac-Le incident.

The Bac-Le Incident. In mid-June 1884, a French force of about nine hundred men under the command of Lieutenant Colonel Alphonse Dugenne was marching northward under instructions to occupy the Vietnamese city of Lang-Son. It was Dugenne's understanding that Lang-Son was to have been evacuated by the Chinese as early as June 6.[1] However, on June 23 his troops encountered a strongly fortified outpost of the imperial army near the village of Bac-Le, approximately eighty kilometers south of the Chinese frontier. Dugenne demanded their withdrawal. Reportedly in a conciliatory tone, the Chinese commanders replied that they knew of the Li-Fournier Convention, and that they had no desire to violate it. But they were in possession of no orders to withdraw, and they asked the French officer to wait until they could get the requisite instructions. The French and Chinese versions usually differ regarding which side first opened fire. In any case, the result was that the French were repulsed, after a three-day fight, with nearly one hundred casualties. The Chinese incurred casualties three times as heavy, but they held their position. This was, in the eyes of both nations, a defeat for the French.[2]

The incident electrified Paris. Jules Ferry informed the

---

[18] CFCS, 15:30, dcmt. 545, decree to Li, May 13, 1884 (KH10/4/19).
[1] See below, p. 135, n. 21.
[2] Alfred Rambaud, *Jules Ferry* (Paris, 1903), pp. 343–344; HR, II, 449–451; CFCS, 19:14b, dcmt. 753, P'an Ting-hsin memorial, June 29, 1884 (KH10/*jun* 5/7); TK, CFCC, IV, 160, P'an Ting-hsin to Li Hung-chang, July 15, 1884 (KH10/*jun* 5/23).

Chamber of the defeat, and termed the Chinese action "a veritable ambush." He further announced that this "violation" of the Li-Fournier Convention would be used as a basis to demand reparations — a declaration that evoked from the deputies cries of "tres bien! tres bien!" [3] The encounter had, in fact, erased all traces of the goodwill created during the meeting of Li and Fournier.

Explanations of the Bac-Le incident have frequently been emotional, biased, and based upon incomplete evidence. Even now, over eighty years after the incident, some aspects of the affair remain opaque. Yet the events that led to the resumption of fighting can now be seen in most of their details.

Despite his initial jubilation after the signing of the Convention, Fournier had become apprehensive that the document was not sufficiently exact regarding the withdrawal of the Chinese forces from Tongking. Therefore, on the afternoon of May 17, the day before his departure for France, Fournier had repaired to the offices of Li Hung-chang. Ostensibly, he had come to bid the governor-general farewell. He had, however, also prepared for the occasion a document — since known as the May 17 Memo — the intent of which was to clarify those articles of the Convention that he felt might be the source of misconstruction. The most important of the three sections of the May 17 Memo was that pertaining to troop evacuations. Fournier declared that the French military would proceed to occupy the areas of Tongking bordering Kwangtung and Kwangsi on June 5, the territory along the Yunnan border on July 1.[4]

What transpired in this meeting between the French and Chinese diplomats will perhaps always remain somewhat conjectural. It is evident that Li was reluctant to agree to an evacu-

[3] Paul Robiquet, ed., *Discours et opinions de Jules Ferry* (Paris, 1893–98), V, 377.
[4] The French and Chinese texts of this document are, respectively, in HR, II, 496–498 and ISHK, CFCC, IV, 100.

ation of the imperial troops within a specified period as Fournier demanded, for he was, as already noted, beleaguered by hostile officials in the capital.

> Just before Fournier was to make his departure [Li later explained to the throne], he suddenly raised the demand that our armies be withdrawn within a specified period of time. . . . Although the provisional treaty we negotiated had received imperial approval, yet officials in the capital were spouting vexatious criticisms; if they learned that Fournier had also requested that our troops withdraw within a specified time, they would surely make an even greater clamor, needlessly creating doubts in the minds of the people.[5]

One may correctly, if cynically, disregard Li's expression of concern regarding the people's state of mind; the fact is that he was rightly convinced that he would be courting political suicide if he conveyed Fournier's demands to Peking. On the other hand, if he did not accept those demands, the recently concluded peace would be nipped in the bud.

Li therefore agreed to the principle of troop evacuations as stipulated in the Memo.[6] But he informed Fournier that, rather

[5] CFCS, 18:22a–b, dcmt. 680, Li memorial, addendum #3, July 5, 1884 (KH10/*jun* 5/13). See also PLHK, CFCC, IV, 14, Li to Ts'en Yü-ying, May 29, 1884 (KH10/5/5) in which Li confided that "I have ventured to do that which was disapprobated in order to conclude the pourparlers, and to resolve the current crisis. But the *ch'ing-i* of those not in positions of responsibility finds fault with many points." Li expressed a similar version of the episode in PLHK, CFCC, IV, 17, Li to Chou Hsiao-t'ang, July 30, 1884 (KH10/6/9).

[6] Whether Li agreed to the precise time limits in Fournier's note, or merely to the general principle of a withdrawal of the troops, is uncertain. Fournier's article, which has otherwise been so revealing regarding this affair, does not elucidate the matter. Li subsequently, at a time when he was more candid than at other times concerning the negotiations, still insisted that he had not agreed to an "immediate" evacuation. (CFCS, 18:22b, dcmt. 680, Li memorial, addendum #3, July 5, 1884 [KH10/*jun* 5/13].) But it is also clear that he had indicated to the Kwangsi troops that the French would advance to their areas in accordance with the dates in the May 17 Memo. (CFCS, 17:16b, dcmt. 603, P'an Ting-hsin telegram, June 16, 1884 [KH10/5/23].) Merely as a matter of conjecture, I am inclined to accept this latter evidence and suggest that Li accepted Fournier's conditions in their entirety.

than request the Tsungli Yamen to order the troop withdrawals, he, Li himself, by virtue of his plenipotentiary powers, would undertake to dispatch the necessary orders. To this, Fournier readily assented, thinking that the arrival of the orders at the front would be more certain than if the bellicose members of the Tsungli Yamen were to act as intermediaries.

Fournier then did one of the most foolish — or at least controversial — things of his career. He took "my primitive note," as he referred to it many years later,[7] and, *with a pencil,* crossed out the article pertaining to the evacuation of the Chinese troops. He certified the alteration with his signature.

Why did Fournier cross out this section when Li had agreed to its conditions? I do not pretend to understand what the man was thinking at the time. On the one hand, he may have thought that Li would transmit the memorandum to the Tsungli Yamen, but crossed out the section regarding troop withdrawals because Li, not Peking, was now to order the Chinese troops out of Tongking, and that section in the Memo therefore no longer concerned the Yamen. On the other hand, Fournier may not have regarded the Memo as an official document at all, but as a private note to Li in which he made more explicit the terms of the formal Convention. In that case, his alteration of the section regarding evacuation of the imperial troops may simply have been a gesture acknowledging that Li would not transmit the purport of that section to Peking.

Fournier carried out his end of the bargain punctually, for that same day, May 17, he informed the commander of the French forces in Vietnam, General Charles Millot, of the details of the arrangement.[8] Li Hung-chang performed his part in a less explicit manner than Fournier could have expected. Li presumed that, because this was the malarial season in Tongking, and because the rivers were still too low to permit ex-

[7] Fournier, p. 786.
[8] HR, II, 443.

tensive navigation, French arms would be unable to accomplish the intended occupation of Tongking.[9] He then made a closely calculated gamble. He informed the frontier commanders of his agreement that their forces should withdraw. However, rather than instructing them actually to withdraw — news of which would surely have reached his enemies in Peking — he merely proposed that the troops maintain their present positions. In the unlikely event that French forces were able to advance as far as their positions, the commanders were to act as the occasion seemed to demand.[10]

Unfortunately, Li made his gamble without full knowledge of the circumstances in Tongking. He believed that the Chinese forces were encamped just outside the Chinese border. In fact, there were troops seventy kilometers farther south than he knew.[11]

On June 16, a telegram from P'an Ting-hsin, the new governor of Kwangsi, reached Tientsin reporting that French troops were approaching the Chinese outposts. One can now only imagine with what trepidation Li received this message. He is reported to have convoked immediately "a sort of cabinet council." [12] Then, after what must have involved much soul-searching, he composed a communication apprising the Tsungli Yamen of the French advance, in addition presenting a relatively accurate account of his commitments to Fournier and of his subsequent attempts to fulfill them.[13]

To Li's consternation, the throne was not disposed to retrieve the situation by ordering the imperial troops to withdraw. On June 18, probably the same day that it learned of Li's report

[9] PLHK, CFCC, IV, 15, Li to Ts'en Yü-ying, May 29, 1884 (KH10/5/5).

[10]*Ibid.;* ISHK, CFCC, IV, 99, July 15, 1884 (KH10/5/23); CFCS, 18:22a–b, dcmt. 680, addendum #3, Li memorial, July 5, 1884 (KH10/jun 5/13).

[11] ISHK, CFCC, IV, 99, June 16, 1884 (KH10/5/23).

[12] Semallé, pp. 208–209.

[13] ISHK, CFCC, IV, 98–99, June 16, 1884 (KH10/5/23).

of the French advance, the throne dispatched a new decree to the commanders at the front. This was a full five days before the fighting at Bac-Le, and a telegram would undoubtedly have reached the front in time to avoid the forthcoming clash. But instead of ordering the troops to evacuate Tongking, the throne commanded them to stand fast. To withdraw, the decree read, would display weakness — though the troops were at the same time instructed not themselves to open hostilities.[14]

Curiously, the Empress Dowager Tz'u-hsi was still wavering in indecision. Li Hung-chang observed now that "Tso Tsung-t'ang has entered the capital and is advocating war. The throne is undecided." [15] Three days later, however, the imperial attitude had clearly hardened. Possibly under the influence of Tso Tsung-t'ang, or possibly because of the intransigent memorials reaching her through the *yen-lu*, Tz'u-hsi had (momentarily) cast off her doubts, and resolved to lay the blame upon the French if fighting did break out.[16] Two days later, the fighting at Bac-Le began.

Explanations of the Bac-Le Incident. Subsequent to the Bac-Le fighting, Fournier declared on numerous occasions, verbally and in writing, that he absolutely had not struck out the passage in the May 17 Memo. He further asserted that Li Hung-chang, during their meeting on May 17, had made no protest to the dates he, Fournier, had set for the evacuation of the Chinese troops.[1]

A furious controversy broke out in the French press over the

[14] CFCS, 17:21 and 21b, dcmts. 607 and 609, decrees to Ts'en Yü-ying and P'an Ting-hsin, June 18, 1884 (KH10/5/25).
[15] TK, CFCC, IV, 151, Li to P'an Ting-hsin, June 19, 1884 (KH10/5/26).
[16] CFCS, 17:24, dcmt. 614, decree to Li, June 21, 1884 (KH10/5/28). The imperial attitude had clearly hardened in three days' time. Cf. CFCS, 17:21, dcmt. 608, decree to Li, June 18, 1884 (KH10/5/25).
[1] HR, II, 502–504; Richard Simpson Gundry, *China and Her Neighbors; France in Indo-China, Russia and China, India and Tibet* (London, 1893), Fournier letter to Ferry, pp. 94–95.

matter, each journal becoming vindictive and personal in its presentation of evidence and interpretation. Fournier himself may have been the author of one of these articles, tendentiously entitled "Les fourberies chinoises" (Chinese Double-dealings).[2] Fournier was so much incensed by the criticisms of one noted journalist, M. Rochefort, that he challenged him to a duel — an act of honor that may have salved the navy captain's overwrought emotions though it left him with a bullet in the thigh.[3] Subsequently Fournier stated that he *could not remember* if he had made the alterations.[4]

Li Hung-chang obfuscated the issue even more when he denied that he had made any commitment on May 17 regarding troop withdrawals.[5] He further justified the presence of the troops at Bac-Le on the grounds that Article II of the May 11 Convention (calling for the immediate withdrawal of Chinese troops from Tongking) actually meant "immediately after the conclusion of the definitive treaty." [6]

As the furor increased, one of Li's secretaries allegedly "found" the controversial document in a drawer where it had been heedlessly left. Li Hung-chang, it was asserted, had not attached any importance to the paper.[7] Later (during the

[2] Semallé, p. 249. Semallé has quoted from a number of the articles from the French journals giving a good representation of both sides of the controversy (pp. 248–253).

[3] *North China Herald,* Nov. 19, 1884, p. 561. The reference was probably to the famous journalist and politician Henri Rochefort, who, however, did not mention the incident in his autobiography, *Les Aventures de ma Vie.*

[4] *North China Herald,* Oct. 15, 1884, p. 410.

[5] CFCS, 18:16, dcmt. 665, Li-Jacquemier conversation, June 30, 1884 (KH10/jun 5/8); CFCS, 18:22a–b, dcmt. 680, addendum #3, Li memorial, July 5, 1884 (KH10/jun 5/13).

[6] ISHK, CFCC, IV, 100, 102, and 103. Article V of the Convention would seem to have verified Li's explanation, for it stipulated that the first four articles of the Convention were to serve as the bases of the definitive agreement. This is just one more example, however, of the imprecision with which the Convention was drafted.

[7] HR, II, 496; Semallé, p. 209; *North China Herald,* Aug. 29, 1884, p. 236.

negotiations with Patenotre), the Chinese confronted the French with the document, complete with the crossed-out section initialed by Fournier, as proof that Li had not agreed to withdraw imperial troops.[8] The French immediately charged that Li had himself crossed out the sections of the Memo, and had then forged Fournier's signature. Subsequently, it was declared that the flourishes of Fournier's hand could not have been reproduced by a Chinese nor by any but a Western specialist. And the *North China Herald* wrote that "the belief in the forgery-theory is now being fast relegated to the limbo of exploded superstitions."[9] Nevertheless, even the eminent Chinese historian, Shao Hsün-cheng, subsequently stated that it was positively a forgery.[10]

In an article he wrote in 1921 — nearly forty years after the events discussed here — Fournier casually, as though it had never been the cause of quarrels, enmities, and a duel, affirmed that it was he who had made the alterations in the Memo.[11] It is inconceivable that the aged Fournier, so far removed from the exigencies of the controversy, would have reversed his story — thus putting himself in a worse light — if it were not true. The controversial alterations on the May 17 Memo had, then, been made by Fournier, just as Li had asserted.

Ironically, the assignment of blame for the Bac-Le incident does not, after all, revolve about the crossed-out passages in the Memo. As already indicated, both Li and Fournier understood that the Convention of May 11 had stipulated that the Chinese forces were to withdraw immediately. These troops should not have been at Bac-Le even had there been no Memo of May 17. That ill-fated document had merely been an attempt by Fournier to define more precisely the dates of the evacuation al-

---

[8] See below, pp. 145–146.
[9] *North China Herald*, Oct. 15, 1884, p. 410; Semallé, p. 206.
[10] Shao Hsün-cheng, p. 143.
[11] Fournier, pp. 786–787.

ready agreed upon. Who, then, was responsible for the tragic fighting at Bac-Le?

It may be stated without qualification that Li Hung-chang had engaged in his talks with Fournier in perfectly good faith — even though his methods do not bear scrutiny. It was with no little vexation that he viewed the Old Buddha's refusal to order a withdrawal of the Chinese forces after he had finally informed her of his commitments to Fournier. She had, Li charged, left the troops in a position to meet the oncoming French out of sheer contrariness (*shang-i fu-ch'i*).[12]

Tz'u-hsi, on her part, was equally unhappy with his conduct in the pourparlers. She accused him repeatedly of deceit and negligence for having withheld full details of his concessions to Fournier.[13] But, once having learned that the treaty agreement demanded an immediate troop evacuation, why did she not acquiesce?

French historians have inclined to the view that the war party, which became dominant after May 11, found the conditions of the agreement unsatisfactory and determined therefore to destroy the pact.[14] Evidence in support of this view is

[12] TK, CFCC, IV, 161, Li to P'an Ting-hsin, July 16, 1884 (KH10/*jun* 5/24). Actually, the decree proscribing a withdrawal did not arrive at the front till one day after the incident had started. (CFCS, 18:2b–3, dcmt. 637, Chang Shu-sheng telegram, June 28, 1884 [KH10/*jun* 5/6].) But the commanders at the front were still under similar orders from a previous decree. (CFCS, 15:30a–b, dcmt. 546, decree, May 13, 1884 [KH10/4/19].) If the decree of June 18 had permitted an evacuation, the whole incident might yet have been averted, however, for the actual defeat of the French at Bac-Le occurred only on June 25, the day after the arrival at the front of the June 18 decree.

[13] CFCS, 17:21, dcmt. 608, decree to Li, June 18, 1884 (KH10/5/25); CFCS, 17:24, dcmt. 614, decree to Li, June 21, 1884 (KH10/5/28); CFCS, 18:12b, dcmt. 660, decree to Li, July 2, 1884 (KH10/*jun* 5/10); Alicia Little, *Li Hung-Chang: His Life and Times* (London, 1903), pp. 139–140.

[14] Examples of this view may be found in Rambaud, pp. 347–348; and Billot, pp. 192–196. A disgruntled diplomat, Semallé, to the contrary, was convinced that the Chinese were acting in good faith. (Semallé, pp. 192–209.)

not lacking. Upon learning the contents of the Li-Fournier Convention, the pro-war officials responded, almost as one, in denouncing the agreement in all its details. They contended that the war effort should be increased, and the recently signed Convention ignored.[15] At the very time that the empress dowager issued the decree forbidding a troop withdrawal, the war-minded Tso Tsung-t'ang was enjoying imperial favor. And when Tso was nominated to the Grand Council in mid-June, some foreign observers were convinced that his influence had been decisive and that Bac-Le had been the work of the war party in Peking.[16]

The evidence is conclusive that the war advocates had temporarily overshadowed Li Hung-chang and the supporters of a peace policy. Does this mean that the throne had determined to overthrow the Li-Fournier agreement? I think not. There is, unfortunately, no way of determining precisely what influence Tso Tsung-t'ang and other critics of the Convention had upon the throne. Their influence was undoubtedly considerable. But Tz'u-hsi had not deliberately destroyed the Li-Fournier Convention. Indeed, she had strictly cautioned the army commanders that they must not start hostilities.[17] Nevertheless, in view of the overwhelming sentiment of *ch'ing-i* and other pro-war officials, she dared not order imperial troops to evacuate in the face of a French threat.[18] Tz'u-hsi therefore blunderingly

[15] Three of many memorials expressing these views are: CFCS, 15: 26–28b, dcmt. 543, K'ung Hsien-chüeh, et al. memorial, May 13, 1884 (KH10/4/19); CFCS, 16:35–36b, dcmt. 591, addendum #1, P'eng Yü-lin memorial, May 22, 1884 (KH10/4/28); CFCS, 17:7–14, dcmt. 599, Shen Shang-i memorial, June 9, 1884 (KH10/5/16).

[16] *North China Herald*, July 18, 1884, p. 62.

[17] CFCS, 17:21 and 21b, dcmts. 607 and 609, decrees to Ts'en Yü-ying and P'an Ting-hsin, June 18, 1884 (KH10/5/25); CFCS, 18:17, dcmt. 668, decree to P'an Ting-hsin, July 2, 1884 (KH10/jun 5/10); CFCS, 19:3b, dcmt. 725, decree, July 16, 1884 (KH10/jun 5/24).

[18] Weng T'ung-ho observed that "The court [*ch'ao-t'ing*] has always desired peace . . . but it is definitely not willing to withdraw the troops." (WJC, CFCC, II, 15, July 4, 1884 [KH10/jun 5/12].)

saddled her troop commanders at the front with inflexible orders that unwittingly set the stage for, though they did not immediately cause, the Bac-Le incident.

The French were not wholly blameless for the resumption of the fighting. Fournier himself recognized that the French commander, Dugenne, had botched the affair by impulsively ordering the assault on a Chinese force that was anxious to avoid a clash of arms.[19] However, Fournier was even more responsible than Dugenne, for he had proved himself to be a uniquely maladroit diplomat. The Li-Fournier Convention is a masterpiece of ambiguity — ambiguity which Li Hung-chang may have nurtured, but which Fournier ought not to have countenanced. The May 17 Memo, to which he had attributed great significance, had not been written in duplicate; the single copy in existence had been allowed to remain in the possession of his Chinese counterpart; and he had crossed out the most crucial, but still valid, passage in the document. A writer for the *North China Herald* made a pointed and accurate appraisal of Fournier's handiwork when he commented that "certainly a more irregular, nondescript, and anomalous piece of penmanship we have never seen claiming the dignity of a political instrument." [20]

Fournier committed another blunder. The May 17 Memo had stipulated that if Chinese troops were encountered in Tongking territory, the French forces were *to wait twenty-four hours* before effecting the required expulsion. But in Fournier's dispatch to General Millot concerning the Memo, he instructed him to "proceed summarily" to expel the unevacuated Chinese troops.[21] Dugenne may therefore have been less guilty of ir-

---

[19] Fournier, p. 787; CFCS, 19:14b–15, dcmt. 753, P'an Ting-hsin memorial, June 29, 1884 (KH10/*jun* 5/7). Cordier criticized Dugenne much as did Fournier. (HR, II, 451.)

[20] *North China Herald*, Aug. 29, 1884, p. 236.

[21] HR, II, 443 and 497. Another inexplicable discrepancy between the Memo and the communication to Millot pertained to the deadlines for

responsible impetuosity than of following, to the letter, Fournier's instructions.

On one level of explanation, there is no gainsaying that the major share of blame for the Bac-Le incident must be assigned first to Li Hung-chang, and secondly to the Chinese throne. And if Fournier had been a more experienced and astute diplomat, there is reason to believe that the entire incident might have been avoided. A more basic explanation, however, would have to include the indirect but potent influence of the war advocates among the Chinese bureaucrats. Their petulant and unremitting criticisms had forced Li Hung-chang to act sub rosa if he were to conclude the peace settlement with Fournier. He had failed. And one reason for his failure was that the throne was indisposed to, or dared not, oppose the prevailing current of thought among the officials. This incident reveals, then, that *ch'ing-i* and its sympathizers constituted one of the chief influences upon the course of Chinese policy.

Negotiations with the French continued after the Bac-Le fighting. But this incident, more than any other during the controversy over Vietnam, created the conditions for the ensuing war. The "ambush" at Bac-Le filled the French with a sense of righteous indignation. They therefore raised their price for a settlement, and to this the Chinese, more emotional and more distrustful of the French than ever before, were by no means willing to accede.

---

the Chinese withdrawal. In the Memo, Fournier informed Li that French troops would be free to occupy Tongking territory contiguous to Kwangtung and Kwangsi on June 5; to Millot, Fournier set June 6. Regarding the territory of Tongking bordering Yunnan, Li was told July 1 was the deadline; the communication to Millot set June 26. These discrepancies were of no consequence in the events that followed, but their existence puts Fournier's efforts in a worse light.

VI

THE TSENG-PATENOTRE NEGOTIATIONS
AND UNDECLARED WAR

Despite the ill-feeling that had been engendered by the Bac-Le incident, the Chinese and French governments continued their preparations for negotiation of the definitive treaty, as the Li-Fournier Convention had stipulated. But the French now introduced a demand for an indemnity. This demand assumed an uncommon urgency for both nations, for the issue at stake was not merely money. The exaction of an indemnity had come to mean for the French, just as the rejection of that demand meant for the Chinese, the assignment of moral culpability in the Bac-Le incident. The demand was therefore as imperative to the French as it was inadmissible to the Chinese.

Paris was averse to engaging the Chinese empire in war — it was already immersed in disputes in Egypt and Madagascar — but it thought a show of force would bring the Chinese to their senses. This situation touched off a policy crisis in the Chinese government. The empress dowager proved that she was able to override majority opinions of both the Grand Council and the Tsungli Yamen; however, she was impotent when regional officials, with their own bases of power, refused to implement her decisions.

Preparations for Renewed Negotiations. When the fighting at Bac-Le erupted, both France and China had begun preparations for the negotiation of a definitive peace settlement on the basis of the Li-Fournier Convention. Li Hung-chang had again been named to negotiate for China. This time, however, the throne not only provided him with instructions to guide his negotiations, but cautioned him that "as soon as the discussions have been concluded, memorialize clearly, wait for an imperial rescript, and then act obediently." In addition, Peking named four officials — two of whom were members of the Ch'ing-liu — to "assist" Li in the impending negotiations.[1] The throne was taking no chances that Li Hung-chang would again exercise initiative as he had done so regrettably in the pourparlers with Fournier!

Meanwhile, Paris had named Jules Patenotre, a career diplomat and nephew of Jules Ferry, as negotiator for France and as the new minister to the court of Peking. Patenotre arrived in Shanghai on July 1, 1884. The Bac-Le fighting had occurred while he was enroute from France, and the Quai d'Orsay had had to reformulate the demands that he would present to the Chinese. Patenotre had now to demand that Peking would not only conform to the Li-Fournier Convention, but would also have to pay heavily for its "bad faith" by rendering an indemnity. The Quai d'Orsay informed Patenotre that it was determined to use force, if necessary, to press home these demands.[2]

Patenotre was joined at Shanghai by Admiral Courbet on July 5. Their intention initially had been to sail to Tientsin for the negotiation of the definitive treaty, using the admiral's fleet as a reminder to the Chinese that they must accept the

---

[1] CFCS, 17:40, dcmt. 631, decree, June 26, 1884 (KH10/*jun* 5/4). The officials were Hsi-chen, Liao Shou-heng, Ch'en Pao-ch'en, and Wu Ta-ch'eng, the latter two being Ch'ing-liu. The throne's instructions to Li were of such a nature that it is clear the two countries were still a long way from a peaceful settlement. Most troublesome of the throne's conditions would have been the demands that the tributary status of Vietnam be expressed clearly and without compromise, and that the disposal of the Black Flags be the responsibility of China.

[2] HR, II, 451, Ferry to Semallé, June 26, 1884.

French demands or fight a war.[3] They now decided instead to conduct the negotiations in Shanghai to avoid undesirable delay, which they were afraid would give the Chinese time for war preparations.[4] There was a delay nevertheless, because Patenotre and Ferry (in Shanghai and Paris, respectively) had a telegraphic squabble whether or not they should declare a deadline for Chinese acceptance of the new demands.[5] Patenotre eventually won, and on July 12 Peking was served the first of a series of three French ultimatums.

The July 12 ultimatum stipulated that Chinese troops must be evacuated from Tongking immediately in accordance with the second article of the Li-Fournier Convention. China must also pay an indemnity of 250 million francs. If these demands were not accepted within seven days, the French warned, they would use force to obtain the guarantees and reparations that they now felt to be their due.[6]

Peking quickly acquiesced on the first point. On July 16 a decree was issued instructing the troops in Tongking to retire to the Chinese frontier.[7] In issuing the order, however, the throne attempted to save some countenance by asserting that the evacuation was not being accomplished because of the French ultimatum, but in accordance with the three-month limit established by the Li-Fournier Convention (a statement that indirectly contradicted the French interpretation of the original Convention, now restated in the July 12 ultimatum, that the troops were to withdraw "immediately").[8]

The Tsungli Yamen protested the French demand for an indemnity. This demand, the Yamen asserted, violated the

[3] HR, II, 452.
[4] HR, II, 460 and 466.
[5] Kiernan, p. 138.
[6] HR, II, 467–468, Semallé to Tsungli Yamen, July 12, 1884.
[7] CFCS, 19:4b, dcmt. 728, decree, July 16, 1884 (KH10/*jun* 5/24); HR, II, 471.
[8] HR, II, 469–470, Tsungli Yamen to Semallé, July 3, 1884.

terms of the Li-Fournier Convention, which stipulated that no indemnity would be exacted. But the threat implied by the presence of Courbet's fleet at Shanghai was seemingly effective. On the final day of grace provided by the ultimatum, France was notified that Tseng Kuo-ch'üan had been granted full powers to treat with them on the matter of the definitive treaty[9] — though the communication conspicuously did not declare Chinese readiness to grant an indemnity. This omission signified little to the poorly informed French government. Ferry and his advisors refused to believe that the Chinese would be recalcitrant. Themselves loath to engage in a war, they chose to believe that the Chinese nomination of a plenipotentiary indicated their acceptance of the principle of an indemnity.[10] The French consequently declared their satisfaction with the Chinese reply, and extended the ultimatum for an additional period of fifteen days, which would allow the plenipotentiaries time to convene in Shanghai.[11]

The chief Chinese negotiator, Tseng Kuo-ch'üan, was one of the empire's most powerful provincial officials. He held the key post of governor-general of the rich Liang-Kiang (Kiangsu, Kiangsi, and Anhwei) provinces, and was concurrently superintendent of trade for the Southern Ports. The younger brother of Tseng Kuo-fan, Tseng Kuo-ch'üan had fought brilliantly against the Taiping rebels, and had won high honors for his capture in 1864 of Nanking, the Taiping capital.[12] He had subsequently served in various high provincial posts, though he was, judging from my own perusal of his writings during the Sino-French controversy, singularly unimaginative in the conduct of foreign affairs. At one point in the discussions with

[9] HR, II, 472. Tseng was named plenipotentiary in a decree dated July 19, 1884 (KH10/*jun* 5/27). (CFCS, 19:17, dcmt. 755.)

[10] Power, p. 174; HR, II, 467, Ferry to Patenotre, July 7, 1884.

[11] HR, II, 472–473.

[12] Tseng's biography is in Hummel, II, 749–751.

Patenotre, Ch'en Pao-ch'en, Tseng's assistant in the negotiations, actually complained to the capital that Tseng was ill-prepared for his diplomatic task, and recommended that Li Hung-chang assume the tasks of negotiator. Ch'en declared that "there is nothing in this affair that Li cannot settle."[13] The throne was still out of humor with Li after his recent bungling of the negotiations with Fournier. It therefore rejected Ch'en's plea, apparently sharing the Grand Council's opinion that Li "is also devoid of any other satisfactory proposals" that might facilitate an entente.[14]

Tseng Kuo-ch'üan had been exceedingly disinclined to accept the unenviable chore of negotiating a peace with the foreigner.[15] But, protesting, he left his viceregal offices at Nanking and went to Shanghai, where Sino-French negotiations recommenced on July 25.

Meanwhile, the Chinese had neglected to inform the French of an extremely important limitation upon Tseng's "plenipotentiary" powers. Tseng was empowered only to negotiate details of the Li-Fournier agreement. The authority to agree to an indemnity had been specifically reserved for the throne.[16]

[13] CFCS, 21:12b, dcmt. 920, Ch'en Pao-ch'en telegram, Aug. 4, 1884 (KH10/6/14); CFCS, 21:19b–20, dcmt. 948, Ch'en telegram, Aug. 6, 1884 (KH10/6/16); CFCS, 22:17b–18, dcmt. 1036, Ch'en telegram, Aug. 12, 1884 (KH10/6/22). This statement sounds out of character for a member of the Ch'ing-liu, but Ch'en had assumed a moderate stance at this time. (LJC, 42:79b, Aug. 13, 1884 [KH10/6/23].)

[14] CFCS, 21:17, dcmt. 933, Grand Council and Prince Ch'un memorial, Aug. 4, 1884 (KH10/6/14).

[15] CFCS, 19:18b, dcmt. 763, Tseng Kuo-ch'üan to Tsungli Yamen, July 20, 1884 (KH10/*jun* 5/28).

[16] Tseng's instructions also specified, inter alia, that the customary tributary status of Vietnam was to be retained, the French were not to dispose of Liu Yung-fu, and a buffer zone was to be created in Tongking. (CFCS, 19:19b, dcmt. 770, decree to Tseng Kuo-ch'üan, July 20, 1884 [KH10/*jun* 5/28].) Peking's interpretation of its instructions to Tseng were stated less ambiguously in a communication to Hart. (CFCS, 19:20, dcmt. 771, addendum #1, Tsungli Yamen to Hart, July 20, 1884 [KH10/*jun* 5/28].)

This limitation placed the inexperienced Chinese negotiator in an untenable position. The French approach to the negotiations was that the matter of the indemnity must be satisfactorily settled first; only then would they consider discussing details of the definitive treaty.[17] Since Tseng was not permitted to negotiate payment of an indemnity, the talks were from the outset fated to an impasse.

The Tseng-Patenotre Negotiations and Chinese Hopes for Foreign Mediation. When Tseng Kuo-ch'üan arrived in Shanghai, he was immediately subjected to strong pressures to grant an indemnity. From Tientsin, Li Hung-chang exhorted him to grant an indemnity, regardless of the lack of justification for the French demand, in order to avoid what he, Li, conceived would be a disastrous rupture with France.[1] From Peking, a member of the Tsungli Yamen, Chang Yin-huan, was urging much the same thing.[2] And in Shanghai, Robert Hart declared to Tseng that all discussions would be fruitless unless the principle of reparations were recognized.[3] Hart's maneuverings in Shanghai were in fact deeply disturbing to the authorities in Peking — "Although Hart has good intentions, he is of small

[17] CFCS, 19:24b, dcmt. 786, Hart to Tsungli Yamen, July 22, 1884 (KH10/6/1); CFCS, 19:26, dcmt. 792, Tseng Kuo-ch'üan to Tsungli Yamen, July 23, 1884 (KH10/6/2); CFCS, 20:12, dcmt. 822, same to same, July 26, 1884 (KH10/6/5).

[1] TK, CFCC, IV, 166, Li to Tseng, July 23, 1884 (KH10/6/2); *ibid.*, p. 171, same to same, July 30, 1884 (KH10/6/9). Li at the same time repeatedly expounded his views to the Tsungli Yamen. See WCSL, 44:5, Li to Grand Council, Aug. 11, 1884 (KH10/6/21); WCSL, 44:6a–b, same to same, Aug. 12, 1884 (KH10/6/22).

[2] LJC, 42:80, Aug. 13, 1884 (KH10/6/23). Chang's views may have been sanctioned by the Tsungli Yamen. See Ho Ping-ti, "Chang Yin-huan shih-chi" (Notes concerning Chang Yin-huan), in Li Ting-i, et al., eds., *Chung-kuo chin-tai-shih lun-ts'ung* (Collection of essays on modern Chinese history; Taipei, 1956), 1st ser., VII, 95.

[3] CFCS, 20:12, dcmt. 822, Tseng Kuo-ch'üan telegram, July 26, 1884 (KH10/6/5).

courage, and we fear that he harms [the negotiations]" — and they requested that he return immediately to the north.[4]

The harm had already been done. Succumbing to the several pressures, Tseng had finally offered Patenotre an indemnity of 3.5 million francs — as compared with the incredible and wholly unreasonable 250 million originally demanded by the French. Even this minuscule sum was offered, not as an indemnity, but under the name of succor to the French victims at Bac-Le.[5] This concession was worse than none at all. Not only would Patenotre not so much as consider submitting the offer to Paris for consideration; it also earned Tseng a severe reprimand from Peking — the throne asserting that the payment of even this amount would needlessly make a laughing stock of China.[6]

In all probability, the throne had never anticipated that Tseng Kuo-ch'üan could conclude a settlement with the French minister. Kuo Sung-tao wrote to Tseng at the time that he "considered the decree [giving Tseng instructions for the negotiations] was only intended to cause a war; everything in it was coercive and nothing could be implemented."[7] Kuo was wrong in assuming that the court was desirous of war. He had discerned correctly, however, that Tseng's instructions had not been intended to facilitate a rapprochement with the French.

Peking had, in fact, placed its money on another horse, and

[4] CFCS, 21:10, dcmt. 909, telegram to Hart, Aug. 3, 1884 (KH10/6/13); CFCS, 21:18b, dcmt. 941, telegram to Li Hung-chang, Aug. 5, 1884 (KH10/6/15). Actually, the Tsungli Yamen disclaimed these motives, but the statement quoted here would seem to belie all professions to the contrary.

[5] CFCS, 20:31, dcmt. 875, Tseng Kuo-ch'üan to Tsungli Yamen, July 31, 1884 (KH10/6/10); HR, II, 473.

[6] CFCS, 20:32a–b, dcmt. 883, decree to Tseng, July 31, 1884 (KH10/6/10).

[7] Kuo Sung-tao, "Yang-chih shu-wu i-chi" (The collected writings of Kuo Sung-tao), CFCC, IV, 584, Kuo to Tseng, no date.

the show of negotiating was probably no more than an attempt to gain time. On July 19, the Yamen sent a communication to the foreign powers designed to obtain from them an offer to mediate the dispute.[8] This strategy caused the French to question Chinese sincerity in the Shanghai negotiations.[9] But the United States minister to China, John Russell Young, was sympathetic to the Chinese cause, and he forwarded to Washington the Yamen's request for arbitration. Washington was slow to reply, and the Yamen had to instruct Tseng Kuo-ch'üan to drag out the negotiations until the United States had made its decision.[10] The United States ultimately agreed to make its good offices available. To Peking's chagrin, France was not willing to submit its case to an impartial judge. On August 7, the French chargé d'affaires, the Comte de Semallé, informed the Chinese that America's offer of mediation had been rejected.[11]

French Bombardment of Keelung and Further Demands. Meanwhile, China's temporizing tactics in the negotiations with Patenotre had already proved unavailing. The second French ultimatum had expired on July 31, and Patenotre notified Tseng two days later that France reclaimed its freedom to obtain satisfaction from China in any way it deemed fit. Even now Patenotre sought to bring the Chinese to terms. If only Tseng would agree to grant "a trifling sum" to France in the form of an indemnity, hostilities could yet be avoided.[1] Peking was

[8] CFCS, 19:15b–17, dcmt. 754, Grand Council memorial, July 19, 1884 (KH10/*jun* 5/27).
[9] CFCS, 20:16, dcmt. 835, Semallé to Tsungli Yamen, July 26, 1884 (KH10/6/5).
[10] WCSL, 43:2b, Tsungli Yamen to Tseng, Aug. 3, 1884 (KH10/6/13).
[11] WCSL, 43:13b, Grand Council to Tseng and Li Hung-chang, Aug. 8, 1884 (KH10/6/18).
[1] CFCS, 21:12, dcmt. 918, Patenotre to Tseng, received at Peking Aug. 3, 1884 (KH10/6/13).

adamant. It was convinced France wished to avoid a rupture, and had resolved it would not give one tael to the French.[2]

Finally, realizing that the Chinese needed some prompting before they would submit, the French gave effect to their threats. On August 5, Admiral Lespès bombarded Keelung on the northern coast of Taiwan, and destroyed the city's gun emplacements. However, to the mortification of the French, an attempt the next day to occupy the city and the nearby coal mines proved abortive. Lespès' troops were badly outnumbered, and he had no alternative but to recall his troops to the ships and abandon the undertaking.[3]

The reluctance of both the Chinese and French to commence hostilities is indicated by the fact that the French assault on Keelung did not mark the beginning of overt warfare. Rather, much as they had done before the incident, the French continued their ill-conceived strategy of bluff in their attempt to obtain an indemnity.[4] This was an approach that displayed the least possible comprehension of the state of mind in China, for if there was anything that the throne and officials held more precious than China's silver, it was self-esteem.[5]

After the French had refused the United States' offer of mediation, China sought relief from its tribulations by presenting to the French and the other powers extended indictments of French crimes and statements of Chinese rectitude.[6] It was

[2] CFCS, 21:14, dcmt. 928, Tsungli Yamen to Tseng Kuo-ch'üan, Aug. 4, 1884 (KH10/6/14); CFCS, 21, 16, dcmt. 932, addendum #1, conversation between Tsungli Yamen and J. R. Young, Aug. 4, 1884 (KH10/6/14).

[3] E. Garnot, *Fa-ch'ün ch'in T'ai shih-mo* ("L'Expedition française de Formose, 1884–1885"; Taipei, 1960), pp. 12–15; H. B. Morse, II, 356.

[4] CFCS, 21:36, dcmt. 988, Tseng Kuo-ch'üan to Tsungli Yamen, Aug. 9, 1884 (KH10/6/19); CFCS, 22:27b, dcmt. 1051, same to same, Aug. 13, 1884 (KH10/6/23).

[5] A statement of the Chinese attitude is in CFCS, 21: 33–34, dcmt. 975, addendum #1, proposed communication to France, Aug. 8, 1884 (KH10/6/18).

[6] *Ibid.*, p. 33; CFCS, 22:4b–5, dcmt. 1004, proposed communication

during this period that the ill-fated May 17 Memo, having gathered dust in the office of Li Hung-chang, was suddenly revealed to the world. Photographic copies of the document were distributed to the diplomatic representatives in Shanghai providing, as Tseng Kuo-ch'üan believed, "iron proof" that the French had been responsible for the hostilities at Bac-Le.[7]

The French were singularly uninterested in China's version of the rights and wrongs of the issue. When, for example, after the Bac-Le incident, an indiscreet French deputy suggested that there might be some justification for the Chinese assertions and proposed that the matter be submitted to arbitration, the wrath of both the majority and the opposition in the Chamber was brought down upon him for unpatriotically believing the word of a Chinese rather than of a Frenchman.[8] The French had come to the East to win an empire, and no evidence the Chinese might produce could nullify the basic truth and righteousness of French destiny.

During the first half of August 1884, Sino-French discussions were being conducted in Peking between Semallé and the Tsungli Yamen; and in Shanghai between Patenotre and Tseng Kuo-ch'üan — not to mention the frequent sallies into diplomacy being made by Robert Hart, both in Shanghai and with Paris through his London agent. But all discussion was fruitless, for the French were utterly insensitive to the Chinese state of mind. They had first thought to frighten the Chinese into a settlement with their attack on Keelung. That effort had failed dismally. Logically, the French should now have moderated their demands. Instead, they again placed their demand

---

to France, Aug. 10, 1884 (KH10/6/20); CFCS, 22:5b–6, dcmt. 1006, proposed communication to the powers, Aug. 10, 1884 (KH10/6/20).
    [7] CFCS, 22:8, dcmt. 1017, Tseng telegram, Aug. 11, 1884 (KH10/6/21); Kiernan, p. 141; HR, II, 495–496. For the May 17 Memo, see above, pp. 126–128.
    [8] Power, p. 176.

for an indemnity at eighty million francs, even though they had indicated previously that fifty million would do.[9]

Chinese Reactions to the Indemnity Demand. The period from mid-July to mid-August was an extraordinarily tense one for the Chinese. Not only were the French voicing threats; their warships were coursing at will in and about the Chinese harbors. On July 14 the first of many reports informed Peking that armed French vessels were assembling in the bay adjoining the Foochow arsenal in Fukien.[1] There, the French revealed their intention to seize the port if Peking did not accede to their demands.[2] The Chinese, displaying a most amazing respect for France's treaty rights, felt they could not deny the warships entry to the bay, even though this provided the French a tactical advantage in anticipated hostilities.[3] The dilemma created by this new development could only have heightened the sense of crisis that was already felt keenly in Peking. Nor would time resolve the dilemma for the planners of imperial policy in the capital. Every few days new arrivals of French warships were being reported, and there were incessant requests from the besieged port for reinforcements.[4]

The French threats acted as a catalyst upon officials' opinions, polarizing sentiment into the extremes of those who would grant the French demand for an indemnity and those who were

[9] WCSL, 43:6a–b, conversation between Tsungli Yamen and J. R. Young, Aug. 4, 1884 (KH10/6/14); WCSL, 44:16, Li Hung-chang to Tsungli Yamen, Aug. 13, 1884 (KH10/6/23); HR, II, 475.

[1] CFCS, 18:39b, dcmt. 709, Chang P'ei-lun to Tsungli Yamen, July 14, 1884 (KH10/*jun* 5/22).

[2] CFCS, 19:1a–b, dcmt. 719, Chang P'ei-lun to Tsungli Yamen, July 16, 1884 (KH10/*jun* 5/24); CFCS, 19:7b, dcmt. 736, Li Hung-chang to Tsungli Yamen, July 18, 1884 (KH10/*jun* 5/26).

[3] John Lang Rawlinson, *China's Struggle for Naval Development, 1839–1895* (Cambridge, Mass., 1967) pp. 110–111; CFCS, 18:39b, dcmt. 709, Chang P'ei-lun to Tsungli Yamen, July 14, 1884 (KH10/*jun* 5/22).

[4] Examples of the Fukien officials' requests are: CFCS, 19:22, dcmt. 775, Ho Ch'ing telegram, July 21, 1884 (KH10/*jun* 5/29); CFCS, 19:25, dcmt. 787, Chang P'ei-lun telegram, July 22, 1884 (KH10/6/1).

unalterably opposed to that course. Li Hung-chang telegraphed from Tientsin, declaring that:

> on my person are heaped calumnies, and I dare not again negotiate with them [the French]. However, the situation is critical and affects China's whole condition. [If we refuse an indemnity now, and enter into hostilities], after the war we would still have to render an indemnity and the amount would be even greater.[5]

And, to those who cared to listen, Robert Hart and J. R. Young were urging that, rather than suffer destruction or loss of the Foochow arsenal, the indemnity should be paid.[6]

Confronted with this advice and with the French threats, the Tsungli Yamen, as reconstituted after the April dismissals, became the most vigorous faction — now and throughout the remainder of the controversy — to advocate compliance with French demands.[7] The members of the Grand Council shared the readiness of the Yamen to conciliate the French. Li Tz'u-ming — who, it will be remembered, abominated the pro-war group led by Chang Chih-tung and company — now exhausted his store of defamatory epithets on these peace advocates as well. They were "slaves of the foreigners," he asserted, their "hearts and gall are utterly broken" and they treat the foreigners like "emperors of heaven." [8]

[5] TK, CFCC, IV, 182, Li to Tsungli Yamen, Aug. 11, 1884 (KH10/6/21).

[6] CFCS, 21:39b, dcmt. 991, addendum #1, Tsungli Yamen conversation with United States chargé d'affaires, Aug. 9, 1884 (KH10/6/19); CFCS, 22:4, dcmt. 1003, addendum #2, Tsungli Yamen conversation with A. E. Hippisley, Aug. 9, 1884 (KH10/6/19).

[7] WJC, CFCC, II, 18, July 21, 1884 (KH10/jun 5/29); ibid., p. 19, July 23, 1884 (KH10/6/2); ibid., p. 21, Aug. 8, 1884 (KH10/6/18).

[8] LJC, 42:66, June 21, 1884 (KH10/5/28); LJC, 42:83, Aug. 20, 1884 (KH10/6/30).

The Yamen membership at this time and during early 1885 was as follows: Prince Ch'ing, Yen Ching-ming, Hsü Keng-shen, Fu-k'un, Hsi-chen, Hsü Yung-i, Liao Shou-heng. The following were dismissed on September 3, 1884: Chou Chia-mei, Wu T'ing-fen, Chou Te-jun, Chang Yin-huan, Ch'en Lan-pin, and K'un-kang. Teng Ch'eng-hsiu was added on September 19, 1884.

The prime mover of this peace faction was Yen Ching-ming. Why Yen should have assumed this role is not clear. He had not had any notable exposure to the West; he was a native of the interior province of Shensi, and what distinction he had was acquired largely during the wars of suppression against the Nien rebels. Nor was he enchanted by the foreigners; he is reported to have declared to a friend that "no gentleman with a sense of honor cared to learn about foreign affairs." [9] Foreign observers knew virtually nothing about him in April 1884 at the time of his promotions to the Grand Council and Tsungli Yamen. However, because he was not renowned as an advocate of war, they interpreted his nomination to these offices as an imperial concession to the foreign powers.[10] Yen Ching-ming did not disappoint the foreigners. He believed that China was militarily incapable of resisting the French. As a consequence, Li Tz'u-ming was convinced, Yen strove "to sell out the country," and "those who seek to flatter the babarians all flock around him." [11]

Counterbalancing the influence of Yen Ching-ming in the Grand Council was the truculent and plain-spoken Tso Tsung-

---

On the Grand Council after April 8, 1884, there were: Prince Li, E-le-ho-pu, Yen Ching-ming, Chang Chih-wan, Sun Yü-wen, and Hsü Keng-shen; and Tso Tsung-t'ang, June–September 1884.

Most closely linked to Yen Ching-ming as the peace faction were Hsü Keng-shen, Chang Yin-huan and Chou Chia-mei. (LJC, 42:66, June 21, 1884 [KH10/5/28]; 42:78b, Aug. 10, 1884 [KH10/6/20]; 42:83, Aug. 20, 1884 [KH10/6/30].) Yen's other colleagues apparently shared his pacific views with the exceptions of Tso Tsung-t'ang, Chou Te-jun, Hsi-chen, Liao Shou-heng and Teng Ch'eng-hsiu. (See Liu Hsiung-hsiang, "Tsung-li ko-kuo shih-wu ya-men chi ch'i hai-fang chien-she" [The Tsungli Yamen and its construction of maritime defenses], in Li Ting-i, et al., eds., *Chung-kuo chin-tai-shih lun-ts'ung* [Collection of essays on modern Chinese history; Taipei, 1956], 1st ser., V, 45, which, however, notes only Chou and Teng as war advocates.)

[9] Quoted from Ssu-ming Meng, p. 77. Yen's biography is in *Ch'ing-shih*, VI, 4908–09.

[10] HR, II, 427.

[11] LJC, 42:86, Aug. 23, 1884 (KH10/7/3); LJC, 43:10, Sept. 26, 1884 (KH10/8/8).

t'ang. Tso in the summer of 1884 had hardly a year to live, but the scarred veteran of innumerable military campaigns was still a force to be reckoned with. The empress dowager placed much faith in this old servant, and his declarations to her that "the French barbarians are nothing to be feared" greatly contributed to her resolution not to grant the French an indemnity.[12]

Tso Tsung-t'ang was also assiduous, despite sickness and the use of only one eye, in attending to his duties in the Grand Council. There, he so consistently obstructed the discussions of the peace advocates that Yen Ching-ming and his colleagues gave up even attempting to talk to the old war horse.[13] Curiously, Tso had incurred the jealousy and disdain of the young war advocates as well.[14] Thus, when Tso in September 1884 gave up his offices in the capital and took command of the military forces in Fukien, few fellow officials grieved his departure.

At lesser levels of the bureaucracy, there was general support of a war policy; what effect this support had upon the decision-making process remains, as always, a matter of sheer speculation. *Ch'ing-i* officials were not unmanned by the French threat in Fukien, and they beseeched the throne to maintain its refusal to pay the French an indemnity. If China were wealthy enough to give an indemnity to France — and some questioned that it was[15] — then the money should be used to carry on the war.[16] The financial condition of the em-

[12] LJC, 42:66b, June 21, 1884 (KH10/5/28). Tso's biography is in Hummel, II, 762–767.

[13] LJC, 42:78b, Aug. 10, 1884 (KH10/6/20).

[14] LJC, 43:3b, Sept. 15, 1884 (KH10/7/26).

[15] CFCS, 21:8, dcmt. 906, Shang-hsien memorial, Aug. 2, 1884 (KH10/6/12).

[16] CFCS, 22:14, dcmt. 1026, Lung Chan-lin memorial, Aug. 11, 1884 (KH10/6/21); CFCS, 22:25b, dcmt. 1041, Liu En-p'u memorial, Aug. 12, 1884 (KH10/6/22).

pire had also disturbed the throne, and it had therefore requested a report on the condition of the national treasury from
the Board of Revenue.[17] The Board's reply demonstrates that
even officials in the most responsible positions in government
were unwilling to single themselves out as opponents of a war
policy:

> Considering the expenditures and income in ordinary years,
> we are able to save very little, and we dare not say there is
> a surplus. But neither dare we say, in times when there are
> continuous foreign complications, that our finances are in-
> adequate in time of war. . . . Now, in discussing finances,
> we do no more than consider whether or not we should
> fight. If we should not fight, we should not start border
> hostilities even though the treasury is full. If we should fight,
> the national prestige should not be sacrificed even though
> the treasury is empty.[18]

What would happen if France received an indemnity? The
war partisans feared that France could then afford to encroach
further on China, and other nations would be encouraged by
the French success to make similar demands on the empire.
As a consequence, reasoned these officials, an indemnity would
not purchase a respite for China, as Li Hung-chang contended,
but would, to the contrary, necessitate increased defense spend-
ing in the future.[19] Furthermore, the French threats were felt
to be mere bluff. The French, one censor argued, do not desire
a port such as Foochow; rather, they require money. France is
deeply in debt, and it now makes these invidious demands of
China in order to obtain means to repay its obligations. If it

---

[17] *Ch'ing-shih-lu*, 187:12, July 28, 1884 (KH10/6/7).
[18] CFCS, 22:32a–b, dcmt. 1067, Board of Revenue memorial, Aug. 14,
1884 (KH10/6/24).
[19] CFCS, 21:9, dcmt. 906, Shang-hsien memorial, Aug. 2, 1884
(KH10/6/12); CFCS, 20:34b, dcmt. 887, Ch'in Chung-chien memorial,
July 31, 1884 (KH10/6/10); CFCS, 22:25, dcmt. 1014, Liu En-p'u
memorial, Aug. 12, 1884 (KH10/6/22).

were not so, reasoned the memorialist, France would have given effect to its threats long ago instead of repeatedly extending the deadline of the ultimatums.[20]

The fruitless assault on Keelung had, in fact, seriously blunted the effect of the French threat to exact reparations from China.[21] Never had *ch'ing-i* been awestruck by French arms, and they conceived of the French forces now as dispirited and critically short of supplies.[22] This was, they thought, the time to attack, not to negotiate. A full-scale assault in the south would recover Tongking from French control and at the same time force the French to withdraw their ships from Foochow.[23] Several officials were also confident that if the French persisted in the attack on Foochow, a victory could be assured if the enemy were bottled up in the harbor, or were enticed from their ships onto land where Chinese arms could easily annihilate them.[24]

At the apex of the government, the attitudes of the Empress Dowager Tz'u-hsi and her chief advisor, Prince Ch'un, offer some insight into the problem of where the power of final policy decision resided. Prince Ch'un's views were highly equivocal. Two weeks after the Bac-Le incident, he flew into a rage when Prince Ch'ing, president of the Tsungli Yamen, argued that China must not get involved in a war. At the time, he considered the recent Li-Fournier Convention so much

[20] CFCS, 21:29b, dcmt. 969, Wan P'ei-yin memorial, Aug. 8, 1884 (KH10/6/18).

[21] CFCS, 22:13b, dcmt. 1026, Lung Chan-lin memorial, Aug. 11, 1884 (KH10/6/21); HR, II, 475.

[22] CFCS, 22:13b, dcmt. 1026, Lung Chan-lin memorial, Aug. 11, 1884 (KH10/6/21).

[23] CFCS, 21:27b, dcmt. 963, Hsü Shu-ming memorial, addendum #2, Aug. 7, 1884 (KH10/6/17); CFCS, 21:31, dcmt. 970, Wu Hsün memorial, Aug. 8, 1884 (KH10/6/18); CFCS, 22:20b, dcmt. 1039, addendum #1, Ch'ü Te-lin memorial, Aug. 12, 1884 (KH10/6/22).

[24] CFCS, 22:14, dcmt. 1026, Lung Chan-lin memorial, Aug. 11, 1884 (KH10/6/21); CFCS, 22:25a–b, dcmt. 1014, Liu En-p'u memorial, Aug. 12, 1884 (KH10/6/22).

"waste paper." [25] But it is very likely that it was on his initiative only a week later that the imperial troops in Tongking were ordered to withdraw, thus facilitating the resumption of negotiations in mid-July.[26] By early August, his views had taken such a turn that he had sided with Prince Ch'ing in opposition to the pro-war contentions.[27]

On the question of an indemnity, too, Prince Ch'un eventually relented. Even among the Chinese officials, he had attained the reputation of being the staunchest opponent of reparations.[28] However, when Li Feng-pao reported from Paris that the indemnity claim might be reduced and could be given under the name of "border [patrol] expenses" rather than as an "indemnity," he felt the payment to be permissible.[29]

Tz'u-hsi, to the contrary, remained steadfast in her resolution not to grant reparations, in any form or in any amount, to the French. On two occasions this resolution faltered in the face of the dark forebodings of Yen Ching-ming.[30] However, throughout most of the summer, 1884, despite threats from the French and warnings from advisors, she remained adamant that "an indemnity is unspeakable; a precedent cannot be established; it cannot be allowed!" [31]

It should not be inferred that Tz'u-hsi had finally determined on a single course of action. She was irresolute whenever she thought a settlement might be arranged without an indem-

[25] WJC, CFCC, II, 15, July 5, 1884 (KH10/*jun* 5/13); *ibid.*, p. 16, July 7, 1884 (KH10/*jun* 5/15).

[26] CFCS, 19:4b, dcmt. 729, Prince Ch'un memorial, July 16, 1884 (KH10/*jun* 5/24).

[27] WJC, CFCC, II, 20, Aug. 1, 1884 (KH10/6/11); *Ch'ing-shih*, VI, 4902.

[28] CFCS, 21:9b, dcmt. 906, Shang-hsien memorial, Aug. 2, 1884 (KH10/6/12).

[29] WJC, CFCC, II, 19, July 30, 1884 (KH10/6/9). The Prince's several oscillations of view toward an indemnity were commented on by Weng T'ung-ho in the same reference, p. 25, Sept. 4, 1884 (KH10/7/15).

[30] WJC, CFCC, II, 21, Aug. 8, 1884 (KH10/6/18); and LJC, 42:86a, Aug. 3, 1884 (KH10/7/3).

[31] LJC, 42:78b, Aug. 10, 1884 (KH10/6/20).

nity. But French demands for reparations merely stiffened her readiness to fight.[32] The fact that China remained militant in the face of French threats demonstrates, therefore, that it was Tz'u-hsi who ultimately made policy decisions. Had Prince Ch'un or the Grand Council been calling the turns of policy, China's course at this juncture would have differed significantly from that plotted by the Old Buddha.

Chinese "Preparations" for a French Attack at Foochow. By mid-August 1884, the French were despairing of a peaceful settlement. As French patience shortened, so did the period of their ultimatums. On August 19, the French chargé, Semallé, presented a third ultimatum to the Tsungli Yamen. Semallé stipulated that the Chinese government must agree to an indemnity in the sum of eighty million francs within forty-eight hours. If Peking remained recalcitrant after this time, he would take leave of Peking, and "Admiral Courbet will immediately take whatever measures seem useful to assure the French government of the reparations that are due it."[1] Two days later, the Yamen handed Semallé his passport, and the two nations prepared for war.

Most scholars who have studied the bombardment of Foochow have been of the opinion that the Chinese did not determine on a war policy until after the French had commenced the shooting. There is evidence to the contrary that, when Peking rejected the final French ultimatum on August 21, it had already determined to conclude the controversy by force of arms. Semallé's departure from Peking was correctly interpreted by the Chinese to mean that the war had begun;[2] and, on August 23, before any reports of the French attack

---

[32] WJC, CFCC, II, 20, Aug. 1, 1884 (KH10/6/11); *ibid.*, p. 23, Aug. 22, 1884 (KH10/7/2).

[1] HR, II, 476.

[2] WCSL, 45:6, Shao Yu-lien to Grand Council, Aug. 23, 1884 (KH10/7/3).

had arrived from Foochow, the throne issued a decree that read, in part:[3]

> French perversity has become extreme. Although We have received from Li Feng-pao [in Paris] a telegram which said that Fournier[4] still speaks of the French desire to negotiate a settlement, We yesterday wired a reply . . . that the demand for an indemnity has put an end to discussion, and that France cannot quickly be brought to terms. We must resolutely prepare for war, and should advance troops into Vietnam and recover Tongking so that the French dare not use their entire body of troops to attack China.

The decree continued by ordering P'an Ting-hsin to lead an attack on Bac-Ninh. It further ordered that militia be formed, and that the telegraph — the lack of which had previously been a severe handicap in coordinating military efforts — be extended from Kwangsi to Yunnan.

It is thus manifest that the throne had tired — for the moment — of grasping at the straws offered by negotiations. Tz'u-hsi, some hours before the French assault at Foochow, had already resolved on a policy of war.

Nevertheless, the French fired the first shot in the subsequent hostilities.[5] For almost six weeks, they had been stretching Chinese hospitality to the utmost. Their warships, singly and in groups, had entered the mouth of the Min River, and then, under the mouths of Chinese cannon placed all along the lower course of the river, steamed approximately twenty miles to Foochow harbor. By mid-August, the French had concentrated a fleet there that could, in terms of firepower,

[3] CSTL, CFCC, V, 511, decree to Chang Shu-sheng, et al., Aug. 23, 1884 (KH10/7/3). Though reports of the French attack arrived on the same day this decree was promulgated, I infer that the throne was yet unaware of the hostilities, for it would then have made note of that fact in the decree.

[4] Fournier was at this time in Paris and in intimate contact with Jules Ferry on matters pertaining to the China problem.

[5] The following account of the bombardment at Foochow is based on Rawlinson, pp. 110–119.

outshoot their complaisant adversary by a ratio of four to three. And, of the seven Gallic warships and two lesser torpedo launches then in the harbor, many were clad with heavy armor. Against this redoubtable flotilla, the Chinese had eleven wooden men-of-war, twelve war junks, miscellaneous steam launches, and rowboats armed with spar-torpedoes — explosives which, as John Rawlinson has suggested, transformed the rowboats into veritable floating, self-destroying powder kegs.

Hostilities in the harbor commenced August 23, exactly two months after the Bac-Le incident. The day before, British and American vessels that had lain at anchor among the vessels of the unfriendly navies abruptly left the future battle arena. The Chinese commanders seemingly discerned nothing ominous in this sudden departure of the neutral vessels, and they made no attempt to remove the imperial ships from their moorings to a place where they could maneuver should the French open fire.[6]

On the morning of the twenty-third, the French brought the 4727-ton *Triomphante* — their heaviest ship in China's waters — up the river on high tide. This was the ace for which they had been waiting; they now played their hand. At two o'clock in the afternoon, French guns opened fire. Within fifteen minutes, all but two ships of the Fukienese fleet were sunk or in flames; only five of the Chinese vessels had even succeeded in clearing their moorings. This initial task accomplished, the French turned their guns on the dockyard, leisurely putting it to ruins. On this afternoon, three thousand Chinese lost their lives, and the damages have been estimated at something like fifteen million dollars. It was an afternoon that forms an unhappy chapter in the history of the Chinese navy, and one

---

[6] There are a number of contemporary accounts averring that the Chinese commanders received from the French an advance declaration of the attack, but that this was wholly ignored. The evidence remains indeterminate. See Rawlinson, p. 118.

whose influence was to be felt throughout the ensuing hostilities with France.

The French attack has been roundly condemned for its treachery by most non-French historians.[7] Indeed, the dispatch of the ships into the harbor for hostile purposes during a period of peace was reprehensible and immoral. As a Chinese official commented, naively perhaps, after he heard of the French attack: "The French are crafty barbarians; but they ought not to have been so lacking in propriety (*wu li*)!"[8]

If one reviews the circumstances preceding the Foochow bombardment, it is manifest that the Chinese had had ample warning. Peking had actually responded to the requests for reinforcements from the Fukien authorities by instructing officials of the several coastal provinces to dispatch assistance to Foochow with all haste. The Kwangtung authorities, P'eng Yü-lin and Chang Chih-tung, had sent both ships and troops in accordance with the imperial decree.[9] Others, notably Li Hung-chang and Tseng Kuo-ch'üan, who had the largest naval contingents at their command, had refused consistently, despite all of Peking's threats and entreaties, to send so much as one ship to the critical area.[10]

In Peking, there had been fright and indecision. If China

[7] For example, Lane-Poole and Dickens, II, 378; H. B. Morse, II, 357–358.

[8] LJC, 42:90b, Aug. 27, 1884 (KH10/7/7).

[9] CFCS, 21:7b, dcmt. 905, decree to P'eng Yü-lin, et al., Aug. 2, 1884 (KH10/6/12); CFCS, 21:28, dcmt. 965, P'eng to Tsungli Yamen, Aug. 8, 1884 (KH10/6/18). Rawlinson (p. 114) has pointed out that the two ships sent from Kwangtung were originally ships of the Fukien navy, which had been sent south in 1882 to join the Kwangtung fleet in Vietnamese waters. (See also CFCS, 19:15b–17, dcmt. 754, Grand Council memorial, July 19, 1884 [KH10/*jun* 5/27].) During the intervening two years, these vessels had been maintained at Fukien's expense, but they had, to all other intents and purposes, become integral parts of the Kwangtung navy.

[10] Examples of the refusals are CFCS, 20:1–2, dcmt. 806, Tseng memorial, July 17, 1884 (KH10/*jun* 5/25); and CFCS, 20:9, dcmt. 817, Li telegram, July 25, 1884 (KH10/6/4). See also Rawlinson, pp. 113–115.

did not agree to the demand for an indemnity, the French warships would bare their cannon. With the throne determined not to grant reparations to the French, would it not be best to attack at Fukien when the enemy was unprepared? The question had the government in a frenzy. Prince Ch'un had strongly advocated offensive action at Foochow before the French could grasp the initiative. "Tomorrow," he informed the Grand Council, "I plan to request that the throne issue a decree strictly commanding the Fukien officials . . . to seize the initiative. Courbet has fallen into a trap!" [11]

In Foochow, Chang P'ei-lun, who shared in the divided command of the defenses there, had noted that the court was hesitating to act upon Prince Ch'un's proposal. Chang too was urging an immediate attack on the French, but the government's vacillation left him distraught. "The Grand Council and the Tsungli Yamen," he declared, "are brave and cowardly by turns." "I am not anxious about the enemy, but am anxious about the government." [12]

The proponents of a policy less extreme than springing the trap on the enemy at Foochow undoubtedly could muster cogent support for their position. Even till the day the French chargé furled his flag at the embassy in Peking, there remained the faint hope that hostilities could yet be avoided. Furthermore, vessels of the other powers were in Foochow harbor, and there was the considerable possibility — which the Chinese wished to avoid — that these would be damaged during the fighting. The Chinese forces in Fukien were also manifestly

[11] I-huan, "Ch'un Ch'in-wang I-huan chih Chün-chi-ch'u ch'ih-tu," CFCC, V, 45, dcmt. 19, Aug. 21, 1884 (KH10/7/1). The presence of the vessels of other powers in the port created an obstacle to this course of action, but the prince would forewarn them so they could remove their ships from the line of fire. See also *ibid.*, p. 44, dcmt. 12, no date.

[12] Chang P'ei-lun, "Chien-yü chi," CFCC, IV, 385–386, Chang to Chang Jen-chün, no date; see also *ibid.*, p. 375, Chang to Li Hung-tsao, no date.

incapable of conducting a sustained fight, as even Chang P'ei-lun acknowledged.[13] With the limited Chinese forces there, it would have been extremely risky to have heeded the advice of Prince Ch'un and Chang P'ei-lun.

Where were the reinforcements that the throne had ordered the superintendents of the Northern and Southern Ports to send? Both Tseng Kuo-ch'üan and Li Hung-chang protested that they did not have any warships to spare from their own defenses. Li furthermore confessed that he was awed by the superiority of the French fleet over his own small and ill-armored "navy." He reasoned that to send his ships to Foochow would have been a foolhardy squandering of China's already meager defense capabilities.[14]

The hot-tempered Chang P'ei-lun, writing virtually in the shade of Gallic guns, viewed the Foochow situation in more urgent terms than did Li or Tseng. Angered beyond temperance when he saw no assistance forthcoming, he proposed that ships' commanders who were dilatory in complying with imperial commands to proceed to Foochow should be summarily executed. This was a transparent threat to the superintendents of trade, for it was manifestly not the officers of the line who had been keeping the ships safe in Shanghai and Tientsin.[15]

Tseng Kuo-ch'üan asserted in reply that his ships were performing essential duties on the Yangtze River, and that, even if they went south, they would be unable to enter Foochow harbor. Besides, he declared, "the French ships are ten times stouter than ours. As soon as our vessels venture outside the harbor, they will be seized by the French." Tseng further pro-

---

[13] *Ibid.*, pp. 376–377, Chang to Chang Jen-chün, no date; *ibid.*, p. 382, Chang to Liu Ming-ch'uan, no date.

[14] TK, CFCC, IV, 177, Li to Tsungli Yamen, Aug. 5, 1884 (KH10/6/15).

[15] WCSL, 44:19, Tseng Kuo-ch'üan telegram, Aug. 14, 1884 (KH10/6/24).

tested that such stringent disciplinary measures as executing ships' commanders would do incalculable damage to naval morale.[16]

Presented with this plethora of objections from the powerful superintendent of trade, the throne relented. The previous decrees ordering ships to Foochow were rescinded, with the throne meekly parroting Tseng Kuo-ch'üan that the Yangtze River defenses were crucial, and that ships, even if sent to Foochow, would be of no assistance to the imperiled port.[17]

This episode is of particular interest for the present study, because it reveals the extent to which the decision-making power of the throne could be limited by the powers-of-execution possessed by the administrative bureaucracy. Since the Taiping Rebellion, certain of the regional officials had become so powerful that they were, to a degree, impervious to the control of Peking. But the limits of power were vague, even fluid, and it may be assumed that the incident related here represented a contest over jurisdictional controls between the throne, on the one hand, and the two governors-general on the other. The fact that Tseng and Li rebuffed the throne with impunity suggests that the throne realized, perforce, that it had impinged too far on the regional interests of the governors-general by ordering their navies to be placed in peril — even though imperial, or national, interests were at stake. The compliance of the Cantonese authorities with the decree to send aid to Foochow undoubtedly accentuated for the throne the desirability of having provincial officials who shared the goals of the throne, or who were too impotent to refuse compliance with imperial orders. But regionalism was a growth that had not taken root in a day — nor was it to be eliminated with a wish.

[16] *Ibid.*, pp. 19a–b.
[17] WCSL, 44:21, decree to Chang P'ei-lun, et al., Aug. 14, 1884 (KH10/6/24).

Ironically, Chang P'ei-lun proved to be the butt of the whole incident. He was strongly censored by the throne for his "improper" suggestions,[18] and, on the day of the bombardment of Foochow, as Fukien ships, unaided, fought and sank, he scurried to ignominious safety in the hills back of the city. This marked the end of his political career. He was sent into exile for three years, and thereafter existed in the penumbra of official life in the service of Li Hung-chang.[19]

Possibly, Li Hung-chang and Tseng Kuo-ch'üan exercised the better part of valor by refusing to send aid to Foochow, and thereby saved their ships from the fate of those now under the waters of the Min River. Nevertheless, had the central government vacillated less, and had the provincial officials been unwilling to sacrifice Foochow for the safety of their own areas of jurisdiction, it is possible that the story of the Foochow incident might now be written differently.

There are many "ifs" in assessing this possibility. If the relatively modern warships of Li and Tseng had joined the wooden vessels at Fukien, Courbet might have relished less the prospect of battle. Or, if Peking had adopted Prince Ch'un's advice to take the French unawares, French naval superiority in Chinese waters might have been dramatically reduced. Nor was this a wholly fantastic possibility. Had the Chinese used the tides to their advantage, as Maurice Loir, a participant in the bombardment, remarked, "the roles would have been reversed, and all the advantages from which the admiral [Courbet] hoped to benefit would have passed into their [the Chinese] hands and been turned against us."[20] But the French admiral knew his enemy well. Loir continued: "There was, however, room to hope that the Chinese, who had not hitherto dared take the initiative during the hostilities, would be no

[18] *Ibid.*
[19] Hummel, I, 48–49.
[20] Maurice Loir, *L'Escadre de l'Amiral Courbet: Notes et Souvenirs* (Paris, 1892), p. 123.

more audacious this time. The admiral could count on the panic that he inspired in them. This was, in any case, a chance to take. Wars are won as much by luck as by daring." [21] Much of Courbet's luck was created by Chinese respect for international law and by their sense of fair play — or, in other terms, by Chinese want of decision, cooperation, and daring at a crucial moment.

Undeclared War: Diplomatic Aspects. The French assault on Foochow on August 23, 1884 marked the beginning of the overt hostilities that are known as the Sino-French War. This war was never declared — creating a situation that has become almost a normal way of life in the mid-twentieth century, but which was relatively anomalous in the nineteenth.

After the Foochow bombardment, the Chinese were unable to launch a campaign of their own, for their forces had withdrawn from Tongking to positions within the Chinese frontier in accordance with the decree issued in July prior to the negotiations with Patenotre.[1] Nevertheless, the throne on August 26 did issue a decree that may be considered a domestic, or informal, declaration of war. "Now the French have violated the treaty and violated their trust," declared the throne; "the people's anger cannot be pacified, and We have no recourse but to go to war." [2] The same day, the Tsungli Yamen observed to the ministers of Britain and Japan that French warships had commenced hostilities at Foochow, and declared that, according to international law, their merchants were not permitted

[21] *Ibid.*

[1] The entire defense force had not been evacuated as the decree had instructed. In early October, Ts'en Yü-ying informed the throne that, because the Black Flags were in a state of virtual collapse at the time he received the decree, he had left some elements of his armies to assist Liu Yung-fu in the defense of Tongking. (WCSL, 47:18b–19, Ts'en memorial, Oct. 5, 1884 [KH10/8/17].)

[2] CSTL, CFCC, V, 518, decree, Aug. 26, 1884 (KH10/7/6).

to sell coal or render aid to French warships.[3] In view of this evidence, it is clear that only the smallest of diplomatic niceties distinguished this conflict from an openly and publicly declared war.

Nevertheless, the fact remains that China had not formally proclaimed to the nations of the world that a state of war existed. Tseng Chi-tse repeatedly apprised his government of this technicality, asserting that "declaring war with gunfire is not the same as declaring war with words." [4] Why Peking permitted this situation to continue can only be speculated. Partially, it may have been due to a limited comprehension of international law, for the Yamen gave evidence that it did in fact consider that a state of war existed, despite Tseng Chi-tse's reminders.[5] A more cogent explanation is that Peking avoided a declaration of war because it hoped to receive aid from non-belligerent nations. The Chinese minister to Germany, Li Feng-pao, observed to the Yamen that large quantities of war matériel already purchased in Europe had not yet arrived in China. He therefore suggested that an immediate declaration of war would be inopportune.[6]

France, too, had compelling reasons for not declaring war. To supply its forces in the East from France, a voyage of six to eight weeks was required, and it was dependent on such places as Ceylon, Singapore, and Hong Kong for the refueling and revictualing of its ships. If all of these were closed to French vessels, problems of logistics would be nearly in-

[3] YNT, IV, 1912, dcmt. 988, Tsungli Yamen to Parkes, Aug. 26, 1884 (KH10/7/6); see also YNT, IV, 1912, dcmt. 987, same to same, same date.

[4] WCSL, 45:29, Tseng to Tsungli Yamen, Aug. 31, 1884 (KH10/7/11). YNT, IV, 2225, dcmt. 1185, same to same, Oct. 20, 1884 (KH10/9/2); CSTL, CFCC, V, 621, Tseng telegram, Oct. 24, 1884 (KH10/9/6).

[5] CSTL, CFCC, VI, 211, conversation between Tsungli Yamen and Parkes, Jan. 3, 1885 (KH10/11/18).

[6] CSTL, CFCC, V, 530, Li Feng-pao telegram, Aug. or Sept. 1884 (KH10/7/?).

superable. There was, it is true, the inconvenience that neutral vessels could not be stopped, even when suspected of carrying supplies to the Chinese, so long as neither nation made a clear declaration of war. On the other hand, nothing prevented the French from taking belligerent action against the Chinese. Another factor deterring Paris from declaring war was that Ferry and his ministry were under heavy attack from the opposition parties at home, and it was not expedient for the premier to admit he was waging a war.[7] The government therefore insisted, despite irrefutable evidence to the contrary, "that no real trouble existed" between the two countries.[8]

The French contention that their policy of "intelligent destruction" against China did not create a state of war was unconvincing to foreign opinion, and legal advisors to the British government rendered the opinion that a war was being fought. Despite this sage judgment, the Foreign Office, for political reasons, decided to accept the myth of peace.[9] This situation continued until late November when, over French protests, the Foreign Office announced that it considered a state of war did exist. As a result, repair and coaling facilities in British ports were henceforth denied the French.[10] Nevertheless, at no time during the Sino-French controversy did either of the combatants make a formal declaration of war.

Undeclared War: Military Aspects. In launching the Foochow assault, the French had once again seriously misjudged their adversary. They presumed Peking had neither the will nor the capability to conduct a prolonged resistance, and that

[7] Power, p. 180; E. Malcolm Carroll, *French Public Opinion and Foreign Affairs, 1870–1914* (New York, 1931), p. 101.

[8] Kiernan, p. 145; Alexander Michie, *The Englishman in China during the Victorian Era* (Edinburgh and London, 1900), II, 331. Billot (pp. 248–249) discusses the French reasons for not declaring war.

[9] Kiernan, p. 146. The law officers were subsequently less certain of their earlier opinion (p. 147).

[10] *Ibid.*, pp. 152–153.

China would hastily sue for a peaceful settlement after a strong show of force.[1] The bombardment of Foochow had, to the contrary, merely added fuel to the Chinese fury. The empress dowager had become so irate that even the word "indemnity" was anathema to her. In early September she decreed that any official with the temerity to propose payment of an indemnity would be committed to the Board of Punishments,[2] and simultaneously issued a flurry of decrees ordering the armies to the attack. Indeed, so strong had the militant spirit become that Tseng Kuo-ch'üan was instructed to make no replies if Patenotre, who remained in Shanghai, should again offer the olive branch.[3]

Perhaps the most remarkable result of the French attack was the display of mass nationalism that was now provoked. News of the Foochow attack, and anticipation of like attacks elsewhere, stirred elements of the common people to frenzied anti-French and anti-foreign sentiment. In Kwangtung, seemingly hysterical bands attacked and demolished Christian chapels — which were the most egregious manifestation of the Westerner — and alien residents warily remained closeted within their homes. Even Chinese tainted by association with the foreigner — doctors and dentists with some Western-style training, and purveyors of foreign manufactures — were assaulted or shunned. Kwangtung for over a month was the storm center of this xenophobic reaction to the Foochow bombardment, but all corners of the empire felt its reverberations.[4]

The rising truculence of the Chinese left the French with no alternative but to continue the attacks. But where? Courbet proposed that strikes against North China would have the

---

[1] Billot, p. 241; Power, p. 174.
[2] *Ch'ing-shih-lu,* 189:29, Sept. 3, 1884 (KH10/7/14).
[3] WJC, CFCC, II, 25, Sept. 4, 1884 (KH10/7/15).
[4] Lloyd Eastman, "The Kwangtung Anti-foreign Disturbances during the Sino-French War," *Papers on China,* 13:13–16 (Harvard, East Asian Research Center, 1959); Lane-Poole and Dickens, II, 381–384.

greatest effect. But Jules Ferry, for a variety of reasons, opposed this course of action, and it was finally decided that the forthcoming military operations should be concentrated against the island of Taiwan.[5] On October 1, Courbet, with a landing force of 2250 men, attacked Keelung. The Chinese defenders under the command of Liu Ming-ch'uan fought gamely, but they were severely handicapped by the lack of weapons and supplies. The city fell into French hands the same day.[6]

On October 23, the French declared a blockade of Taiwan, hoping thereby to cut off all aid to the defenders. (Despite French insistence that this was a "pacific blockade," Britain took this as the cue to proclaim that it considered that an actual state of war existed.)[7] Sir Harry Parkes, referring to the blockade in January 1885, observed that the blockade "was very serious to foreigners, but almost harmless to the Chinese," for junks had no difficulty avoiding the blockading vessels.[8] In fact, however, both communication and supply to Taiwan was exceedingly difficult and a source of real concern to Peking.[9]

Efforts to thwart the French blockaders were essayed. In November, a British vessel employed by the Chinese success-

[5] The dispute between Ferry and Courbet seems to have been a heated one. From a military standpoint, Courbet's proposal held much merit. However, Ferry's purpose was merely to obtain a territorial gage that would be relinquished when the Chinese had rendered an indemnity — and Ferry was afraid that an eventual evacuation from an area thus occupied on the mainland would easily be construed by the Chinese to be a victory over the French. Furthermore, Ferry was opposed to operations in the north, because he was anxious not to disturb the interests of the neutral powers, *and because he did not wish to alienate Li Hung-chang* by attacking that official's regional base. Billot, pp. 239, 249–254; Garnot, pp. 16–18.

[6] Garnot, pp. 18 and 22–24.

[7] Kiernan, pp. 152–153.

[8] *Ibid.*, p. 172.

[9] YNT, IV, 2236, dcmt. 1197, Hart to Tsungli Yamen, Oct. 25, 1884 (KH10/9/7); CSTL, CFCC, V, 627, Liu Ming-ch'uan to Tsungli Yamen, Oct. or Nov. 1884 (KH10/9/?); CSTL, CFCC, VI, 204, Liu Ming-ch'uan memorial, Dec. 28, 1884 (KH10/11/12); CSTL, CFCC, VI, 223–224, Liu Ming-ch'uan memorial, Jan. 7, 1885 (KH10/11/22).

fully made the passage to the island, put eight hundred Chinese troops ashore, and safely made the return trip. Another venture, on a larger scale, ended less gloriously.[10] Immediately after Courbet imposed the blockade of Taiwan, the throne commanded Tseng Kuo-ch'üan and Li Hung-chang to send to Taiwan a relief expedition to be formed of five ships from each of their navies. Just as prior to the Foochow incident less than three months earlier, the two governors-general refused to comply with the imperial commands. This time, however, the throne threatened them with punishment, and ultimately they relented. That is, Tseng did. Li, only partially compliant, sent but two ships. By early December, the fleet of seven vessels had assembled for the projected passage to Taiwan.

On December 10, however, Li Hung-chang learned of an attempted coup d'état in Korea,[11] and he requested permission from the Tsungli Yamen to recall his two new British-built cruisers for what he conceived to be more urgent duty than breaking the blockade of Taiwan. Peking agreed that the Korean development warranted attention, and it instructed that two ships of the relief force should be released for duty in the north. But in what was an obvious attempt to demonstrate that it, not Li, possessed the authority to deploy naval forces, the throne ordered Li's ships to remain with the relief expedition. Instead, two of Tseng's warships were to be detached for service in Korean waters. By the time these instructions reached Shanghai, Li's two cruisers were already steaming northward. Without waiting for imperial permission, Li had recalled them to his own jurisdiction.[12]

Tseng Kuo-ch'üan's five ships had now to attempt passage

[10] The following account of this venture is based on Rawlinson, pp. 120–127.

[11] See below, pp. 196–197.

[12] WCSL, 50:6, Li to Tsungli Yamen, Dec. 14, 1884 (KH10/10/27); ibid., p. 6, decree to Li, same date; ibid., p. 9b, Li to Grand Council, same date.

to Taiwan alone. They left Shanghai in late December — but they did not proceed directly to Taiwan. Rather, two full weeks were consumed with training and coaling, preoccupations that kept the fleet ever within view of the coast of the mainland. Finally, by the latter part of January 1885, everything was in readiness; still the passage to Taiwan was not attempted. Instead, the fleet commander searched for a way to learn how effectively the French actually had the island isolated — he thought of spreading false rumors, and of making an initial probe with a merchant ship. Meanwhile, the fleet meandered southward along the coast; they meandered northward along the coast — never were their prows pointed toward the beleaguered island.

February 13 put an end to the comedy — nearly three months after the decree had initially ordered formation of the convoy. The day was foggy, and Courbet's fleet loomed suddenly within view. The Chinese ships immediately took flight, but the two slowest were overtaken and sunk. The three others were pursued by the French to Chen-hai, a harbor near Ningpo in Chekiang, sufficiently fortified so that the French were deterred from pursuing their quarry farther. The relief force got no closer to Taiwan. The three ships remained bottled up in Chen-hai until the armistice in April.

Li Hung-chang and Tseng Kuo-ch'üan had opposed the relief expedition from the start. Korean troubles opportunely provided Li with an excuse to avoid participation in the venture. Tseng had no such pretext, and he outwardly complied with Peking's instructions. However, the expedition was conducted with such pusillanimity that the suspicion inevitably arises that Tseng devised his own stratagems to avoid contact with Courbet. Peking had on this occasion demonstrated that the regional navies were, theoretically, within the sphere of imperial jurisdiction. In practice, however, Li and Tseng had again cushioned the impact of imperial interests upon their own regional ones.

While the relief expedition had been cruising the waters near the mainland, conditions on the embattled island worsened. Reports from Liu Ming-ch'uan were so gloomy that Prince Ch'un asserted that Liu should be less pessimistic in his communications to the capital, so that the advocates of peace would not have support for their contentions.[13]

In late January 1885, reinforcements from Vietnam enabled Courbet to increase the scope of his operations. He briefly imposed a blockade on Ningpo, and rice destined for North China was, in February, declared a contraband of war in a desperate effort to exert direct pressure on Peking. Finally, in March, an offensive was mounted in Taiwan that broke the Chinese encirclement of Keelung, and that established the French in a commanding position on the Tamsui River — though they never succeeded, despite courageous efforts, in capturing the city of Tamsui. Later the same month, the French flag was raised over the barren Pescadore Islands.[14]

During the seven months of the Taiwanese campaign, France had been able to accomplish no more than the occupation of a number of towns on the northern coast and of the Pescadore Islands, and to impose a blockade that was only partially effective.[15] If its operations were considered by some to be a success, it was a strictly limited and indifferent victory. Cordier has observed: "The fact that the French had taken nearly three months to occupy two such worthless places as Keelung and Tamsui [sic] gave the impression [to the Chi-

---

[13] I-huan, "Ch'un Ch'in-wang I-huan chih Chün-chi-ch'u ch'ih-tu," CFCC, V, 41, dcmt. 4.

[14] Garnot, pp. 80–81 and 98–104; H. B. Morse, II, 362.

[15] WCSL, 49:1b, Li Hung-chang to Grand Council, Nov. 15, 1884 (KH10/9/28); WCSL, 49:14, same to same, Nov. 25, 1884 (KH10/10/8).

nese] that they were incapable of undertaking a serious operation." [16]

While the French were pressing the attack in Taiwan, the
Chinese were implementing a plan, long a favorite of bellicose officials, of attacking in Tongking as a means of prevent-
ing the French from diverting their entire strength in the campaign against the China Coast. Immediately after the Foochow
bombardment, the throne had named Liu Yung-fu a general-
in-chief (t'i-tu) in the Chinese army, bestowed on him a Pea-
cock Feather, and ordered him to the attack.[17] In the following
months, the imperial troops were repeatedly ordered to advance against Tongking. But Chinese forces met with even less
success there than their enemy was having in Taiwan. Liu
Yung-fu opposed his orders, arguing that the weather was
unfavorable for operations.[18] The principal factors that de-
bilitated the Chinese war machine were not those of weather,
however, but illness and shortages of supplies. Lacking both
equipment and money, the southern commanders frequently
had no alternative but to confine their efforts to defensive operations. Despite the remonstrances of ch'ing-i officials and the
instructions of the throne, they did not possess the capabilities
necessary to mount a full-scale offensive.[19] Even without encountering the enemy, mortalities rose into the thousands.
Troops not acclimated to the miasmic wastelands of Tongking
were decimated by malaria and other diseases that seemed
to rise out of the "poisonous waters" of the region. One unit,
that consisted originally of two thousand men, buried fifteen
hundred of its number who died of disease. Ts'en Yü-ying

[16] HR, II, 512. Cordier erred here in asserting that Tamsui had been
captured. See Garnot, p. 29.
[17] CSTL, CFCC, V, 518, Aug. 26, 1884 (KH10/7/6).
[18] Shao Hsün-cheng, p. 171.
[19] CSTL, CFCC, VI, 131, Chang Chih-tung telegram, Nov. 13, 1884
(KH10/9/26); CSTL, CFCC, VI, 150, Ts'en Yü-ying memorial, Nov. 21,
1884 (KH10/10/4).

warned the throne that one-half of all reinforcements to the south would be cut down and rendered useless for combat by what appeared to be the principal enemy, pestilence.[20]

Despite these adverse conditions, P'an Ting-hsin, governor of Kwangsi, had personally led a large body of troops into Tongking and established headquarters at Lang-Son. From there, he had directed elements of his army to advance to positions as much as 140 kilometers outside the Chinese frontier. In response, the French launched a counteroffensive against P'an's advance units in early February 1885. The Chinese collapsed before the onslaught. While the French were still twenty kilometers from Lang-Son, P'an pulled his headquarters back to the border, and on February 14 the French occupied the defenseless city. The French pressed their advantage. They actually took the Chinese border town of Chennan-kuan on the twenty-third, although after putting the town to flames they withdrew to Lang-Son. At this same time, the Black Flags were put into retreat after a defeat near Tuyen-Quang. The Chinese military situation along the entire front showed no prospects of success.

For his unheroic withdrawal from Lang-Son, P'an Ting-hsin was relieved of his command. The imperial forces soon displayed a renewed vigor, inspired partly by the courage of the famous Feng Tzu-ts'ai, and perhaps partly by the fact that some retreating comrades had been beheaded by their commanders. On March 21, the Chinese launched a fresh attack; a week later they reoccupied Lang-Son and were advancing along the whole front. The French commander at the front, General François de Négrier, was seriously wounded in battle on March 28, and he was succeeded at the head of the French forces by a highly excitable lieutenant colonel who had been

[20] TK, CFCC, IV, 216, Li Hung-chang to Tsungli Yamen, Dec. 18, 1884 (KH10/11/2); CSTL, CFCC, VI, 150, Ts'en Yü-ying memorial, Nov. 21, 1884 (KH10/10/4); WCSL, 44:6b, P'eng Yü-lin, et al. memorial, Aug. 12, 1884 (KH10/6/22).

in Tongking only three months. Deprived of effective leadership, the Europeans panicked.[21] In a moment of unreasonable trepidation, the French commander in chief, Louis Brière de l'Isle, fired off a telegram to the Ministry of War stating that he still hoped to be able to defend the area around Hanoi — a hope that instilled in Paris more concern than confidence. Brière de l'Isle subsequently realized he had been overly pessimistic. But the Chinese were, in fact, making preparations for assaults against Bac-Ninh and Hung-Hoa, not far from Hanoi — when suddenly orders arrived from Peking announcing an armistice.[22]

The Sino-French War had been fought, not essentially for territory, nor money, nor commercial rights, but for national *amour propre*. Four and one-half thousand Frenchmen, and many times that many Chinese, gave their lives during the seven months of the war[23] — a price an ordinary citizen must

[21] The role of this officer, Lieutenant Colonel Paul Gustave Herbinger, has recently been the subject of a revisionist study by Cecil E. Spurlock. Spurlock points out that Herbinger was a brilliant officer: he had graduated first in his class at Saint Cyr; had fought with distinction against Germany in 1870; and was a professor of infantry tactics at the École Supérieure at the time of his transfer to Vietnam. Spurlock contends, not entirely unconvincingly, that Herbinger's command to withdraw from Lang-Son was a result, not of panic, but of a calculated decision to retire to strongly fortified positions at Kep and Chu. This was, Spurlock concludes, "militarily a prudent and proper" decision. "The First French Defeat in Vietnam: The Retreat from Langson and Its Consequences" (unpublished seminar paper, Harvard, 1963), pp. 18–27.

Herbinger's contemporaries did not deny his brilliance, but they were convinced that, having arrived but recently from France, he panicked in the face of the Chinese attack. See, for example, Georges Taboulet, II, 846–850, quoting extracts from Lecomte, *Langson, combats, retraite, négociations*, pp. 470–512. Even a participant of the fighting who was strongly sympathetic with Herbinger concluded that "this evacuation would not, certainly, have taken place under the command of General de Négrier." (Captain Armengaud, *Lang-Són: journal des opérations qui ont précédé et suivi la prise de cette citadelle* [Paris, 1901], p. 69.)

[22] Huang Ta-shou, II, 67; HR, II, 516–518 and 522–524. Brière de l'Isle's telegram is quoted in Taboulet, II, 850.

[23] Jules Ferry, *Le Tonkin et la mère-patrie*, pp. 359–364. No figures of Chinese mortalities are available. But imperial casualties in combat

expect to pay for the prideful blunderings of his political leaders.

were invariably much higher than those of the French. See Garnot and HR, *passim*. These are French sources, but from scattered evidence in the Chinese materials, I believe their assessment of Chinese losses is roughly accurate.

VII

PRELUDE TO PEACE

The French demand for an indemnity had stiffened the opposition of the throne and of the overwhelming majority of officials to a negotiated settlement with the French. This reaction to their demands forced the French to expand their military operations from Tongking to the coast of South China and to Taiwan. In March 1885, after seven months of sanguinary warfare, the French seemed to have the upper hand in Taiwan, but their armies in Tongking were in disorderly retreat before a Chinese offensive. Seemingly at mid-point, the drama was brought to an end. The multifarious forces acting upon Chinese policy had created a sudden and often criticized denouement.

The Court Conference of October 28, 1884. Admiral Courbet's devastation of Foochow on August 23 and his occupation of Keelung on October 1 had not diminished the militancy among the Chinese officials. On October 26, however, Peking learned of Courbet's blockade of Taiwan. Tseng Kuo-ch'üan, reporting the blockade, observed that the fate of the entire island hung in the balance, and that the outcome would be determined imminently.[1] This news added immeasurably to the sense of crisis pervading Peking, and the Empress Dowager Tz'u-hsi immediately ordered a court conference for October 28 to discuss the military situation in Taiwan and Tongking.[2]

[1] CSTL, CFCC, V, 627, received in Peking Oct. 26, 1884 (KH10/9/8).
[2] CSTL, CFCC, VI, 1, Oct. 26, 1884 (KH10/9/8).

The tone of the conferees memorials was, expectedly, strongly pro-war. Of especial interest were their reactions to two documents that they discovered in the archives of the Grand Secretariat, for they reflect typical conservative thinking in late Ch'ing China. The two documents in question were proposals for a negotiated settlement of the dispute with France.

The first proposal had been submitted by that avid amateur diplomat, Gustav Detring. Detring had, avowedly on his own initiative, asked Captain Fournier in Paris what conditions the French government would now consider as a satisfactory basis for a peaceful settlement of the controversy.[3] On the basis of Fournier's cabled reply, Detring had drafted a four-article proposal which he in turn presented to the Tsungli Yamen.[4] Paris was still content that the Li-Fournier Convention form the basis of a peace settlement. What distinguished this new proposal was French willingness to forego an indemnity — by this time they realized that this demand caught in the Chinese craw. In lieu of an indemnity, the French would accept temporary control of the customs and mining rights in Keelung and Tamsui. If the Chinese remained reluctant to accept this condition, the entire matter of reparations might be submitted to the arbitration of a third power. Detring's proposals were not unreasonable; the section allowing arbitration of the dispute, in particular, suggests that the French wished to end the hostilities.

The participants of the court conference, however, viewed Detring's proposals with hearty and virtually unanimous disapprobation. Even Chou Chia-mei, one of Yen Ching-ming's closest associates, allowed that they would be "exceedingly

[3] CSTL, CFCC, VI, 3, Detring conversation with Tsungli Yamen, Oct. 28, 1884 (KH10/9/10).
[4] Detring's version of the proposal is in CSTL, CFCC, VI, 4–6, Detring to Tsungli Yamen, Oct. 28, 1884 (KH10/9/10).

difficult to permit." [5] The new demand for French control of the customs and mining rights on Taiwan was a blatant and ill-disguised substitute for an indemnity, and the memorialists were as opposed to the one as to the other. Furthermore, the prospect of French control exercised on Chinese territory was intolerable, and the memorialists were dubious that France would be willing to retrocede those rights to China. It was manifest to these officials that the French lusted after the whole of the island. Keelung and Tamsui would therefore merely serve as convenient bases for further aggression — either through the use of force or of that equally invidious instrument of the French, Christianity.[6]

The conferees' reactions to the proposal that a third power arbitrate the question of reparations are especially noteworthy. The premise upon which the officials responded was that the principal foreign powers would not act disinterestedly regarding Chinese interests. How pervasive this sentiment was is difficult to determine — certainly Chinese xenophobia is not an invention of the Communists. A reader in the Grand Secretariat, Yen-mao, viewed the likely nominees for the task of arbitration — Britain, Russia, Germany and the United States — as part of a coalition with France against China. "They are all of the same species," he asserted, "and have long ago joined France in their villainous schemes." [7]

Yen-mao's castigation of the major foreign powers in China might suggest to a modern reader that he was a rabid, narrow-minded, chauvinistic reactionary. His apprehensions appear

[5] CSTL, CFCC, VI, 24, Chou memorial, Oct. 31, 1884 (KH10/9/13).
[6] CSTL, CFCC, VI, 29, Chou Te-jun memorial, Oct. 31, 1884 (KH10/9/13); CSTL, CFCC, VI, 37–38, Hsü Shu-ming memorial, same date; CSTL, CFCC, VI, 34, Yen-mao memorial, same date.
[7] CSTL, CFCC, VI, 34, Yen-mao memorial, Oct. 31, 1884 (KH10/9/13). Yen-mao was obviously unaware that the Tsungli Yamen was considering offering the task of arbitrator to Austria. (CSTL, CFCC, VI, 18, Detring and Hart conversation with Tsungli Yamen, Oct. 30, 1884 [KH10/9/12] quoting Parkes.)

less excessive, however, when juxtaposed with advice given the Tsungli Yamen by Robert Hart and Gustav Detring. Hart (a Britisher) and Detring (a German) declared that they favored "the mediation of Austria rather than that of England, as the latter, like Germany, is supposed to be interested in the prolongation of French difficulties in China." [8] Perhaps, then, Yen-mao's aversion to the intervention of these major foreign powers had a substantial basis in fact.

Yen-mao's views were somewhat atypical in that they stressed the unity and concord among the major foreign powers. Most officials in the 1880's, to the contrary, emphasized the enmities and discord characterizing the relationships of the foreigners. The time-tested concept of playing one foreigner off against another (*i-i chih-i*)[9] therefore remained the officials' favored formula of defensive strategy.

Despite the strained relations that some officials discerned between France and its fellow imperialists, they asserted that arbitration would not produce an equitable settlement. The other powers also coveted the riches of Taiwan. Therefore, "how do we know," inquired one official, "that at the time of arbitration each foreign power will not harbor selfish aspirations and have no regard for right and wrong?" [10] Li Feng-pao, acting minister to France and Germany and intimate of Li Hung-chang, was also disinclined to accept German mediation for much the same reason. He observed that Germany lusted after Taiwan and trade within China just as did France. Hence, if Germany were asked to mediate the dispute with France,

[8] Kiernan, p. 153.

[9] Wang Erh-min, "Tao-Hsien liang-ch'ao Chung-kuo ch'ao-yeh chih wai-chiao chih-shih" (Chinese knowledge of foreign relations, 1821–1861), *Ta-lu tsa-chih* ("The continent magazine"), 22.10:11 (May 15, 1961); Immanuel Hsü, p. 11.

[10] CSTL, CFCC, VI, 38, Hsü Shu-ming memorial, Oct. 31, 1884 (KH10/9/13). Ch'in Chung-chien believed that the United States would procure for China a just settlement, but he doubted that France would accept that country's arbitration. (CSTL, CFCC, VI, 65, Oct. 31, 1884 [KH10/9/13].)

it would probably demand these as compensation for its efforts.[11] In short, sentiment against foreigners was intense, and most of the officials felt it would be unwise to place trust in barbarians who were essentially untrustworthy.

The second set of proposals had been inspired by those from Detring. Sheng Hsüan-huai, *taotai* in charge of the Tientsin customs, and Paul Ristelhueber, French consul at Tientsin, had together composed a new draft of a settlement. From the Detring version, they had excised the patently unacceptable clause pertaining to French controls in Taiwan, and substituted articles of their own invention.[12]

> *Article 5 read:* China will agree to borrow from France, at a fair rate of interest, twenty million taels to be repaid over a forty-year period. Initially, the Maritime Customs will serve as security. However, if China constructs a railroad, that railroad may, with the approval of France, serve instead as the required security.
>
> *Objection:* The conferees calculated that the total interest on the loan would be equivalent to the amount the French had previously been demanding in the form of an indemnity. This fact, in itself, was sufficient reason to reject the proposal.[13]
>
> *Article 6 read:* Of the twenty million taels, one-half will be used to purchase from France, at a fair price, war matériel and railroad equipment. The remaining half of the loan will be given to China in the form of ready cash, and will be used for the construction of railroads, etc.
>
> *Objections:* Some officials doubted that France had even ten million taels at its command to loan China.[14] This ob-

[11] YNT, IV, 2218, dcmt. 1184, Li Feng-pao to Tsungli Yamen, Oct. 20, 1884 (KH10/9/2).

[12] Sheng presented the proposals to the Tsungli Yamen on Oct. 25, 1884. (CSTL, CFCC, V, 626–627 [KH10/9/7].)

[13] CSTL, CFCC, VI, 29, Chou Te-jun memorial, Oct. 31, 1884 (KH10/9/13); CSTL, CFCC, VI, 49, Hui Yen-pin memorial, same date; CSTL, CFCC, VI, 65, Ch'in Chung-chien memorial, same date.

[14] CSTL, CFCC, VI, 72, T'ang Ch'un-sen memorial, Oct. 31, 1884 (KH10/9/13).

jection aside, the officials reacted strongly to the proposal that China engage itself to purchase matériel from France, for they feared that France would only sell inferior goods, or acceptable goods at exorbitant prices. China would thus be placing itself in the position that "if it wanted to buy, it must buy; and if it did not wish to buy, it still must buy." [15]

Significantly, the officials reacted most strongly against the Sheng-Ristelhueber proposal concerning railroads. Most of them were afraid that, if France loaned money to construct railroads, France was certain that it would somehow benefit from those railroads — and "if it will benefit the French barbarians, then it will not benefit China." [16] The possibility that railroads could be of mutual advantage to the two nations seems not to have occurred to the officials. There were, however, more specific objections. Railroads would put China's transport workers out of work with the probable result that, reduced to starvation, they would rise in rebellion.[17] Also, with the Taiping and Nien Rebellions still etched deeply in their memories, there was the trenchant concern that rebels would be able to seize trains and dash to the attack of distant cities before imperial forces could establish countermeasures.[18]

Above all, the officials feared that the introduction of the "iron roads" would weaken the empire's defenses against the barbarians. They recognized that trains could be of strategic value in the event of a foreign invasion. Yet the general feeling was that the foreigner would be able to outsmart them in the use of the railroads. A foreign aggressor would be able to cut the tracks so that the railroads would be useless to the de-

[15] CSTL, CFCC, VI, 49, Hui Yen-pin memorial, Oct. 31, 1884 (KH10/9/13). See also CSTL, CFCC, VI, 40, Shen Yüan-shen memorial, same date; CSTL, CFCC, VI, 72, T'ang Ch'un-sen memorial, same date.

[16] CSTL, CFCC, VI, 52, Ch'en Hsüeh-fen memorial, Oct. 31, 1884 (KH10/9/13).

[17] Ibid.; CSTL, CFCC, VI, 71, Feng Ying-shou memorial, same date.

[18] CSTL, CFCC, VI, 30, Chou Te-jun memorial, Oct. 31, 1884 (KH10/9/13).

fenders.[19] Illogically, they did not argue that they could themselves cut the tracks to prevent the invader's sudden ingress to the interior.

These protests strikingly reveal that most officials held no more enlightened views regarding railroads in 1884 than they had seventeen years earlier. In 1867, a considerable discussion had been provoked over the question of the introduction of railroads, and the objections in 1884 displayed much the same antipathies and prejudices that had previously resulted in the postponement of railroad construction in China.[20]

Though a student in the twentieth century may belittle the anxieties of these officials, it must be admitted that they instinctively and accurately predicted the ill-effects that would ensue from the introduction of railroads. They sensed that France might attempt to acquire control of the roads, and, then, control of Chinese territory. The fact that a Frenchman had proposed that the railroads serve as security for the loan seemed to the memorialists adequate evidence of their intentions.[21] "The barbarians have previously used this method to rule other peoples," asserted Chou Te-jun, and the French could now "use it to place China under their control" [22] — an astute insight revealing that the officials were not wholly ignorant of the tactics of the imperialists in other parts of the world. The officials further recognized that special privileges granted to France would evoke similar demands from the other powers, with perhaps dire consequences for the dynasty.[23]

[19] CSTL, CFCC, VI, 40, Shen Yüan-shen memorial, Oct. 31, 1884 (KH10/9/13); CSTL, CFCC, VI, 51–52, Ch'en Hsüeh-fen memorial, same date; CSTL, CFCC, VI, 72, T'ang Ch'un-sen memorial, same date.

[20] See Knight Biggerstaff, "The Secret Correspondence of 1867–1868: Views of Leading Chinese Statesmen Regarding the Future Opening of China to Western Influence," *Journal of Modern History*, 22:129–130 (June 1950).

[21] CSTL, CFCC, VI, 34, Yen-mao memorial, Oct. 31, 1884 (KH10/9/13).

[22] CSTL, CFCC, VI, 30, Chou memorial, Oct. 31, 1884 (KH10/9/13).

[23] CSTL, CFCC, VI, 62, Hung Liang-p'in memorial, Oct. 31, 1884

Ten years elapsed before the Chinese learned how wrong they had been regarding the usefulness of the railroads. This was demonstrated to them during the Sino-Japanese War.[24] On the other hand, it was nearly twenty years until they learned how right they had been regarding the insidious nature of foreign control of their railroads — revealed to them during the first decade of the twentieth century.

Despite the threat of obloquy, there was a scattering of officials who guardedly supported the Detring and Sheng-Ristelhueber proposals. Hui Yen-pin, who held a sinecure as deputy supervisor of instruction, suggested that, out of consideration for the welfare of the people, China should at least essay one more attempt at an understanding with France. He thought that Detring's proposal to allow the French temporary rights in Taiwan was the more acceptable of the two proposals. Railroads, he reasoned, would enable the French to gain access to the heartland of China, whereas in Taiwan they were at least confined to the borders. He admonished, however, that if the French "make intolerable demands, how can we readily submit and thereby increase the burdens of the people?" In such an event, he believed China would have no alternative but to continue fighting.[25]

Chou Chia-mei was of all the memorialists the least confident regarding the military situation, and he believed the Sheng-Ristelhueber proposals offered the most acceptable conditions that China could expect. He shared the widespread belief that France was in even greater financial straits than China. However, it was necessary for China to maintain large defensive forces, while the French navy could, with a relatively

---

(KH10/9/13); CSTL, CFCC, VI, 65, Ch'in Chung-chien memorial, same date.

[24] H. B. Morse, III, 81.

[25] CSTL, CFCC, VI, 48–50, Hui memorial, Oct. 31, 1884 (KH10/9/13). See also CSTL, CFCC, VI, 70–72, Feng Ying-shou memorial, same date.

small force, make quick strikes against China's weak points. French expenditures were therefore much smaller than those of the empire. Liu Ming-ch'uan on Taiwan had recently scored some small successes. Chou suggested that these gave China enough military prestige so that it could negotiate a settlement now without undue loss of national dignity.[26]

Li Hung-chang, the arch spokesman for the peace faction, had adopted a surprisingly reserved attitude toward the two proposals. On October 24, the Tsungli Yamen, having heard rumors, asked Li if he knew of the existence of a set of peace proposals. Only after he was presented with this direct query did he inform Peking of the general purport of the documents. Even in doing so, he pointedly observed that he had not made any commitments regarding Detring's articles. Indeed, Detring subsequently told the Yamen members that Li had refused his, Detring's, request to convey the proposal to the capital.[27] With regard to the articles composed by Sheng and Ristelhueber, Li assured the Yamen that he had done no more than instruct Sheng to present them to the Grand Council. He did suggest, nevertheless, that in view of the critical situation a decision be made immediately.[28] Two days later, he more courageously offered the opinion that construction of a railroad, and its management by whatever nation, would be an effective means of dispelling the enmity that existed between France and China.[29]

Li Hung-chang had conducted himself with utmost circumspection in regard to the two sets of proposals. He knew that, now when his prestige was at its nadir, and when the war

[26] CSTL, CFCC, VI, 23–25, Chou memorial, Oct. 31, 1884 (KH10/9/13). A similar view was expressed by Weng T'ung-ho, et al. (WCSL, 48:16b–18, same date.)

[27] CSTL, CFCC, VI, 3, Detring conversation with Tsungli Yamen, Oct. 28, 1884 (KH10/9/10). See also Kiernan, p. 149.

[28] TK, CFCC, IV, 210, Li to Tsungli Yamen, Oct. 25, 1884 (KH10/9/7).

[29] TK, CFCC, IV, 211, Li to Tsungli Yamen, Oct. 27, 1884 (KH10/9/9).

partisans reigned in Peking, to be caught violating the imperial proscription of indemnity proposals could be fatal. He had, in fact, even cast doubt on the trustworthiness of the Sheng-Ristelhueber proposals, declaring that they were not worth further consideration.[30] Despite his attempts to avoid identification with the proposals, officials in Peking thought they discerned in them his traitorous hand. It was not, several memorialists insisted, Detring, Ristelhueber, or Sheng who were guilty of this effrontery to the throne, but rather Li Hung-chang. He should, therefore, they proposed, be punished for ignoring the imperial interdiction.[31]

There is no documentary evidence to show that Li had initiated either of the proposals; still, I think that the officials' suspicions of Li were well-founded. Both Detring and Sheng were Li's men: the intimate relationship between Li and the German was common knowledge, and Sheng Hsüan-huai had long been associated with Li as his manager of various Western-style industrial enterprises. Furthermore, the ascendancy of the war advocates in the policy councils in Peking had not lessened Li's desire to end a war that threatened his political and military sources of power; he simply had to act more warily in offering the throne alternatives to war. He had done so by acting through intermediaries, scrupulously avoiding becoming personally identified with the peace propositions. The episode demonstrates the "witch hunt" character that *ch'ing-i* had assumed by 1884 — and how Li Hung-chang tried to cope with it.

The Hart Negotiations. The court conference of October 28, 1885 had resulted in an expression of almost unanimous rejection of the peace proposals and of support of the govern-

[30] WJC, CFCC, II, 29, Oct. 28, 1884 (KH10/9/10).
[31] CSTL, CFCC, VI, 43, Lung Chan-lin memorial, Oct. 31, 1884 (KH10/9/13); CSTL, CFCC, VI, 53, Ch'en Hsüeh-fen memorial, same date; CSTL, CFCC, VI, 54, Sheng-yü memorial, same date.

ment's policy of war. But the fighting in Vietnam and Taiwan had been indecisive, and the throne could feel no complacency about the outcome. It had long been the fervent expectation of the Chinese that, in the event of a war, Britain and Germany would join the hostilities against France. These hopes were to be utterly quashed, just as Robert Hart had forewarned a year earlier.[1] In late October 1884, both Britain and Germany apprised China that, though they were not well-disposed toward France, they were not prepared to force a rupture with that country and come to the assistance of China.[2]

The throne had also to consider in its policy formulations the possibility that Russia and Japan might join France in a concerted attack on the empire. The dispute with Russia over Ili had ended officially in February 1881 with the signing of the Treaty of St. Petersburg. Nevertheless, an aura of ill-feeling and suspicion enveloped the relations between the two nations. Russian troops did not withdraw from the Chinese portion of Ili until 1883; Russian gold prospectors continued to violate Chinese territory; and the frontier of the southern Ussuri district remained undefined.

Peking's concerns were exacerbated by the fear of Russian aggression against Manchuria and Korea. Actually, as reputable scholarship has shown, Russia's commercial interests in Korea were still inchoate in 1884, and its policy in East Asia was essentially one of indifference throughout this period — although, like Japan, it would have liked to see Korea attain independence.[3] Of the relative benignity of Russian policy, the Chinese

---

[1] See above, p. 93.

[2] YNT, IV, 2218, dcmt. 1184, Li Feng-pao to Tsungli Yamen, Oct. 20, 1884 (KH10/9/2); YNT, IV, 2225, dcmt. 1185, Tseng Chi-tse to Tsungli Yamen, same date.

[3] Andrew Malozemoff, *Russian Far Eastern Policy, 1881–1904; with Special Emphasis on the Causes of the Russo-Japanese War* (Berkeley and Los Angeles, 1958), pp. 15–17.

were unaware, and the worst was feared.[4] Russia's designs remained, therefore, a huge imponderable, and Peking could not discount the possibility of trouble with the czar's forces anywhere along a frontier stretching from Central Asia to the Pacific Ocean. No crisis coalesced in Sino-Russian relations during this period. Many Chinese as well as Russians apprehended, however, that war was in the offing.[5]

Japan was a source of even greater uncertainty and concern than was Russia. The reform movement in Korea, supported by impassioned Japanese liberals, had made significant inroads on the traditionally conservative and pro-Chinese government on the peninsula during 1883 and early 1884. Japanese influence was also increasing as Japanese technicians arrived to assist nascent Korean industries. At the same time, the Korean king dismissed Chinese advisors who had been serving as instructors in the army.[6]

Meanwhile, Japanese liberals perceived that Chinese involvement in Vietnam made this an especially propitious time for direct action in Korea. Thinking that the French would look kindly upon anti-Chinese activities in Korea, these Japanese approached the French minister in Tokyo seeking monetary and material assistance for a pro-independence coup in Korea. This would have the virtue, in French eyes, of diverting Chinese forces from the south. The Japanese liberals were not disappointed. After several months of negotiations in early 1884, the French minister promised that "if the opportunity

---

[4] *Ch'ing Kuang-hsü ch'ao Chung Jih chiao-she shih-liao* (Historical materials relating to Sino-Japanese relations in the Kuang-hsü period, 1875–1908; Peiping, 1932), 6:4b, dcmt. 253, Shang-hsien memorial, Dec. 19, 1884 (KH10/11/3); Ch'en Han-sheng, et al., eds., *Chung-kuo hai-kuan yü Chung Fa chan-cheng* (The Chinese Maritime Customs and the Sino-French war; Peking, 1957), dcmt. 49, p. 180, Hart to Campbell, Dec. 22, 1884.

[5] Malozemoff, p. 21.

[6] Hilary Conroy, *The Japanese Seizure of Korea: 1868–1910* (Philadelphia, 1960), p. 141.

comes, there will be a fund of one million yen and a warship to meet the need." [7]

The Japanese government, too, recognized the opportunity presented to it by the Sino-French conflict. However, it was less willing than the liberals to essay direct action in Korea. The government decided, therefore, to venture no more than its previous covert efforts to pry Korea away from Chinese control.[8] An alliance between Japan and France was, therefore, never formed. Occasionally, in fact, Japanese consuls in China provided the Chinese with information about French military movements. Nevertheless, the Chinese inevitably remained fearful that Tokyo would adopt a hostile attitude during the fighting in Vietnam and Taiwan.[9]

In late October, the Chinese learned to their gratification that neither Japan nor Russia was, as they had feared, bound to France by a treaty that would demand its involvement in the conflict with France. Nevertheless, Peking at the end of 1884 had been informed of two ineluctable facts: (1) it could not disregard the possibility that it would have to face simultaneous assaults from more than one adversary; and (2) it must resist its adversaries without foreign assistance.

During the second week of November, Tseng Chi-tse, still minister at the Court of St. James, informed Peking that Jules Ferry had become exceedingly anxious for an armistice.[10] This news prompted a new peace probe — though pacifism in Paris did not imbue the Chinese with a strong sense of the need for conciliation. With imperial approval of the new peace overtures, the Tsungli Yamen on November 11 communicated to the British the conditions upon which that government might attempt mediation of the dispute.[11]

[7] Conroy, pp. 142–143.
[8] Conroy, p. 144.
[9] T. F. Tsiang, p. 84.
[10] WJC, CFCC, II, 29, Nov. 5, 1884 (KH10/9/18); WJC, CFCC, II, 30, Nov. 9, 1884 (KH10/9/22).
[11] WJC, CFCC, II, 30, Nov. 9 and 11, 1884 (KH10/9/22 and 24).

These proposals never had any issue, for the British foreign secretary, Lord Granville, declined to submit them to the French on the ground that they had no chance of acceptance.[12] Granville was undoubtedly correct. France would, according to the terms of the Chinese proposal, be denied all claims to a protectorate in Vietnam. The French might continue to trade in Vietnam, but they were to interfere neither in Vietnamese government nor in the presentation of tribute by that state to its northern overlord. Regarding the military situation, France must immediately withdraw its forces from Keelung, though Chinese troops in Tongking were to remain in their positions until the negotiations were concluded. As a final insult to the French, the Chinese text of the treaty was to be official — though, in the interests of friendship, China would graciously waive all its rightful claims to an indemnity from France! [13] The Chinese conditions were preposterous, and they could only have been indited on the assumption that the French were now desirous of peace at any price.

In early December, the climate of opinion in the court changed. The French Chamber had granted new credits to support the war effort;[14] and the Japanese were again muddying the waters in Korea, reinforcing their armed contingent, and apparently preparing to throw down the gauntlet to Peking. Whether or not these were the motivating factors, Princes Ch'un and Ch'ing had become eager by this time to reach an understanding with the French. After urgent entreaties, Tz'u-hsi yielded to their advice. Weng T'ung-ho, on December 8, made the revealing entry in his diary that "the French affair has hitherto been conducted according to the

---

[12] Kiernan, p. 155.

[13] CSTL, CFCC, VI, 101–103, Nov. 10, 1884 (KH10/9/23). The Chinese government subsequently emended the proposals but made no substantive changes in the meaning. CSTL, CFCC, VI, 103, Nov. 12, 1884 (KH10/9/25); and ibid., pp. 103–104, Nov. 15, 1884 (KH10/9/28).

[14] Documents diplomatiques. Affaires de Chine et du Tonkin, 1884–1885, p. 172, dcmt. 152.

views of [officials in] the court. But Prince Ch'ing vigorously opposed this policy, and finally the throne ceased to heed the war advocates." [15] With Tz'u-hsi no longer disinclined to listen to talk of peace, the principal problem for the advocates of peace was to discover a formula that would satisfy each of the two nations without jarring the sensibilities of the other.

The new attitude prevailing in the court was immediately noticed by Robert Hart, who grasped the occasion to offer his personal mediation between the two warring nations. The story of Hart's patient and subtle conduct of the subsequent negotiations has been told in detail elsewhere.[16] It will therefore suffice here to give but a brief account of the events preceding the signing of the peace protocol on April 4, 1885.

Hart suggested to the Tsungli Yamen that China accept the Li-Fournier agreement, with the additional understanding, inter alia, that Vietnam might continue optionally to send tribute to China. The Yamen accepted the proposal on about December 14,[17] and Hart's European agent, James Duncan Campbell, finally found a means to present it to Jules Ferry on January 24, 1885. Ferry rejected the proposals. Hart had anticipated this eventuality, however, and he had prepared an alternative set of proposals — which had not received the sanction of the Yamen. In these, the French premier expressed interest. Hart now had what he wanted: contact with Ferry, and support of the Chinese government for a set of proposals

---

[15] WJC, CFCC, II, 31, Dec. 8, 1884 (KH10/10/21). This is a loose paraphrase of Weng's elliptic phrase. Prince Ch'ing appears to have been one of the most consistent and vigorous proponents of a peace policy in the court during the final phases of the controversy. This observation leads me to believe that Ssu-ming Meng was guilty of overstatement when he asserted that Prince Ch'ing was the "figurehead" of the Yamen, and that "He had neither the personal or official power, nor the desire, to take any initiative in China's foreign affairs." (p. 55).

[16] Stanley Fowler Wright, pp. 517–534; Shao Hsün-cheng, pp. 193–209; Billot, pp. 335–409.

[17] Ch'en, *Chung-kuo hai-kuan*, dcmt. 136, p. 62, Hart to Campbell, Dec. 14, 1884.

that served as a start in a diplomatic barter. The subsequent negotiations in Paris were long and worrisome; not the less so, Hart felt, because Li Hung-chang, Tseng Chi-tse, and the new Chinese minister to France and Germany, Hsü Ching-ch'ing, were anxious to grasp a share of the honors for ending the war. There were, however, even greater difficulties. Anti-foreign disturbances in the port cities of the empire; the French blockade, instituted in late February, of Chinese rice shipments to North China; and foreign protests against the French blockade of Taiwan — one or all of these could suddenly blow up and wreck the negotiations. Despite these problems, Hart had brought the Chinese and French governments to an agreement on all but minute details by late March.

Then, in a moment, events suddenly threatened to undo his handiwork. The recapture of Lang-Son by imperial forces[18] contributed to Jules Ferry's resignation on March 30, the treaty still unsigned. Could the signing of the pact wait for the formation of a new ministry? Hart feared not, knowing that the war advocates in Peking, inspired by the recent successes, might force the government to renounce its commitment to peace.[19] The French president, Jules Grévy, recognized the urgency of the situation, and he therefore took the extraordinary action of ordering that the protocol be concluded without waiting for the formation of a new ministry. On April 4, 1885, signatures were formally attached to the armistice.

The protocol was a simple document, for it was essentially a reaffirmation of the agreement between Li and Fournier in May of the previous year. Beyond the terms of that Convention, the French agreed to make no further demands on the empire. An accompanying interpretative note specified details of troop withdrawals, of the termination of the blockade of

[18] Noted above, pp. 171–172.
[19] Ch'en, *Chung-kuo hai-kuan,* dcmt. 246, p. 98, Hart to Campbell, Apr. 3, 1885.

Taiwan, and of arrangements for the conclusion of a definitive treaty.[20]

The armistice was only a first step toward the conclusion of a final settlement. Each feared that through an act of bad faith on the part of the other, or as a result of a chance misunderstanding, the agreement of April 4 might be wrecked as had been its predecessor, the Li-Fournier Convention. Indeed, Paris had to wait until April 9 to receive confirmation of Chinese imperial sanction — a delay that caused some anxiety on the Quai d'Orsay.[21]

Reactions to the Peace. In China, opposition to the agreement was muted; *ch'ing-i* remained silent — a sharp contrast to the reception the same Convention had received in May 1884. This unwonted and abject acquiescence in an unfavorable peace settlement, particularly at a time when imperial military fortunes had improved, demands explanation. Had the *ch'ing-i* spirit dissipated because officials had tired of the war? Or did the officials think this was as favorable a settlement as could be obtained against a mighty France? Unlikely! The explanation seems to lie, rather, in the changed attitude of the empress dowager. Having determined on peace, the remonstrances and admonitions of the war advocates would be inconvenient to her. She therefore closed the *yen-lu*.

Revocation of the privilege of addressing the throne on policy matters (*yen-lu*) was not an action to be undertaken lightly. The *yen-lu* was a traditional institution, and early emperors of the dynasty had sternly proclaimed it to be inviolable.[1] Tz'u-hsi therefore had to move with caution, and she had a ready pretext to hand. Factional politics had assumed outrageous proportions during the preceding year, and, as early

[20] The full texts of the protocol and of the accompanying interpretative note may be found in HR, II, 525–526.

[21] Stanley Fowler Wright, p. 532.

[1] *Ch'ing-shih-lu,* 200:1b, Jan. 31, 1885 (KH10/12/16).

as the spring of 1884, she had given evidence that she was wearying of the remonstrances and denunciations that were constantly brought to her through the *yen-lu*. At that time she had merely admonished the officials that memorials motivated by factional rivalries and personal rancor would not be tolerated.[2] It was undoubtedly more than coincidence that she chose this time, when she was preparing for a peace settlement, to begin meting out punishments to *ch'ing-i* spokesmen.

Muzzling of the *ch'ing-i* began in mid-January 1885. Hsü Chih-hsiang, a sub-chancellor in the Grand Council, had submitted a memorial in which he averred that those who propose and support railway construction "are sycophants if they are not traitors." [3] Hsü did not, in this onslaught on railroads, posit any arguments against a peace settlement with France. However, it was at this time no secret in the court that peace probes were being essayed,[4] and indirection was not alien to Hsü's mode of expression.[5] It may be speculated, therefore, that Hsü, assuming that the proposed settlement would include a railroad clause as did the Sheng-Ristelhueber articles, intended to denounce indirectly the government's attempts to establish an entente with France. Whatever Hsü's motives, the throne on January 10 replied:

> The court originally opened the *yen-lu* with the hope that the officials would correct Our oversights, and that, by realistically searching for the truth, We might attain to the highest principles. Officials who discuss current affairs

---

[2] *Shih-erh ch'ao tung-hua-lu,* Kuang-hsü reign, III, 1650, Apr. 8, 1884 (KH10/3/13); LJC, 42:48b, June 15, 1884 (KH10/5/22).

[3] Hsü Chih-hsiang, "Chia-ting hsien-sheng tsou-i" (Memorials of Hsü Chih-hsiang), in Hsia Chen-wu, ed., *Chia-ting Ch'ang-pai erh hsien-sheng tsou-i* (Memorials of Hsü Chih-hsiang and Pao-t'ing; place of publication unknown, 1901), 2:16, Jan. 10, 1885 (KH10/11/25).

[4] WJC, CFCC, II, 32, Dec. 23, 1884 (KH10/11/7).

[5] Compare his memorial of Oct. 31, 1884, in which he discussed the Sheng-Ristelhueber proposals, but never mentioned the proposals nor their relation to a peace settlement. (Hsü Chih-hsiang, 1:11b–14 [KH10/9/13].)

should, in accordance with the facts, speak out forthrightly regarding the rights and wrongs of government. But the practice of rashly submitting unfounded opinions and making slanderous accusations without a sense of responsibility cannot be extended.[6]

The obloquies delivered by Hsü Chih-hsiang had not been more extreme than those of innumerable other memorialists. But the wrath of the throne had been stirred; Hsü was demoted three steps in rank and assigned to a new post.

Officials interpreted the degradation of Hsü Chih-hsiang as an attack on the privilege of offering advice to the throne, and protests were made. The throne was adamant. The *yen-lu* was being closed tightly — though the throne insisted that it had no wish to interfere with moderately phrased memorials.

Less than two weeks after punishment had been inflicted on Hsü, a relatively unknown possessor of a metropolitan sinecure rushed to Hsü's rescue, charging that Hsü had been punished because he had dared to discuss imperial policy. The official, Fan Kung-hsü, further warned the throne that officials now suspected their counsels would no longer receive imperial attention.[7]

The decree in response to Fan's admonition was a direct denial of what was in fact being accomplished:

The reason a decree was issued ordering the punishment of Hsü Chih-hsiang was because he had made slanderous accusations. It was surely not because he had discussed current affairs. If you officials who are charged to discuss affairs hold firm views on government policy, you should speak out directly, concealing nothing. If it is said that the *yen-lu* has been impeded by the punishment of Hsü, how is it that Fan Kung-hsü has now submitted this memorial . . . ? The court listens eagerly to the opinions of all and seeks the truth about conditions. It had been hoped that there would be

[6] *Ch'ing-shih-lu*, 198:10b, Jan. 10, 1885 (KH10/11/25).
[7] *Ch'ing-shih-lu*, 199:7, Jan. 22, 1885 (KH10/12/7).

real benefits derived from employing the opinions of many men in the administration of government. You officials should each purify your hearts and tremblingly obey the repeated imperial commands to reveal your loyal counsels. But you must not irresponsibly offer personal opinions.[8]

Fan Kung-hsü was then degraded and transferred to a new post.

The imperial farce was not yet ended. A week later, Teng Ch'eng-hsiu, a central figure in the Ch'ing-liu, protested against the punishment of Hsü and Fan. The result was only to add the name of Teng to the list of recently demoted officials. While decreeing the degradation of Teng, however, the throne maintained that it was observing the instructions of the imperial ancestors to permit officials to submit their views for imperial consideration. The throne had, the decree read, recently retained for perusal or discussion the memorials of several other officials, which was "clear proof" that the *yen-lu* remained open. It was added, however, that the "unseemly expression of personal opinions or the introduction of private conjectures" would not be tolerated.[9] This arbitrary — and, indeed, specious — standard of what constituted proper and improper policy criticisms produced the effect the empress dowager desired. The *yen-lu* was closed; *ch'ing-i* spokesmen were cowed.

There was, nevertheless, a small but vocal stronghold of opposition to the peace protocol formed by a few of the officials and commanders who had been close to the fighting in Vietnam. After their recent smashing successes and deep penetrations into Tongking, they were loath to return to the Chinese frontier and give up the fruits of their victories. One detail of the agreement in particular caused consternation. The French had originally demanded a guarantee that there would be no mishaps in the execution of the troop withdrawals. Hart knew

[8] *Ch'ing-shih-lu,* 199:7a–b, Jan. 22, 1885 (KH10/12/7).
[9] *Ch'ing-shih-lu,* 200:1b, Jan. 31, 1885 (KH10/12/16).

that the insertion of the word "guarantee" would be inadmissible to the Chinese. He therefore proposed that French forces remain in Taiwan until after the Chinese forces had completed their evacuation of Tongking. This would in fact be an effective guarantee, but would avoid use of the objectionable terminology. This concession did not escape the notice of several members of Chinese officialdom. They placed no trust in the French word — French duplicity was still thought to be the cause of the Bac-Le incident[10] — and they feared that, after Chinese troops had evacuated Vietnam, the French would be unwilling to leave Taiwan.[11]

Pao Ch'ao, one of the outstanding commanders in the suppression of the Taiping Rebellion, presented a memorial that exemplifies the highly emotional reaction of front-line commanders to the peace settlement. Pao informed the throne that his subordinate officers had come to him pleading that they be permitted to press the attack. Pao had condoled with them, but repeatedly emphasized to the disconsolate soldiers that they must obey the imperial instructions and withdraw accordingly. However, when it was learned that the French were not required to withdraw, "all the men exploded with anger; they gathered around my tent, wringing their hands and in unison requesting that they be allowed to fight, declaring that if they fought and were not victorious . . . they would gladly submit to martial law for not heeding the imperial commands. I ordered them, and they did not respond; I commanded them and they did not leave; they performed the kowtow without cease and they were so excited they were in tears." Pao was hardly less emotional than were his men, aver-

[10] CSTL, CFCC, VI, 40, Shen Yüan-shen memorial, Oct. 31, 1884 (KH10/9/13); ibid., p. 50, Hui Yen-pin memorial, same date.
[11] CSTL, pp. 405–406, Chao Erh-sun memorial, Apr. 17, 1885 (KH11/3/3); ibid., p. 412, Tso Tsung-t'ang memorial, Apr. 18, 1885 (KH11/3/4).

ring that he could neither sleep nor eat thinking of the money and men that would have been expended in vain were his forces to comply with the order to withdraw.[12]

Pao Ch'ao was not alone in opposing the peace settlement. Ts'en Yü-ying, Feng Tzu-ts'ai, and P'eng Yü-lin, to mention but a few of the commanders and officers in the south, all protested the surrender of territory that they had fought to preserve.[13] By far the most irate critic of the peace was Chang Chih-tung, now governor-general of Kwangtung-Kwangsi. His arguments did not differ essentially from those of the other critics, but he was certainly the most vociferous. On the very day that he heard of the April protocol, he dispatched a protest to Peking, and from that time until the final treaty was signed two months later, he kept the telegraph wires to the north singing with his condemnations of the "wolf-hearted," "insatiable," and "unscrupulous" French.[14]

The policy-makers in Peking were unmoved by these arguments against the peace. Hart commented that "the Prince [Ch'ing] has stuck to me splendidly" during the course of the negotiations.[15] The Tsungli Yamen as a whole was also "relieved and delighted" when it was informed that the protocol had finally been signed.[16]

Nor had the sudden victory at Lang-Son altered Tz'u-hsi's will to honor the peace settlement. Viewed from Peking, the situation looked much different than it did to most of the commanders in Tongking, still flushed with their triumph. The fighting in Taiwan had been going badly, a French offensive

[12] CSTL, pp. 466–470, May 24, 1885 (KH11/4/11).
[13] CSTL, pp. 427–429, Ts'en Yü-ying memorial, Apr. 27, 1885 (KH11/3/13); ibid., p. 422, Chang Chih-tung memorial, Apr. 22, 1885 (KH11/3/8); ibid., pp. 425–427, P'eng Yü-lin memorial, Apr. 27, 1885 (KH11/3/13).
[14] Chang's memorials may be found in ibid., pp. 384–538 passim.
[15] Stanley Fowler Wright, p. 529.
[16] Ibid., p. 531.

there in early March having forced the defenders to relinquish considerable areas on the northern coast of the island.[17] Furthermore, only three days after the Chinese recapture of Lang-Son, the Pescadore Islands had fallen to Courbet. The Chinese navy, too, had not been able to break the French blockade in order to supply the hard-pressed defenders on Taiwan.

Even from Tongking, the throne received disheartening news. In a memorial that arrived in Peking on the day after the protocol had been signed, Ts'en Yü-ying reported that only about one-half of his Yunnanese troops possessed breech-loading rifles. Even these, though purchased from abroad, were inferior to those used by the French. Ts'en also complained that ammunition was scarce, money lacking, and food supplies depleted. It was, on the whole, an extraordinarily discouraging report, and the throne could only reply that "We have long been thoroughly cognizant of the logistical difficulties in Tongking." [18]

Complications with other foreign powers also made a peace settlement in April 1885 highly desirable. Russian armies along the northern frontier were being reinforced, and the defenses there had become a matter of sharp concern.[19]

Relations with Japan were also abrasive. Tension between that country and the empire had come close to the rupture point in December 1884 after an attempted coup d'état in Seoul brought the armies of the two countries into a brief but bloody clash.[20] The Korean reformers had felt that they were losing their influence, and that the government was heading

[17] See above, p. 169.
[18] WCSL, 55:30–31b, Ts'en Yü-ying memorial, Apr. 5, 1885 (KH11/2/20); *Ch'ing Kuang-hsü ch'ao Chung Jih chiao-she shih-liao*, 6:4b, dcmt. 253, Shang-hsien memorial, Dec. 19, 1884 (KH10/11/3).
[19] WCSL, 56:19a–b, Hsi-yüan memorial, Apr. 15, 1885 (KH11/3/1).
[20] Conroy, pp. 139–158; Hummel, I, 468 and II, 950–951; H. B. Morse, III, 11.

toward closer ties with China. Time was apparently working against them and they were becoming desperate. They therefore conceived a plot to kill several high officials and to seize control of the government. On December 4, Japanese legation guards occupied the royal palace, the king was taken prisoner by the reformers, and eight high government officials were put to death. The Chinese became involved two days later, on December 6. Yüan Shih-k'ai, chief of staff of the Chinese garrison, responded to a request from Korean anti-reform officials, and with approximately two thousand men[21] attacked the palace, which was defended by some two hundred Japanese. The defenders killed over forty Chinese soldiers while losing thirty of their own number.[22] The Japanese were vastly outnumbered, however, and the hapless Korean king was restored to Chinese hands. Leaving their legation in flames, the Japanese retreated from Seoul and sought refuge on a ship in Chemulpo harbor. Order was restored, and, with the Chinese again in control, the conservatives were restored to power.

The incident brought relations between Japan and the empire to a critical turn. Popular sentiment in Japan became strongly pro-war after the fighting, and the Japanese garrison in Seoul was quickly reinforced[23] — although reports of these reinforcements received in Peking were highly exaggerated.[24] In China, there were murmurs in favor of war. Chang Chih-tung was almost gleeful at the prospect of a fight with Japan. He did indeed recognize it would be best if hostilities did

[21] Hummel, II, 950–951. T. F. Tsiang (p. 80) states that there were only fifteen hundred Chinese troops in Korea at the end of 1884.

[22] *Ch'ing Kuang-hsü ch'ao Chung Jih chiao-she shih-liao*, 6:27, dcmt. 280, addendum #1, Dec. 28, 1884 (KH10/11/12); *ibid.*, p. 1, dcmt. 246, Dec. 17, 1884 (KH10/11/1).

[23] Kiernan, pp. 160–171; WCSL, 49:26b–27, Li Hung-chang to Tsungli Yamen, Dec. 10, 1884 (KH10/10/23); *ibid.*, pp. 27–28b, same to same, Dec. 11, 1884 (KH10/10/24).

[24] *Ch'ing Kuang-hsü ch'ao Chung Jih chiao-she shih-liao*, 6:31, dcmt. 281, decree, Dec. 28, 1884 (KH10/11/12).

not erupt. But he asserted China must not shy away from a conflict, for Japan would then increase its demands. Furthermore, he confidently predicted that a defeat of the Japanese would not only secure the defenses of North China, but would break the spirit of the French.[25]

Those who now dominated policy in Peking were, fortunately, less rash than Chang Chih-tung. To the throne and the Tsungli Yamen, it did not seem at all certain that a war with Japan would have the happy effect of dispiriting the French as Chang predicted.[26] Rumors that the French were planning to assist the Japanese in operations in the north increased their anxieties, and the Yamen began seeking means to prevent an alliance of these two adversaries.[27] Peking was further deterred from taking a belligerent stand toward Japan by the fear that a war in the north would provide an opening for the encroachments of Russia in Korea.[28]

Despite popular pressure, government leaders in Tokyo retained their moderate views. For the moment, they were content merely to negotiate a means to prevent a repetition of the December 6 clash with Chinese troops, and in mid-March Ito Hirobumi arrived in China to conclude the settlement famous for its provision that both Japan and China would withdraw all their forces from Korea. The Chinese were naturally fearful that Ito brought with him extortionate demands,[29] and they knew Ito enjoyed a real advantage in the negotiations as long

[25] *Ibid.*, p. 5, dcmt. 254, Chang Chih-tung memorial, Dec. 19, 1884 (KH10/11/3).

[26] *Ibid.*, 5:36b, dcmt. 245, decree, Dec. 16, 1884 (KH10/10/29); Ch'en, *Chung-kuo hai-kuan*, dcmt. 49, p. 180, Hart to Campbell, Dec. 22, 1884.

[27] *Ch'ing Kuang-hsü ch'ao Chung Jih chiao-she shih-liao*, 6:32, dcmt. 284, Li Hung-chang telegram, Dec. 29, 1884 (KH10/11/13); Ch'en, *Chung-kuo hai-kuan*, dcmt. 137, p. 62, Hart to Campbell, Dec. 14, 1884.

[28] Ch'en, *Chung-kuo hai-kuan*, dcmt. 49, p. 180, Hart to Campbell, Dec. 22, 1884.

[29] *Ch'ing Kuang-hsü ch'ao Chung Jih chiao-she shih-liao*, 7:7b, dcmt. 338, addendum #1, Li Hung-chang letter, no date.

as the fighting in the south continued. The Yamen was consequently extremely anxious that the conflict with France be terminated before the Japanese could take advantage of the empire's other preoccupations.[30] Li Hung-chang shared the Yamen's conviction, and, just two days before the protocol of April 4, he reminded the throne:

> While we are occupied with the French difficulties, Japan uses the opportunity to grasp advantages in Korea, and knavishly creates incidents. The situation is deplorable. If the French affair is quickly settled, we can use reason to expose their pretexts, and, making slight compromises, it should be easy to bring them to terms. The crux of the Korean situation seems to lie not in resisting Japan, but in settling the controversy with France.[31]

Chinese historians and propagandists have frequently condemned the final peace settlement with France as an ignoble and unwarranted surrender. These writers stress the recent victories in Tongking, and assert that the empire had victory in the palm of its hand.[32] Such an interpretation is wrong, because it fails to take into consideration the totality of China's political and military situation. In fact, the throne and its advisors correctly recognized that they needed a peace settlement — and urgently! Russian movements in the north were suspect; the situation in Taiwan had become critical; and the paucity of supplies in Tongking suggested that the recent

[30] Ch'en, *Chung-kuo hai-kuan*, dcmt. 56, p. 184, Hart to Campbell, Mar. 17, 1885.

[31] WCSL, 55:10, Li's report of Mar. 23, 1885, transmitted to the throne on Apr. 2, 1885 (KH11/2/17).

[32] Examples are Shu Shih-ch'eng, *Chung Fa wai-chiao-shih* (History of Sino-French relations; Shanghai, 1928), p. 49; Lo Tun-yung, "Chung Fa ping-shih pen-mo" (Sino-French hostilities), in Tso Shun-sheng, comp., *Chung Fa chin-pai-nien shih ts'ai-liao* (Materials relating to the history of the past hundred years of Sino-French relations; Shanghai, 1928), p. 357; A. Ying, ed., *Chung-Fa chan-cheng wen-hsüeh ch:* (A collection of literature during the Sino-French war; Peking, 1957), introductory section, p. 3; Hu Sheng, p. 88.

dramatic victories might be only ephemeral. These alone were compelling and sufficient reasons why Peking might have determined to end the war with France. It was, however, the dispute with Japan that tipped the scales of policy influence in favor of the peace advocates.[33] Li Hung-chang and Ito Hirobumi commenced their negotiations of the Korean problem on April 3, the day before the peace protocol was signed in Paris. Tz'u-hsi undoubtedly recognized the good fortune that Robert Hart had completed his diplomatic work when he did. She was not, therefore, going to revive the war with France when the negotiations with Japan were in progress, despite the victory at Lang-Son.

The Final Peace Settlement. Subsequent to the signing of the peace protocol, Hart and Campbell continued to work at their diplomatic task. It fell to them, together with the diplomats on the Quai d'Orsay, to draft a definitive treaty of peace and commerce, because it was felt that, for reasons of secrecy, the negotiations should be conducted in Paris rather than in China. Thereafter the chief negotiators in Tientsin, Li Hung-chang and Patenotre, had only to smooth out details in the final treaty.[1]

On April 22, Li Hung-chang received full powers to conclude the definitive treaty. The throne was still mistrustful of Li — the fact that he was ordered to engage in the negotiations at all suggests the degree to which Tz'u-hsi was de-

---

[33] Alexander Michie (II, 334) wrote that Tz'u-hsi "recked nothing of the success of her brave troops on the outskirts of the empire, but thought only of the enormous expense of the war, which had been unpleasantly brought home to her, and of matters affecting her own convenience. She therefore had no thought of going back on the treaty, but was even more urgent than before to have it promptly signed and ratified." I believe that Michie was unduly harsh on the Old Buddha, and that important matters of state weighed more heavily in her quest for peace than did her personal inconvenience.

[1] Stanley Fowler Wright, pp. 532–533.

pendent upon him in diplomatic matters — and admonished him not to enter carelessly into an agreement that would produce further complications "as you did last year when Fournier was making his departure." [2] To ascertain that Li kept his cards on the table, the throne named two members of the Tsungli Yamen, Hsi-chen and Teng Ch'eng-hsiu (also a member of the Ch'ing-liu), to participate in the negotiations.[3]

The final treaty was signed in Tientsin on June 9, 1885.[4] The provisions of this document are of interest, because they reveal that neither nation reaped diplomatic gains as a result of the warfare since the Bac-Le Incident. In particular, it may be noted that the French protectorate over Vietnam had been reaffirmed, and that Vietnam was to conduct its relations with other countries only through the intermediary of France — a stipulation that implicitly severed its tributary ties with China. The barriers that shielded the southern interior provinces from foreign trade were now also broken down. The treaty of June 9 stipulated that trade would be conducted through a minimum of two ports of entry, in accordance with the trade regulations established in other treaty ports. (Two years later, in June 1887, these limited commercial concessions were substantially revised. Three more ports of entry were opened, and customs duties were fixed at rates less than those in force in the coastal treaty ports.)[5]

The definitive treaty further stipulated that France would undertake to provide China with material and technical assistance whenever the empire should decide to commence railroad construction. This phrase was clearly a vestige of the

[2] CSTL, CFCC, VI, 418, decree to Li Hung-chang, et al., Apr. 22, 1885 (KH11/3/8).
[3] Ibid.
[4] The full text of the treaty is in HR, II, 531–535; and MacNair, pp. 486–489.
[5] HR, II, 572–573. During the two years after June 1885, additional agreements were concluded between the two countries, covering details of commerce and border delimitation. (HR, II, 552–575.)

Sheng-Ristelhueber proposals. Just as in the previous year, however, the Chinese were determined to forestall French efforts to obtain a favored position within the empire by means of influence on Chinese railroads. The final agreement, therefore, pointedly declared: "It is . . . understood that this clause shall not be looked upon as constituting an exclusive privilege in favour of France." [6] The time when the European powers would establish spheres of exclusive influence was not yet!

After the conclusion of the treaty of June 9, 1885, Robert Hart observed: "I don't think any one will say that China comes badly out of the year's trial, and, as for the work that reestablished peace, I, looking at it critically, as if it were another man's performance, pronounce it [a] good . . . bit of work!" [7] Eighty years later, one may well make the same assessment of the Sino-French War and the final peace settlement. The Chinese, although fettered by outmoded techniques and shortages of supplies, had fought the French to a stalemate. China lost, it is true, its claim to sovereignty over Vietnam, and that country remained under French domination until 1954. But the French had been denied an indemnity; railroad construction had been averted; and imperial control of the southern boundaries and of the rich natural resources lying within those boundaries had not been broken. In short, China was not much changed by the war. This is the reason, I think, why historians have tended largely to ignore this, the third war that the Chinese fought with Europeans. This tendency is unfortunate, for the controversy was historically significant *precisely because* it permitted the Chinese throne and mandarins to lapse again into apathy and self-contentment.

It is tempting to speculate that *defeat* in the war would have *saved* China from the humiliations that it has experienced in

---

[6] Article VII of the treaty. (MacNair, p. 488.)

[7] Private letter from Hart, dated June 28, 1885, quoted in MacNair, p. 489.

the twentieth century. A more bruising denouement of this war might have imparted a renewed impetus to the modernization efforts that had lost momentum after the 1860's. Between 1885 and 1895, the forces of imperialism were markedly weaker than they were during the decade after the Sino-Japanese War. There was, then, still time after the Sino-French controversy for China to work out its own salvation — if its leaders had been inspirited to adopt a policy of change.

I confess that this possibility seems extremely remote. The mandarins in Peking were probably, in any event, psychologically incapable of pursuing a thoroughgoing policy of change. A more credible sequence of events, as a result of a defeat in 1885, would have been an earlier quickening of mass nationalism, with the result that the Ch'ing dynasty would have collapsed a decade or more before the Revolution of 1911. Would a premature fall of the Ch'ing order have aborted the development of the regional forces that produced the era of warlords during the first half of the twentieth century? Might China have then remained politically unified? If so, what would be the role of Communism in China today? There are no certain answers to these questions, but they do suggest the weighty significance of the issues hinging upon the Sino-French controversy.

On the other hand, I do not see that a decisive Chinese victory in 1885 would have smoothed the path of China's development during the late-nineteenth and twentieth centuries. Cultural isolation has become an historical curiosity, and the Chinese could not permanently have prevented the interplay of their culture with the cultures of the rest of the world. Indeed the longer China's entrance into the mainstream of international life was postponed — which is probably the result a Chinese victory would have had — the more painful and traumatic was its transition to modernity fated to be.

Still, victory or defeat is in the eyes of the beholder. Sun

Yat-sen was convinced that China had been humiliated by the French and betrayed by the Manchus. His revolutionary sentiments were therefore sparked by the same war that had left most officials unperturbed.[8] K'ang Yu-wei was also deeply moved by events of the war, and thirty-five years later he recalled: "I was twenty-seven in Kuang-hsü Chia-sen [1884–1885]. French troops threatened the City of Rams [i.e., Canton]. For safety's sake I lived in . . . Yin-t'ang village, north of the Hsi-ch'iao hills. Aroused by the nation's calamity and commiserating the people for their plight, I wrote the *Ta-t'ung Shu.*"[9]

A number of less well-known Chinese were also influenced by the events of 1884–1885, so that the Sino-French War was actually a highly significant milestone in the intellectual and political development of modern China. These intellectuals — most notable among whom were Cheng Kuan-ying and Ho Kai (or Ho Ch'i) — recognized as a result of the war that the primarily military orientation of the self-strengthening policy was sterile, ineffectual, and shortsighted. And, during the decade 1885–94, they elaborated a program of reform that urged not only economic modernization, but political innovation, in-

[8] Lyon Sharman, *Sun Yat-Sen, His Life and Its Meaning: A Critical Biography* (New York, 1934), pp. 28–29; and Sun Yat-sen, *Memoirs of a Chinese Revolutionary* (Taipei, 1953), p. 143. There is disagreement among historians whether Sun became a revolutionary immediately after the Sino-French War, or if he remained a reformist until 1894. See Harold Zvi Schiffrin, "Sun Yat-sen and the Origins of the Chinese Revolution," chap. i, n. 52 of unpublished manuscript (to be published by University of California Press).

[9] Kung-chuan Hsiao, "K'ang Yu-wei and Confucianism," *Monumenta Serica*, XVIII, 110–111 (1959). Brackets and ellipses are Hsiao's. The *Ta-t'ung shu* (Book of the Grand Unity) was a utopian work, radically iconoclastic in nature. K'ang could not possibly have written the *Ta-t'ung shu* when he said he did (*ibid.*, pp. 105–113; Richard C. Howard, "K'ang Yu-wei [1858–1927]: His Intellectual Background and Early Thought," in Arthur F. Wright and Denis Twitchett, eds., *Confucian Personalities*, pp. 295–296). Nevertheless, the fact that K'ang attributed the work to the influence of the Sino-French War indicates the profound impression that the war had made upon him.

cluding parliaments. These reformers in the years preceding the Sino-Japanese War asserted that the common people were of greater importance than the emperor. They further insisted that a political solution was a precondition for an effective defense against foreign aggression. The character of Chinese reformism was therefore dramatically changed by the Sino-French War, and, indeed, the demands for political reform after 1885 may be regarded as the opening shots of the revolution against the Manchus.[10]

[10] Lloyd E. Eastman, "The Early Institutional Reformers, 1890–1895" (paper presented at the meetings of the Association for Asian Studies in New York, Apr. 4, 1966).

VIII

CH'ING-I AND THE CHINESE STATE

Throughout much of history, Chinese political philosophers and reformers believed that the opinions of the Confucian literati were one of the most powerful of political forces. Men like Fan Chung-yen in the eleventh century, and Huang Tsung-hsi in the seventeenth, looked to the articulation of that opinion as the surest means of preserving the traditional practices of government, of curbing the powers of the imperial institution, and of guaranteeing the Confucian orientation of governmental policy.[1] Historians of Chinese government have lately tended to make light of this force. They have stressed instead the increasingly despotic practices of the emperors. They have depicted the Confucian literati as slavish servitors of the throne, devoid of both the will and the means to oppose imperial wishes. Confucian doctrine, we are told, had become so distorted by the official interpretations of Neo-Confucianism, and the officials had become so dependent upon the throne for prestige, wealth, and office, that they forfeited all independent standards of judgment.

Tz'u-hsi's closure of the *yen-lu* in January 1885 might be taken as evidence for this point of view. Yet clearly the throne's domination over the officials was by no means com-

[1] James T. C. Liu, "An Early Sung Reformer: Fan Chung-yen," p. 124, and W. T. de Bary, "Chinese Despotism and the Confucian Ideal: A Seventeenth-Century View," p. 194, in John K. Fairbank, ed., *Chinese Thought and Institutions* (Chicago, 1957).

plete. At the end of the imperial period, the literati displayed an amazing vitality and exercised an influence upon imperial policy which belie neat theories of the "abject servility" of the officials.

Ch'ing-i Influences. That *ch'ing-i* influenced imperial policy is certain; the extent of its influence remains a moot point. It is clear that occasionally a memorial from a *ch'ing-i* official would directly influence governmental policy. In late 1884, for example, an offensive was ordered in Vietnam as a result of a memorial from a subexpositor of the Hanlin Academy.[1] On a number of occasions, also, the throne dispatched copies of *ch'ing-i* memorials to Li Hung-chang during the course of his several negotiations with the French, suggesting that these contained "many points that can be adopted."[2]

Such instances of specific policy proposals being adopted or heeded by the throne are rare. One may nevertheless infer that Tz'u-hsi was highly sensitive to the formless, but real, pressures created by *ch'ing-i*. The belligerence and determination to resist French advances in Vietnam displayed so rashly in the court's declaration of November 16, 1883 presumably resulted from the throne's wish to appease *ch'ing-i*. The same reasoning may have caused Tz'u-hsi's refusal to withdraw imperial troops from Bac-Le, even after Li Hung-chang had informed her of his commitments to Fournier. And her curious obstinacy regarding an indemnity after the Bac-Le incident may also have been a consequence of the pressure of literati opinion. Other instances could be mentioned, but it must be confessed that there is no possible way of determining to what extent Tz'u-

[1] CSTL, CFCC, VI, 111–112, decree, Nov. 12, 1884 (KH10/9/25). The memorial mentioned is from Lung Chan-lin (pp. 113–114, same date).
[2] CFCS, 15:5b–6, dcmt. 514, decree to Li, May 8, 1884 (KH10/4/14); *ibid.*, p. 37, dcmt. 557, decree to Li, May 16, 1884 (KH10/4/22).

hsi's policy calculations at any one time were directly influenced by this "current of thought."

The influence of individual *ch'ing-i* officials upon imperial policy is more easily demonstrable. Li Tz'u-ming commented in December 1883 that "the empress dowager was quick to heed advice. However, the incoherent babble of the grand councilors was impossible to implement, so she committed her affairs to two or three green youths who then called their buddies (*p'eng-t'u*). They have since frivolously and dangerously ruined things. It is lamentable!" [3] Almost a year later, Li Tz'u-ming was still convinced that this "pack of rats" must be killed, or there would be no end to China's afflictions.[4] The influence of these "green youths," most notable among whom were the paladins of Ch'ing-liu, Chang Chih-tung, and Chang P'ei-lun, continued to grow until after the humiliating defeat at Foochow in August 1884. Thereafter, Tz'u-hsi did not trust their bellicose advice. The only members of the Ch'ing-liu to survive the Foochow fiasco politically were Chang Chih-tung and Teng Ch'eng-hsiu. The rest faded into obscurity for the reremainder of their careers.[5]

Thus far, I have remarked only about the direct influences of *ch'ing-i* and *ch'ing-i* officials on Chinese policy. *Ch'ing-i* also wielded indirect and far more insidious influences. One of its instruments was intimidation. Many officials, convinced that China had no alternative to conciliating the French, forbore from expressing their views for fear of drawing upon themselves the attacks of *ch'ing-i*. Kuo Sung-tao observed this fact, lamenting that "officials who know this principle

[3] LJC, 41:56, Dec. 25, 1883 (KH9/11/26).

[4] LJC, 38:5, June 23, 1882 (KH8/5/8); LJC, 42:48, June 14, 1884 (KH10/5/21); LJC, 42:48b, June 15, 1884 (KH10/5/22).

[5] Ayers, pp. 132–133. Ayers remarks that only Chang remained in a position of influence, but, in fact, Teng also remained politically active until his early death in 1891. In 1886, he was especially instrumental in negotiations with the French regarding demarkation of the border between China and Vietnam. (*Ch'ing-shih*, VI, 4938.)

[that peace should be made quickly to protect the people's livelihood] are few, and those who know do not dare memorialize [their views]."[6] Even Li Hung-chang, who had more courage than most when it came to advancing an unpopular opinion, was ultimately cowed by his political opponents. In late 1884, Detring observed that Li refused to convey to Peking a new peace proposal, declaring that "I dare not speak of mediation — I know only that we are fighting."[7]

Officials who did not yield before the flood of literati opinion often suffered for their views. Wang Wen-shao, for example, was senior vice-president of the Board of Revenue until impeachment by war advocates in the summer of 1883; and Chou Chia-mei, Wu T'ing-fen, and Chang Yin-huan were members of the Tsungli Yamen until they were dismissed following their impeachment by a war partisan in October 1884.[8] In this political atmosphere, even Li Hung-chang's former protégés and associates were apostatizing and joining the cause of war.[9]

Many officials adopted a *ch'ing-i* attitude, not out of fear, but because they sensed that this was a sure means to obtain favor and office. Some deplored this phenomenon, and occasionally one encounters in their private correspondence criticisms of officials who "toady to Ch'ing-liu in order to maintain honor and favor," or who "cheat the emperor in order to obtain honor."[10] However, the pressure of literati opinion became so strong in 1884 that one high official memorialized urging a belligerent measure, but he declared privately that

[6] Kuo Sung-tao, "Yang-chih shu-wu i-chi," CFCC, IV, 594. See also *ibid.*, p. 584; and Chou Chia-mei, "Ch'i-pu-fu chai ch'üan-chi," CFCC, IV, 547.

[7] CSTL, CFCC, VI, 3, Detring conversation with Tsungli Yamen, Oct. 28, 1884 (KH10/9/10).

[8] Chou Chia-mei, "Ch'i-pu-fu chai ch'üan-chi," CFCC, IV, 542; *Ch'ing-shih*, IV, 2806 and VI, 4904.

[9] Wu Ju-lun, "T'ung-ch'eng Wu hsien-sheng ch'üan-shu" (The complete writings of Wu Ju-lun), CFCC, IV, 634.

[10] *Ibid.*, p. 633; Chou Chia-mei, "Ch'i-pu-fu chai ch'üan-chi," CFCC, IV, 542; LJC, 42:48b, June 15, 1884 (KH10/5/22).

"I recognize clearly that this cannot be carried out, but I have no alternative to speaking thusly." [11]

When even the highest officials of the realm, as a result of the pressure of *ch'ing-i,* were urging action that they admitted was impossible of implementation, the government had abandoned sanity. It is indeed wondrous, therefore, that the dynasty did not crumble before the forces of domestic rebellion and foreign encroachment sooner than it did.

The political atmosphere generated by *ch'ing-i* sharply narrowed the range of opinions that were expressed to the throne, for it was a rare official who would venture to advise peace or caution to the empress dowager. The consequences in the decision-making process were serious, for the policy alternatives available to the throne were limited in proportion to the intensity and uniformity of literati opinion. In Ch'ing dynasty China, where the role of the throne in policy formation was more often that of passive arbiter than of active inaugurator, such limitations upon proposals reaching the throne patently tended to impose a policy upon it.

Still, *ch'ing-i* never succeeded in suppressing all divergent opinions. Even when war fever was highest, some officials with greater political security than most — men like Prince Ch'un and Prince Ch'ing — or with more daring than most — men like Li Hung-chang and Sheng Hsüan-huai — were able to bring alternative points of view to the empress dowager's attention. The effect upon policy was vacillation and inconsistency.

The Throne and Policy Vacillation. Officials repeatedly expressed their dissatisfaction with the throne's indecisive conduct of affairs. Weng T'ung-ho, an opponent of a war policy, epitomized the despair of the officials when he bemoaned that

---

[11] Chou Chia-mei, "Ch'i-pu-fu chai ch'üan-chi," CFCC, IV, 542.

"In the morning an order is issued; in the evening it is changed. Unavoidably outsiders will laugh. But there is nothing that can be done about it." [1] Li Hung-chang became so disgusted with Peking's vacillation that, in the wake of the Son-Tay defeat in December 1883, he momentarily abandoned his penchant for peace. He denounced officials who cried for war when the country was at peace, but who, as soon as the armies received a defeat, timidly talked of peace. He therefore implored the throne to follow resolutely one policy, and not be disheartened by a single defeat. [2]

Ch'ing-i officials were, of course, even more critical of the throne's failure to maintain a consistent policy. "The throne sets the tone for officialdom," reads a typical *ch'ing-i* memorial. "If the empress dowager and the emperor will resolutely say 'fight,' then the court and the provincial officials will also say 'fight.'" The memorialist added that the officials acted indecisively even when they received a command to fight, for they knew the throne might soon countermand the original orders. [3]

These protests shared the assumption that the throne alone could impart positive direction to policy. For the historian, it is tempting to attribute the inconsistencies of imperial policy to the changing moods and personality foibles of this remarkable lady. Such an explanation would be specious. The Old Buddha was possessed of a mercurial temperament that may at times have beclouded her judgment. Still, she was a woman of genuine perspicacity, and a master of the game of politics. The basic reason, therefore, that she did not impart consistency to her policy against the French must be found in her relations with the officials.

[1] WJC, CFCC, II, 7, Dec. 21, 1883 (KH9/11/22).
[2] See above, p. 99.
[3] CFCS, 22:13b, dcmt. 1026, Lung Chan-lin memorial, Aug. 11, 1884 (KH10/6/21).

In deciding a policy, the French were but one of the factors that Tz'u-hsi had to weigh. The reader will recall that her primary value goal was the maximization of her power as embodiment of the dynasty. From her point of view, the reactions of the officials to her decisions could be an even more weighty consideration than the effect of those decisions upon the French. She had to predict, therefore, the reactions of the various power-holders in the bureaucracy. Would Li Hung-chang, for example, be willing to send the troops or money that would be necessary for the successful implementation of a policy? Or would *ch'ing-i* create a furor that might subvert her claims to supreme authority?

Tz'u-hsi's quandary resulted from the fact that, to repeat Herbert A. Simon's metaphor, she had to take the bus where the passengers wished to go, or they would leave her.[4] But not all the passengers, in this case the officials, desired the same destination. She therefore had to act flexibly, first shifting to mollify officials whose power at the time impinged most forcefully upon her own power interests, then turning to prevent the influence of those same officials from threatening her predominant position.

Ch'ing-i was particularly useful to the Old Buddha in the latter function. She depended heavily upon the high officials for their administrative, diplomatic, and military abilities. Men like Li Hung-chang were, in fact, indispensable to her. Nevertheless, she feared their challenge to her monopoly of government, and she therefore sought to control them with *ch'ing-i*. Evidence that Tz'u-hsi used *ch'ing-i* in this way is circumstantial. The Communist historian Mou An-shih, who was one of the first scholars to suggest this interpretation, supported his contention by quoting the remark of a late nineteenth-century political writer, Cheng Kuan-ying, to the effect that "China uses *ch'ing-i* to maintain the general situation" (*Chung-kuo i*

[4] Simon, p. 134.

ch'ing-i wei-ch'ih ta-chü).[5] This phrase is certainly too vague to bear the entire weight of Mou's hypothesis. However, a remark by Kuo Sung-tao is more explicit: "The provincial officials are utterly ignorant of foreign affairs, but they impose their ignorant ideas on the court under the guise of *kung-lun* [i.e., *ch'ing-i*]. The court encourages them to do this and itself uses *kung-lun* as a gloss for its own purposes." [6]

Tz'u-hsi's use of *ch'ing-i* as a counterbalance to the power of her felt political rivals was, of course, antithetic to the highest ideals of Confucianism.[7] Nevertheless, to deny that the Old Buddha was capable of manipulating *ch'ing-i* in order to maintain her dominance in domestic politics would be to underestimate grossly her political skills. She resorted to these stratagems not merely because she loved, and was an adept at, intrigue. They were also a necessity of her political existence; a means of preserving the power of final decision from a power-hungry bureaucracy and self-engrossing mandarins. (Another master of this technique of encouraging competition among subordinates, incidentally, was President Franklin D. Roosevelt.)[8]

[5] Mou An-shih, *Yang-wu yün-tung* (The foreign affairs movement; Shanghai, 1956), p. 27. The complete quotation is in Cheng Kuan-ying, "Sheng-shih wei-yen" (Warnings to a seemingly prosperous age), in Chien Po-tsan, et al., eds., *Wu-hsü pien-fa* (The 1898 reform movement; Shanghai, 1957), I, 97.

[6] Kuo Sung-tao, *Yang-chih shu-wu ch'üan-chi* (Collected works of Kuo Sung-tao; 1892), 11:3b. The translation is adapted from that in Ssu-yü Teng and John K. Fairbank, *China's Response to the West: A Documentary Survey, 1839–1923* (Cambridge, Mass., 1961), p. 100. Regarding the equivalence of *kung-lun* to *ch'ing-i*, see p. 17, n. 1.

[7] W. T. de Bary (p. 197) writes of Huang Tsung-hsi, whose goal was a traditional Confucian one: "the ideal is not a balance of interests or an equilibrium of countervailing powers. . . . The only secure system is one which places its reliance on men of character and ability."

[8] Arthur M. Schlesinger, Jr., wrote regarding Roosevelt that: "His favorite technique was to keep grants of authority incomplete, jurisdictions uncertain, charters overlapping. The result of this competitive theory of administration was often confusion and exasperation on the operating level; but no other method could so reliably insure that in a

Other than the general reasons why the Chinese throne was dependent upon the officials (viz., for the administrative effectiveness and ideological legitimation of its rule), there were three further reasons why Tz'u-hsi's position, in particular, was insecure vis-à-vis the officials. First, Tz'u-hsi recognized that her authority — that is, the legitimacy of her rule — was not beyond challenge. She was a woman. And the house laws of the Manchus, patterned after those of the Ming dynasty, specifically prohibited the regency of an empress dowager. Pao Chao Hsieh has remarked in his study of Ch'ing government that "Some doubt may be raised as to the legal effects of the edicts issued by the Empress Dowager Tsu Hsi which read 'By order of the Empress Dowager, the Emperor issues this edict. . . .' *Legally the patriarchal character of the government permitted no woman at the helm.*" [9]

Even the weighty authority of the Confucian classics could be evoked against Tz'u-hsi's rule, for in the *Classic of Documents (Shu Ching)* there is the following grim, if quaint, warning against the rule of women: "The hen does not announce the morning. The crowing of a hen in the morning indicates the subversion of the family." [10] It is impossible to ascertain to what extent Tz'u-hsi's violation of these interdictions lessened her legitimacy in the eyes of the officials. However, Tz'u-hsi was herself poignantly aware that her authority might be questioned, and for many years therefore she avoided flaunting her actual role in government.[11]

---

large bureaucracy filled with ambitious men eager for power the decisions, and the power to make them, would remain with the President." (*The Age of Roosevelt* [Boston, 1959], II, 528.)

[9] Pao Chao Hsieh, p. 37 (italics added). See also Lien-sheng Yang, "Female Rulers in Imperial China," *Harvard Journal of Asiatic Studies,* 23:56 (1960–61); Bland and Backhouse, *China under the Empress Dowager,* p. 37.

[10] James Legge, tr., *The Chinese Classics* (Hong Kong, 1960), III, 302–303, quoted in Lien-sheng Yang, p. 52.

[11] Bland and Backhouse, *China under the Empress Dowager,* pp. 51–52. One possible reason that Tz'u-hsi looked kindly upon the Ch'ing-liu,

A second source of Tz'u-hsi's political weakness was that she had not won the esteem of the officials. One will never know how much credence to lend to the reports of orgies, profligacy, and corruption in Tz'u-hsi's court; or to the tales that the eunuch An Te-hai was not indeed a eunuch, and that he had fathered a son by Tz'u-hsi; or to the stories of her intimacies with the handsome Manchu nobleman Jung Lu; or to the rumors that she had murdered, first, the widow of her son T'ung-chih and then her coregent, the Empress Dowager Tz'u-an.[12] The question here is not whether or not this catalog of licentiousness and atrocities is true. What is significant is that

---

for a time at least, was that they had materially assisted her at a critical time during her consolidation of power. In 1875 her son, the T'ung-chih Emperor (Tsai-ch'un) died, and she succeeded in having the Kuang-hsü Emperor (Tsai-t'ien) named the adopted son and successor of the childless T'ung-chih. However, Kuang-hsü was a cousin of, and hence of the same generation as, his adoptive father T'ung-chih. This confusion of generations in the imperial succession blatantly disregarded the laws of the dynasty. Any other arrangement, however, would have bestowed the position and authority of empress dowager upon T'ung-chih's wife, the Empress Hsiao-che, and hence have marked the end of Tz'u-hsi's political career. (Hummel, I, 297.) Many officials were filled with righteous, Confucian indignation at Tz'u-hsi's solution of the succession question, and in 1879 a lesser official, Wu K'o-tu, committed suicide as an expression of protest. (Hummel, II, 875.) Tz'u-hsi's legitimate exercise of authority was sharply challenged by this *coup de théatre*. However, members of the Ch'ing-liu now came to her aid, providing her with an acceptable Confucian ratification of the imperial succession. The crisis thus passed, and Tz'u-hsi may justifiably have felt a debt of gratitude to the Ch'ing-liu. One of the Ch'ing-liu, Chang Chih-tung, for example, received five new posts during the year following the Wu K'o-tu crisis, two appointments again in 1881, and a governorship in 1882. (Ayers, pp. 93–98.)

This incident demonstrates the tenuous character of her rule during the early years of her regency. It also suggests, though the evidence is circumstantial, that the Ch'ing-liu gained from the incident an extraordinary position from which to influence Tz'u-hsi's policy decisions.

[12] Books of Bland and Backhouse are particularly rich sources of this kind of contemporary gossip. See especially *China under the Empress Dowager*, Ch. 6, and E. Backhouse and J. O. P. Bland, *Annals and Memoirs of the Court of Peking* (Boston and New York, 1914), Ch. 20. Also see Harry Hussey, whose biography of Tz'u-hsi reflects Manchu court gossip.

these stories circulated widely and persistently among the officials during the 1880's.

Harold D. Lasswell and Abraham Kaplan have asserted in their study of politics that "respect enjoyed independently of authority status is . . . an important factor in determining the weight of authority exercised." [13] In other words, even if Tz'u-hsi's formal authority could be questioned, her actual power might have been unchallengeable had she enjoyed the unqualified honor and respect of the officials. This was not the case. She was ridiculed; her character was denigrated. Some officials did, of course, hold her in high esteem. But the fact that her reputation was tainted placed a strain upon the officials' loyalty to her, and consequently made her position more tenuous.

Much could have been forgiven Tz'u-hsi if she had crowned her rule with success. However, the third and most critical source of Tz'u-hsi's weakness was the fact that the throne in the 1880's was enveloped in failures. This became more apparent to the officials after the French conflict. Yet, even before, the throne's charisma had begun to pale. Max Weber has observed that a charismatic leader must constantly *prove* his right to rule.[14] Overtly, the officials continued to express their obeisance to the throne; but some of the officials' criticisms of policy during the controversy betrayed an underlying lack of respect for the throne that could not have escaped Tz'u-hsi. She knew that the correctness of her policy decisions was seriously questioned by the officials.

In short, Tz'u-hsi's power rested upon a shaky foundation.

[13] Lasswell and Kaplan, *Power and Society: A Framework for Political Inquiry* (New Haven and London, 1950), p. 135.

[14] Reinhard Bendix, *Max Weber: An Intellectual Portrait* (New York, 1962), pp. 418–419. The charismatic quality of a Chinese emperor's rule is remarked in Max Weber, *The Religion of China*, tr. and ed. Hans H. Gerth (Glencoe, Ill., 1962), p. 143; S. N. Eisenstadt, *The Political Systems of Empires* (New York, 1963), p. 227.

She had, consequently, to compromise with other power-holders in the government in a way that a ruler like K'ang-hsi, who in his later years was more certain of the officials' allegiance and support, had not needed to do.

In pointing out Tz'u-hsi's weaknesses, I have not forgotten that she had acted forcefully, indeed despotically, in suing for peace with the French after having closed the *yen-lu*. But this incident was an exception, proving only that the forces with which we are treating here were relative and exceedingly complex; it does not demonstrate that Tz'u-hsi could always determine policy, regardless of literati opinion. In fact, Tz'u-hsi could have decided to suppress the war advocates and to support a peace policy only after advisors like Prince Ch'ing convinced her that a prolongation of the fight against the French would have been more destructive of her power than would commercial and territorial concessions in distant South China and Vietnam.

Nevertheless, Tz'u-hsi had been given a clear mandate — for example, by the court conference of October 28, 1884 — to pursue the war in Vietnam. By acting contrary to the will of these officials, did she not have reason to fear that she would lose their ideological and administrative support? The answer is "yes." But she sued for peace and closed the *yen-lu* only after she became convinced that momentary alienation of these officials would be less costly to her power than would continuation of the war with France. Even in closing the *yen-lu*, she had been at pains to pacify the officials by contending that the *yen-lu* remained open. In fact, the *yen-lu* was reopened soon after the peace treaty with France had been concluded.[15]

---

[15] Continued vitality of *ch'ing-i* was particularly apparent in the controversy that erupted in 1889 over the proposed construction of a railroad from Tientsin to the neighborhood of Peking. See Wu To, "Ching-t'ung t'ieh-lu te cheng-i" (The dispute over the Tientsin-Tungchow railroad), *Chung-kuo chin-tai ching-chi-shih yen-chiu chi-k'an* (Researches on the modern economic history of China), 4.1:67–132 (May 1936).

The throne would have responded more creatively and more effectively to the Western challenge in the nineteenth century if it had not needed to conciliate *ch'ing-i* and like-minded officials. Tz'u-hsi was not, to the same extent as were the *ch'ing-i* officials, antagonistic to changes in the Confucian state — with its existing relations among social strata, dominance of familistic considerations, and the conception of China as the center of a world order. This is demonstrated by her backing of the self-strengtheners after 1860. She actually intimated sometime prior to 1898 that she had long desired greater reforms in the empire. And, later, after the Boxer humiliation, she personally gave impetus to the imperial reform movement that promised to alter even the relations between the ruler and the ruled. However, Chinese tradition continued to have a strong attraction for her, to a large extent because she considered that the traditional system of societal relations and moral values served as a bulwark of imperial authority and prestige. Nevertheless, the evidence is strong that she was capable of recognizing that technological and ultimately even political innovations might be used to perpetuate her own power and that of the dynasty.[16]

However, Tz'u-hsi did not fully comprehend the implications of Westernization for her power position. Her imagination in this respect was obviously limited by her training, her environment, and her restricted contacts with the non-Chinese world. Nevertheless, she did reveal a spark of detachment from tradition that, fanned by her determination to maximize her power, might have burst into a flame of modernization if she had been able to act unrestrained by other political considerations. The modernization of Meiji Japan is an example of what might

[16] Tz'u-hsi's attitudes toward Westernization are described masterfully in Hsiao, "Weng," pp. 142–143. I differ from Hsiao here in giving greater emphasis to the point that Tz'u-hsi's adherence to traditional values resulted, at least partially, from the realization that those values contributed to her power.

occur when a country's leaders are moved largely by political values.[17]

Tz'u-hsi was never free to give unstinting support to efforts to modernize China, even if she had clearly perceived their value. She knew that to do so would alienate officials upon whom she was dependent. The officials, therefore, seemed to represent a more awesome threat to her power, even if only potentially, than did the encroachments of the imperialists. Her judgment may have been myopic. Nevertheless, the fact that she assessed the threats in that order shows that the officials, imbued with the ideal of Confucianism and tremulous at the prospect of change, were to a large extent responsible for the fate of modern China. Their influence upon the throne and upon state policy was considerable, and this influence was generally uncreative and retardative. The power-oriented drives of the throne and its like-minded advisors, that might have caused China to formulate an effective response to the Western challenge, were therefore diverted and blunted.

A prominent characteristic of the throne-mandarin relationship has been perpetuated by the Chinese Nationalists and Communists. We have noted how the throne tolerated discussion and criticism of policy by the officials, but that there were specific policies that the ruler decreed to be incontestable. During the Sino-French controversy, for instance, Tz'u-hsi interdicted proposals to pay an indemnity to the French and suppressed criticism of her decision to sue for peace. In other words, literati were permitted a considerable latitude of expression, but policy that directly involved the personal commitment and prestige of the ruler, or the power and stability of the throne, was not discussible.

[17] Albert M. Craig, *Choshu in the Meiji Restoration* (Cambridge, Mass., 1961), pp. 372–374. Japan's successful modernization did not, of course, result merely from the value orientation of the Meiji oligarchs. A multiplicity of factors were involved that make the study of change in modern Japan, as in China, extraordinarily complex.

One sees this principle operating in Taiwan today, where the Nationalist government officially endorses the principle of democracy, and tolerates criticism upon such wide-ranging themes as economic and educational policies, the activities of the secret police, and military training in the universities. Reports of corruption within the bureaucracy are particularly in evidence, even in the government-sponsored press — a fact suggesting that this form of criticism may be officially encouraged as a means of maintaining discipline within the political structure in a way analogous to Tz'u-hsi's use of *ch'ing-i* to check the ambitions of Li Hung-chang. Restrictions upon criticism are, however, sharp and immutable. Taiwanese-mainlander relations and the possibility of returning to the mainland are topics not open to discussion. The suppression in 1960 of the *Free China* fortnightly, and the imprisonment of the editor, Lei Chen, give testimony to the continuing determination of a Chinese ruler, in this case Chiang Kai-shek, to maintain inviolate the ideological and practical bases of his personal power.[18]

In Communist China, Mao Tse-tung has given the traditional distinction between discussible and non-discussible policy an unprecedentedly clear definition. In his *On the Correct Handling of Contradictions among the People,* Mao asserted that there may be friendly differences of opinion ("non-antagonistic contradictions") between the formulators of state policy and the mass of the people in a socialist society. To remove these contradictions, Mao urged full discussion and criticism of governmental policies and practices. "Marxists should not be afraid of criticism from any quarter," Mao declared. "Quite the contrary, they need to steel and improve themselves . . . in the teeth of criticism and the storm and stress of struggle.

[18] John Israel, "Politics on Formosa," pp. 3–11, and Mei Wen-li, "The Intellectuals on Formosa," pp. 65–74, in *China Quarterly,* 15 (July–Sept. 1963).

. . . Carrying out the policy of letting a hundred flowers blossom and a hundred schools of thought contend will not weaken but strengthen the leading position of Marxism in the ideological field." [19] At the same time, however, Mao stipulated that statements that tended to undermine the leadership of the Communist Party, or that were harmful to the socialist transformation of Chinese society, resulted from "antagonistic contradictions." Hence they are wrong, and, in practice, they are not tolerated.[20]

Mao's statement in *On the Correct Handling of Contradictions* that the policies of the leaders may differ from the views of the led, and that the led should be permitted to criticize those policies, has been widely recognized as an original contribution to Communist doctrine. It is, Arthur Cohen has written, "unprecedented in Communist literature and practice. These ideas have no Soviet paternity and they represent Mao's contribution . . . to the Communist discussion of contradictions under 'socialism.'" [21]

[19] Mao Tse-tung, *On the Correct Handling of Contradictions among the People* (Peking, 1960), pp. 52–53.

[20] Mao Tse-tung, p. 56. A full discussion of Mao's attitudes toward criticism would have to take into account the discrepancies between the original text of Mao's lecture on contradictions, delivered in February 1957, and the revised version that was published in June 1957. It would be necessary also to delineate the greater limitations that have been put upon public discussions in Communist China since the "wilting" of the Hundred Flowers Movement in June 1957. However, the Hundred Flowers Movement persists, although in modified form, and Mao continues to adhere to the principle portrayed in this paragraph.

(These paragraphs were written before Mao's proclamation of the New Cultural Revolution, and the emergence of the Red Guards in 1966. It is still too early to ascertain whether or not the principle outlined here has persisted under the impact of this new political phenomenon in Communist China.)

[21] Arthur A. Cohen, *The Communism of Mao Tse-tung* (Chicago and London, 1964), p. 156. See also Stuart R. Schram, *The Political Thought of Mao Tse-tung* (New York and London, 1963), pp. 51 and 68–69; G. F. Hudson, "China and the Communist 'Thaw,'" in Roderick MacFarquhar, ed., *The Hundred Flowers Campaign and the Chinese Intellectuals* (New York, 1960), p. 307. Benjamin Schwartz has asserted

If this concept is original within the corpus of Marxist-Leninist literature, one thing remains eminently clear: the concept is firmly rooted in Chinese tradition. It merely represents a specific formulation of the throne-official relationship during the imperial period, exemplified by the relations between *ch'ing-i* and Tz'u-hsi.

---

that the concept of contradictions between the leaders and the people in a socialist society actually dates from Lenin. Schwartz nevertheless agrees that Mao made an "important innovation" in specifying that "leaders," and not just "bureaucrats," could be in contradiction to the masses. See Schwartz, "New Trends in Maoism?" in *Problems of Communism*, 6.4:4 (July–Aug. 1957).

GLOSSARY

BIBLIOGRAPHY

INDEX

BIBLIOGRAPHY

A Ying 阿英 , ed.　Chung Fa chan-cheng wen-hsüeh chi　中法
　　戰爭文學集 (A collection of literature during the Sino-
　　French war).　Peking, 1957; 470 pp.

Alcock, Rutherford.　"China and Its Foreign Relations, "
　　Contemporary Review, 38:1000-24 (December 1880).

Armengaud, Captain.　Lang-Son: Journal des opérations qui ont
　　précédé et suivi la prise de cette citadelle.　Paris, 1901; 76 pp.

Ayers, Thomas William.　"Chang Chih-tung and Chinese Educational
　　Change. "　Ph. D. thesis; Harvard, 1959.

Backhouse, E. and J. O. P. Bland.　Annals and Memoirs of the
　　Court of Peking.　Boston and New York, 1914; 531 pp.

Balázs, Etienne.　"La Crise Sociale et la Philosophie à la fin des
　　Han, "　T'oung Pao, 34:83-131 (1950).

----- Chinese Civilization and Bureaucracy: Variations on a Theme,
　　ed. Arthur F. Wright, tr. H. M. Wright.　New Haven and
　　London, 1964; 309 pp.

Beer, Samuel H. et al.　Patterns of Government: The Major
　　Political Systems of Europe.　Rev. ed. ; New York, 1962;
　　780 pp.

Bendix, Reinhard.　Max Weber: An Intellectual Portrait.
　　New York, 1962; 522 pp.

Biggerstaff, Knight.　"The Secret Correspondence of 1867-1868:
　　Views of Leading Chinese Statesmen Regarding the Further
　　Opening of China to Western Influence, " Journal of Modern
　　History, 22:122-136 (June 1950).

Billot, Albert. L'Affaire du Tonkin; Histoire diplomatique de
l'établissement de notre protectorat sur l'Annam et de
notre conflit avec la Chine, 1882-1885. Paris, 1888; 430 pp.

Bland, J. O. P. and E. Backhouse. China under the Empress
Dowager: Being the History of the Life and Times of Tzu Hsi.
Philadelphia, 1910; 525 pp.

Bodde, Derk. "Feudalism in China," in Rushton Coulborn, ed.,
Feudalism in History, pp. 49-92. Princeton, 1956.

Boulger, Demetrius C. The Life of Sir Halliday Macartney.
London, 1908; 515 pp.

Brunnert, H. S. and V. V. Hagelstrom. Present Day Political
Organization of China. Shanghai, 1912; 572 pp.

Buttinger, Joseph. The Smaller Dragon: A Political History of
Vietnam. New York, 1958; 535 pp.

Cady, John F. The Roots of French Imperialism in Eastern Asia.
Ithaca, 1954; 322 pp.

Carroll, E. Malcolm. French Public Opinion and Foreign Affairs,
1870-1914. New York, 1931; 348 pp.

CFCC: Chung Fa chan-cheng 中法戰爭 (The Sino-French war),
ed. Shao Hsün-cheng 邵循正 et al. 7 vols.; Shanghai, 1957.

CFCS: Ch'ing Kuang-hsü ch'ao Chung Fa chiao-she shih-liao 清光
緒朝中法交涉史料 (Historical materials relating
to Sino-French relations in the Kuang-hsü period, 1875-1884).
22 chüan; Peiping, 1932-1933.

Chang Chih-tung 張之洞. "Chang Wen-hsiang Kung ch'üan-chi"
張文襄公全集 (The complete writings of Chang Chih-tung);
in Chung Fa chan-cheng, IV, 437-536.

Chang P'ei-lun 張佩綸. "Chien-yü chi" 澗于集 (The collected
writings of Chang P'ei-lun); in Chung Fa chan-cheng, IV,
241-420.

Chao I 趙翼. Nien-erh-shih cha-chi 廿二史劄記 (Studies from the twenty-two dynastic histories). 2 vols.; Taipei, 1958.

Ch'en Han-sheng 陳翰笙 et al., eds. Chung-kuo hai-kuan yü Chung Fa chan-cheng 中國海關與中法戰爭 (The Chinese Maritime Customs and the Sino-French war). Peking, 1957; 248 pp.

Cheng Kuan-ying 鄭觀應. "Sheng-shih wei-yen" 盛世危言 (Warnings to a seemingly prosperous age); in Chien Po-tsan 翦伯贊 et al., eds., Wu-hsü pien-fa 戊戌變法 (The 1898 reform movement), I, 39-129. Shanghai, 1957.

Ch'in-ting Ta-Ch'ing hui-tien 欽定大清會典 (Collected statutes of the Ch'ing dynasty, Kuang-hsü reign). 100 chüan; Taipei, 1963.

Ch'ing-chi wai-chiao shih-liao, see WCSL.

Ch'ing Kuang-hsü ch'ao Chung Fa chiao-she shih-liao, see CFCS.

Ch'ing Kuang-hsü ch'ao Chung Jih chiao-she shih-liao 清光緒朝中日交涉史料 (Historical materials relating to Sino-Japanese relations in the Kuang-hsü period, 1875-1905. 88 chüan; Peiping, 1932.

Ch'ing-shih 清史 (History of the Ch'ing dynasty). 8 vols.; Taipei, 1961.

Ch'ing-shih-lu: Ta-Ch'ing li-ch'ao shih-lu 大清歷朝實錄 (Veritable records of successive reigns of the Ch'ing dynasty). Tokyo, 1937-1938.

Cho Huan-lai. Les Origines du Conflit Franco-Chinois à propos du Tonkin jusqu'en 1883. Paris, 1935; 228 pp.

Chou Chia-mei 周家楣. "Ch'i-pu-fu chai ch'üan-chi" 期不負齋全集 (The complete writings of Chou Chia-mei); in Chung Fa chan-cheng, IV, 541-547.

227

Chung Fa chan-cheng, see CFCC.

"Chung Fa Yüeh-nan chiao-she tzu-liao," see CSTL.

Cohen, Arthur A. The Communism of Mao Tse-tung. Chicago and
   London, 1964; 210 pp.

Colquhoun, Archibald R. China in Transformation. Rev. ed. ;
   London and New York, 1912; 299 pp.

Conroy, Hilary. The Japanese Seizure of Korea, 1868-1910: A
   Study of Realism and Idealism in International Relations.
   Philadelphia, 1960; 544 pp.

Cordier, Henri. Histoire des relations de la Chine avec les
   puissances occidentales, 1860-[1902]. See HR.

Craig, Albert M. Choshu in the Meiji Restoration. Cambridge,
   Mass. , 1961; 385 pp.

Creel, H. G. Chinese Thought: From Confucius to Mao Tse-tung.
   New York, 1960; 240 pp.

CSTL: "Chung Fa Yüeh-nan chiao-she tzu-liao" 中法越南
   交涉資料 (Materials relating to Sino-French-Vietnamese
   relations); in Chung Fa chan-cheng, Vols. 5-7.

De Bary, W. T. "Chinese Despotism and the Confucian Ideal:
   A Seventeenth-Century View," in John K. Fairbank, ed. ,
   Chinese Thought and Institutions, pp. 163-203. Chicago, 1957.

Der Ling, Princess. Old Buddha. New York, 1928; 347 pp.

Djang Chu. "War and Diplomacy over Ili," Chinese Social and
   Political Science Review, 20. 3:369-392 (October 1936).

Documents diplomatiques
   Affaires du Tonkin, Première Partie, 1874-Décembre 1882.
      Paris, 1883.
   Affaires du Tonkin, Deuxième Partie, Décembre 1882-1883.
      Paris, 1883.

Affaires du Tonkin, Exposé de la situation, Octobre 1883.
Paris, 1883.

Affaires de Chine et du Tonkin, 1884-1885. Paris, 1885.

Dorland, A. A.   "A Preliminary Study of the Role of the French
Protectorate of Roman Catholic Missions in Sino-French
Diplomatic Relations." M. A. thesis; Cornell, 1951.

Eastman, Lloyd.   "The Kwangtung Antiforeign Disturbances during
the Sino-French War," Papers on China, 13:1-31 (1959).
East Asian Research Center, Harvard University.

-----"The Early Institutional Reformers, 1890-1895." Paper
presented at the meetings of the Association for Asian Studies
in New York, April 4, 1966.

Eisenstadt, S. N.   The Political Systems of Empires.   London, 1963;
524 pp.

Evans, Brian Llewellyn.   "The Attitudes and Policies of Great
Britain and China toward French Expansion in Cochin China,
Cambodia, Annam, and Tongking, 1858-1883." Ph. D. thesis;
University of London, 1961.

Fairbank, John K.   Trade and Diplomacy on the China Coast: The
Opening of the Treaty Ports, 1842-1854.   Cambridge, Mass.,
1953; 489 pp.

-----and Kwang-Ching Liu.   Modern China: A Bibliographical Guide
to Chinese Works, 1898-1937.   Cambridge, Mass., 1950; 608 pp.

-----and Ssu-yü Teng.   Ch'ing Administration: Three Studies.
Cambridge, Mass., 1960; 246 pp.

Fan Wen-lan 范文瀾.   Chung-kuo chin-tai-shih 中國近代史
(Modern Chinese history).   Peking, 1961; 432 pp.

Fan Yeh 范曄.   Hou Han shu 後漢書 (History of the latter Han
dynasty).   120 chüan; Shanghai, 1894.

Ferry, Jules.   Le Tonkin et la mère-patrie: Témoignages et
documents. Paris, 1890; 406 pp.

Fournier, François-Ernest.   "La France et la Chine au traité
Tien-Tsin," Revue des Deux Mondes, 65:755-790 (Oct. 15,
1921).

Garnot, E. Fa-chün ch'in T'ai shih-mo 法軍侵臺始末
(L'Expédition française de Formose, 1884-1885). Taipei,
1960; 125 pp.

Gervais, A. "Diplomatie chinoise: Li Hung-chang et le commandant
Fournier," Revue politique et littéraire (Revue Bleue), 34.15:
449-457 (Oct. 11, 1884).

Gundry, Richard Simpson.   China and Her Neighbors; France in
Indo-China, Russia and China, India and Tibet. London,
1893; 408 pp.

Hao Yen-p'ing 郝延平 . "T'ung-Kuang hsin-cheng-chung te so-wei
'ch'ing-i'" 同光新政中所謂的清議 (The so-called
ching-i during the reforms of the T'ung-chih and Kuang-hsü
reigns). Bachelor's thesis; Taiwan National University, 1958.

-----"A Study of the Ch'ing-liu Tang: The 'Disinterested' Scholar
Official Group, 1875-1884," Papers on China, 16:40-65 (1962).

Ho Ping-ti 何炳棣. "Chang Yin-huan shih-chi"張蔭桓事蹟
(Notes concerning Chang Yin-huan); in Li Ting-i 李定一
et al., eds., Chung-kuo chin-tai-shih lun-ts'ung 中國近
代史論叢 (Collection of essays on modern Chinese history),
1st ser., VII, 91-113. Taipei, 1956.

-----The Ladder of Success in Imperial China: Aspects of Social
Mobility, 1368-1911. New York and London, 1961; 385 pp.

Howard, Richard C.   "K'ang Yu-wei (1858-1927): His Intellectual
    Background and Early Thought, " in Arthur F. Wright and
    Denis Twitchett, eds. , Confucian Personalities, pp. 294-316.
    Stanford, 1962.

HR: Henri Cordier.   Histoire des relations de la Chine avec les
    puissances occidentales, 1860-[1902]. 3 vols.; Paris,
    1901-1902.

Hsiao I-shan 蕭 一 山 .   Ch'ing-tai t'ung-shih 清代通史 (A
    comprehensive history of the Ch'ing period). 5 vols.; Taipei,
    1962.

Hsiao Kung-chuan.   "Weng T'ung-ho and the Reform Movement of
    1898, " Tsing Hua Journal of Chinese Studies, new ser. ,
    1. 2:111-243 (April 1957).

-----"K'ang Yu-wei and Confucianism, " Monumenta Serica,
    18:96-212 (1959).

Hsieh Pao Chao.   The Government of China, 1644-1911. Baltimore,
    1925; 414 pp.

Hsü Chih-hsiang 徐致祥. "Chia-ting hsien-sheng tsou-i"
    嘉定先生奏議 (Memorials of Hsü Chih-hsiang); in Hsia
    Chen-wu 夏寰武 , ed. , Chia-ting Ch'ang-pai erh hsien-sheng
    tsou-i 嘉定長白二先生奏議 (Memorials of Hsü
    Chih-hsiang and Pao-t'ing). 1901.

Hsü, Immanuel, C. Y.   China's Entrance into the Family of Nations:
    The Diplomatic Phase, 1858-1880. Cambridge, Mass. , 1960;
    255 pp.

Hu Sheng.   Imperialism and Chinese Politics. Peking, 1955; 308 pp.

Huang Fen-sheng 黃奮生 .   Pien-chiang cheng-chiao chih yen-chiu
    邊疆政教之研究 (Researches on administration and
    education in the frontier areas). Shanghai, 1947; 136 pp.

Huang Hai-an 黃海安. Liu Yung-fu li-shih ts'ao 劉永福歷史草 (Draft history of Liu Yung-fu), ed. Lo Hsiang-lin 羅香林. Taipei, 1957; 293 pp.

Huang Hsien-fan 黃現璠. Sung-tai t'ai-hsüeh-sheng chiu-kuo yün-tung 宋代太學生救國運動 (National salvation movement of students of the Imperial Academy during the Sung dynasty). Shanghai, 1936; 136 pp.

Huang Ta-shou 黃大受. Chung-kuo chin-tai-shih 中國近代史 (Modern Chinese history). 3 vols.; Taipei, 1955.

Hucker, Charles O. "The Tung-lin Movement of the Late Ming Period," in John K. Fairbank, ed., Chinese Thought and Institutions, pp. 132-162.

-----"Confucianism and the Chinese Censorial System," in David S. Nivison and Arthur F. Wright, eds., Confucianism in Action, pp. 182-208. Stanford, 1959.

Hudson, G. F. "China and the Communist 'Thaw,'" in Roderick MacFarquhar, ed., The Hundred Flowers Campaign and the Chinese Intellectuals, pp. 295-308. New York, 1960.

Hummel, Arthur W., ed. Eminent Chinese of the Ch'ing Period, 1644-1912. 2 vols.; Washington, 1943.

Hussey, Harry. Venerable Ancestor: The Life and Times of Tz'u Hsi. Garden City, N.Y., 1949; 354 pp.

I-huan 奕譞 (Prince Ch'un 醇親王). "Ch'un ch'in-wang I-huan chih Chün-chi-ch'u ch'ih-tu" 醇親王奕譞致軍機處尺牘 (Letters from I-huan, Prince Ch'un, to the Grand Council); in Chung Fa chan-cheng, V, 39-71.

Iriye Akira. "Public Opinion in Late Ch'ing China." Paper presented to a conference on the 1911 Revolution, sponsored by the Joint Committee on Contemporary China of the American

Council of Learned Societies and the Social Science Research
Council, August 1965); 37 pp.

Israel, John. "Politics on Formosa," China Quarterly, 15:3-11
(July-September 1963).

Kiernan, E. V. G.   British Diplomacy in China, 1880-1885.
Cambridge, England, 1939; 327 pp.

Ko Kung-chen 戈公振 . Chung-kuo pao-hsüeh shih 中國報
學史 (History of Chinese journalism). Peking, 1955; 378 pp.

Ku Hung-ming. The Story of a Chinese Oxford Movement: With
Letter from Chinese Official to German Pastor and Appendices.
Shanghai, 1912; 125 pp.

Kublin, Hyman. "The Attitude of China during the Liu-ch'iu
Controversy, 1871-1881," Pacific Historical Review,
18:213-231 (May 1949).

Kuo Sung-tao 郭嵩燾 . "Yang-chih shu-wu i-chi" 養知書
屋遺集 (The collected writings of Kuo Sung-tao); in Chung
Fa chan-cheng, IV, 571-594.

-----Yang-chih shu-wu ch'üan-chi 養知書屋全集 (Collected
works of Kuo Sung-tao). 55 chüan; 1892.

Kuo T'ing-i et al., eds. Chung Fa Yüeh-nan chiao-she tang.
See YNT.

Lane-Poole, Stanley and F. V. Dickens. The Life of Sir Harry
Parkes. 2 vols.; London, 1894.

Lasswell, Harold D. and Abraham Kaplan. Power and Society:
A Framework for Political Inquiry. New Haven and London,
1963; 295 pp.

Le Than-Khoi. Le Viet-Nam: Histoire et Civilisation. Paris,
1955; 587 pp.

Legge, James, tr. The Chinese Classics, with a Translation,
Critical and Exegetical Notes, Prolegomena, and Copious
Indexes. 5 vols.; Hong Kong, 1960.

Levenson, Joseph R. Confucian China and Its Modern Fate.
3 vols.; Berkeley and Los Angeles, 1958-1965.

Li Hung-chang 李鴻章 . "Li Wen-chung Kung ch'üan-chi 李文
忠公全集 (The complete writings of Li Hung-chang); in
Chung Fa chan-cheng, IV, 1-256.

Li Tz'u-ming. Yüeh-man-t'ang jih-chi. See LJC.

Lin, T.C. "Li Hung-chang: His Korea Policies, 1870-1885,"
Chinese Social and Political Science Review, 19.2:202-233
(July 1935).

-----"Manchurian Trade and Tribute in the Ming Dynasty: A Study
of Chinese Theories and Methods of Control over Border
Peoples," Nankai Social and Economic Quarterly, 9.4:855-892
(January 1937).

Lin Yu-tang. A History of the Press and Public Opinion in China.
Chicago, 1936; 179 pp.

Little, Alicia Helen Neva (Bewicke) (Mrs. Archibald Little).
Li Hung-chang: His Life and Times. London, 1903; 356 pp.

Liu Ch'ang-yu 劉長佑 . "Liu Wu-shen Kung i-shu" 劉武慎
公遺書 (The collected writings of Liu Ch'ang-yu); in
Chung Fa chan-cheng, I, 55-146.

Liu Hsiung-hsiang 劉熊祥 . "Tsung-li ko-kuo shih-wu ya-men
chi ch'i hai-fang chien-she" 總理各國事務衙門及
其海防建設(The Tsungli Yamen and its construction of
maritime defenses); in Li Ting-i et al., eds., Chung-kuo
chin-tai-shih lun-ts'ung, 1st ser., V, 33-55. Taipei, 1956.

Liu, James T.C. "An Early Sung Reformer: Fan Chung-yen,"
in John K. Fairbank, ed., Chinese Thought and Institutions,
pp. 105-131.

234

Liu K'un-i 劉坤一． "Liu Chung-ch'eng Kung i-chi" 劉忠誠
公遺集 (The collected writings of Liu K'un-i); in Chung Fa
chan-cheng, I, 147-162.

-----Liu K'un-i i-chi 劉坤一遺集 (The collected writings of
Liu K'un-i). 6 vols.; Peking, 1959.

LJC: Li Tz'u-ming 李慈銘． Yüeh-man-t'ang jih-chi 越縵
堂日記 (Diary of Li Tz'u-ming). Peking, 1922.

Lo Tun-yung 羅惇曧 ． "Chung Fa ping-shih pen-mo" 中法
兵事本末 (Sino-French hostilities); in Tso Shun-sheng
左舜生, comp., Chung-kuo chin-pai-nien shih tzu-liao
中國近百年史資料 (Materials relating to the history of
the past hundred years of Sino-French relations), pp. 321-357.
Shanghai, 1928.

Loir, Maurice. L'Escadre de l'Amiral Courbet: Notes et
Souvenirs. Paris, 1892; 370 pp.

MacIver, Robert Morrison. The Web of Government. New York,
1947; 498 pp.

MacNair, Harley Farnsworth, ed. Modern Chinese History:
Selected Readings. Shanghai, 1923; 910 pp.

Malozemoff, Andrew. Russian Far Eastern Policy, 1881-1904,
with Special Emphasis on the Causes of the Russo-Japanese
War. Berkeley and Los Angeles, 1958; 358 pp.

Mao Tse-tung. On the Correct Handling of Contradictions among
the People. Peking, 1960; 70 pp.

Maruyama Masao. Thought and Behavior in Modern Japanese
Politics, ed. Ivan Morris. London, 1963; 344 pp.

Masson André. Hanoi pendant la période héroique (1873-1888).
Paris, 1929; 262 pp.

-----, ed.   Correspondance politique du Commandant Henri
    Rivière au Tonkin.   Paris and Hanoi, 1933; 322 pp.

Mei Wen-li.   "The Intellectuals on Formosa, " China Quarterly,
    15:65-74 (July-September 1963).

Meng Ssu-ming.   The Tsungli Yamen: Its Organization and Functions.
    Cambridge, Mass. , 1962; 146 pp.

Merriam, Charles Edward.   Political Power: Its Composition and
    Incidence.   New York and London, 1934; 331 pp.

Michie, Alexander.   The Englishman in China during the Victorian
    Era, As Illustrated in the Career of Sir Rutherford Alcock,
    K. C. B. , D. C. L. , Many Years Consul and Minister in China
    and Japan.   2 vols.; Edinburgh and London, 1900.

Morse, Hosea Ballou.   The International Relations of the Chinese
    Empire.   3 vols.; London, 1918.

Mote, Frederick W.   "Confucian Eremitism in the Yüan Period, "
    in Arthur F. Wright, ed. , The Confucian Persuasion, pp. 202-
    240.   Stanford, 1960.

-----"The Growth of Chinese Despotism: A Critique of Wittfogel's
    Theory of Oriental Despotism as Applied to China, " Oriens
    Extremus, 8. 1:1-41 (August 1961).

Mou An-shih 牟安世 .   Yang-wu yün-tung 洋務運動 (The
    foreign affairs movement).   Shanghai, 1956; 230 pp.

Nelson, M. Frederick.   Korea and the Old Orders in Eastern Asia.
    Baton Rouge,1945; 326 pp.

Neustadt, Richard E.   Presidential Power: The Politics of
    Leadership.   New York, 1964; 221 pp.

Nimier, H.   Histoire Chirurgicale de la Guerre au Tonkin et à
    Formose (1883-1884-1885).   Paris, 1889; 178 pp.

Nivison, David S. "Introduction," in David S. Nivison and Arthur F.
    Wright, eds., Confucianism in Action, pp. 3-24.

-----"Ho Shen and His Accusers: Ideology and Political Behavior
    in the Eighteenth Century," in David S. Nivison and Arthur F.
    Wright, eds., Confucianism in Action, pp. 209-243.

Norman, Charles Boswell. Tonkin, or France in the Far East.
    London, 1884; 343 pp.

North China Herald. 1883-1884.

Ochi Shigeaki 越智重明 . "Shingi to kyōron" 清議と郷論
    (Ch'ing-i and village opinion); Tōyō gakuhō 東洋学報
    (Journal of oriental studies), 48:1-48 (June 1965).

"Pavillons-Noirs, Les," Annales de L'Extrême Orient et de
    L'Afrique, 6:69-73 (1883-1884).

Power, T. F., Jr. Jules Ferry and the Renaissance of French
    Imperialism. Morningside Heights, N. Y., 1944; 222 pp.

Rambaud, Alfred. Jules Ferry. Paris, 1903; 553 pp.

Rawlinson, John Lang. China's Struggle for Naval Development,
    1839-1895. Cambridge, Mass., 1966.

Robiquet, Paul, ed. Discours et Opinions de Jules Ferry, pub.
    avec commentaires et notes. 7 vols.; Paris, 1893-1898.

Rochefort, Henri. Les Aventures de ma Vie. 5 vols.; Paris, 1898.

Schlesinger, Arthur M., Jr. The Age of Roosevelt. 3 vols.;
    Boston, 1957-1960.

Schram, Stuart R. The Political Thought of Mao Tse-tung.
    New York and London, 1963; 319 pp.

Schwartz, Benjamin. "New Trends in Maoism?" in Problems of
    Communism, 6.4:1-8 (July-August 1957).

-----In Search of Wealth and Power: Yen Fu and the West. Cambridge, Mass., 1964; 298 pp.

Semallé, Marie Joseph Claude Edouard Robert, comte de. Quatre ans à Pékin, août 1880-août 1884: Le Tonkin. Paris, 1933; 267 pp.

Shao Hsün-cheng 邵循正 . Chung Fa Yüeh-nan kuan-hsi shih-mo 中法越南關係始末 (Relations between China, France, and Vietnam). Peiping, 1935; 215 pp.

-----et al., eds. Chung Fa chan-cheng. See CFCC.

Sharman, Lyon. Sun Yat-sen, His Life and Its Meaning: A Critical Biography. New York, 1934; 418 pp.

She I-tse 余貽澤 . Chung-kuo't'u-ssu chih-tu 中國土司制度 (The Chinese system of tribal chieftains). 1944; 222 pp.

Shih-erh ch'ao tung-hua-lu 十二朝東華錄 (Tung-hua documents of twelve reigns). 30 vols.; Taipei, 1963.

Shu Shih-ch'eng 束世澂. Chung Fa wai-chiao shih 中法外 交史 (History of Sino-French relations). Shanghai, 1928; 142 pp.

Simon, Herbert A. Administrative Behavior: A Study of Decision-Making Processes in Administrative Organization. New York, 1949; 259 pp.

Spector, Stanley. Li Hung-chang and the Huai Army: A Study in Nineteenth-Century Chinese Regionalism. Seattle, 1964; 359 pp.

Spurlock, Cecil E. "The First French Defeat in Vietnam: The Retreat from Langson and Its Consequences." Seminar paper, Harvard, 1963.

Sun Yat-sen. Memoirs of a Chinese Revolutionary. Taipei, 1953; 206 pp.

Ta-Ch'ing li-ch'ao shih-lu, see Ch'ing-shih-lu.

Taboulet, Georges. La Geste Française en Indochine. 2 vols.;
Paris, 1955-1956.

T'ang Chang-ju 唐長孺 . Wei Chin Nan-pei ch'ao shih lun-ts'ung
魏晉南北朝史論叢 (Collected essays on the history
of the Chin, Wei, and Northern and Southern dynasties).
Peking, 1955; 452 pp.

T'ang Chen 湯震. "Wei-yen" 危言 (Words of warning); in
Chien Po-tsan et al., eds., Wu-hsü pien-fa, I, 177-180.

Teng Ssu-yü and John K. Fairbank. China's Response to the West:
A Documentary Survey, 1839-1923. Cambridge, Mass., 1961;
296 pp.

Translation of the Peking Gazette for 1884. Shanghai, 1885; 184 pp.

Tseng Chi-tse 曾紀澤. "Tseng Hui-min Kung i-chi" 曾惠敏
公遺集 (The collected writings of Tseng Chi-tse); in
Chung Fa chan-cheng, IV, 257-269.

"Tseng Chi-tse yü Fa wai-pu wang-lai chao-hui" 曾紀澤與法
外部往來照會 (Communications between Tseng Chi-tse
and the French Foreign Ministry); in Chung Fa chan-cheng,
V, 79-85.

Tseng Kuo-ch'üan 曾國荃 . "Tseng Chung-hsiang Kung ch'üan-
chi" 曾忠襄公全集 (The complete writings of Tseng
Kuo-ch'üan); in Chung Fa chan-cheng, IV, 271-320.

Tseng Kuo-fan 曾國藩 . Tseng Wen-cheng Kung ch'üan-chi
曾文正公全集 (The complete works of Tseng Kuo-fan).
50 ts'e; Changsha, 1876.

Tsiang, T. F. "Sino-Japanese Diplomatic Relations, 1870-1894,"
Chinese Social and Political Science Review, 17.1:1-106
(April 1933).

Wang Erh-min 王爾敏 . "Tao-Hsien liang-ch'ao Chung-kuo ch'ao-yeh chih wai-chiao chih-shih" 道咸兩朝中國朝野之外交知識 (Chinese knowledge of foreign relations, 1821-1861); Ta-lu tsa-chih 大陸雜誌 (The Continent magazine), 22.10:8-12 (May 15, 1961).

WCSL: Ch'ing-chi wai-chiao shih-liao 清季外交史料 (Historical materials concerning foreign relations in the late Ch'ing period, 1875-1911). Peiping, 1932-1935.

Weber, Max. "The Presuppositions and Causes of Bureaucracy," in Robert King Merton et al., eds., Reader in Bureaucracy, pp. 18-27. Glencoe, Ill., 1960.

-----The Religion of China, tr. and ed. Hans H. Gerth. Glencoe, Ill., 1962; 308 pp.

Weng T'ung-ho. "Weng Wen-kung Kung jih-chi" See WJC.

Wiens, Herold J. China's March toward the Tropics. Hamden, Conn., 1954; 441 pp.

WJC: Weng T'ung-ho 翁同龢. "Weng Wen-kung Kung jih-chi" 翁文恭公日記 (Diary of Weng T'ung-ho); in Chung Fa chan-cheng, II, 1-40.

Wright, Mary C. The Last Stand of Chinese Conservatism: The T'ung-chih Restoration, 1862-1874. Stanford, 1957; 426 pp.

-----"The Adaptability of Ch'ing Diplomacy: The Case of Korea," Journal of Asian Studies, 17.3:363-381 (May 1958).

Wright, Stanley Fowler. Hart and the Chinese Customs. Belfast, 1950; 949 pp.

Wu Hsiang-hsiang 吳相湘 . Wan-Ch'ing kung-t'ing shih-chi 晚清宮庭實紀 (Records of the court during the latter part of the Ch'ing dynasty). Taipei, 1952; 258 pp.

Wu Ju-lun 吳汝綸. "T'ung-ch'eng Wu hsien-sheng ch'üan-shu" 桐城吳先生全書 (The complete writings of Wu Ju-lun);

    in Chung Fa chan-cheng, IV, 633-634.

Wu To 吳鐸 . "Ching-T'ung t'ieh-lu te cheng-i" 津通鐵路的
    爭議 (The dispute over the Tientsin-Tungchow railroad);
    Chung-kuo chin-tai ching-chi-shih yen-chiu chi-k'an 中國
    近代經濟史研究集刊 (Researches on the modern
    economic history of China), 4.1:67-132 (May 1936).

Yang Lien-sheng. "Female Rulers in Imperial China," Harvard
    Journal of Asiatic Studies, 23:47-61 (1960-1961).

Yao Hsin-an 姚欣安 . "Hai-fang yü sai-fang te cheng-lun"
    海防與塞防的爭論 (The controversy over naval and
    internal frontier defenses); in Li Ting-i et al., eds., Chung-kuo
    chin-tai-shih lun-ts'ung, 1st ser., V, 206-215.

YNT: Kuo T'ing-i 郭廷以 et al., eds. Chung Fa Yüeh-nan chiao-
    she tang 中法越南交涉檔 (Tsungli Yamen archives
    relating to relations between China, France, and Vietnam).
    7 vols.; Taipei, 1962.

Yü Ying-shih 余英時 . "Han Chin chih chi shih chih hsin tzu-chüeh
    yü hsin ssu-ch'ao" 漢晉之際士之新自覺與新思潮
    (Self-awareness of the literati and the new intellectual trend in
    China in the second and third centuries); Hsin-ya hsüeh-pao
    新亞學報 (New Asia journal), 4.1:25-144 (Aug. 1, 1959).

An Te-hai 安德海

Annam 安南

Bac-Le 北黎

Bac-Ninh 北寧

Cao Bang 高平

Chang Chih-tung 張之洞

Chang Chih-wan 張之萬

Chang Jen-chün 張人駿

Chang K'uei-chai 張簣齋

Chang P'ei-lun 張佩綸

Chang Shu-sheng 張樹聲

Chang Yin-huan 張蔭桓

Chao Erh-sun 趙爾巽

ch'ao-t'ing 朝廷

Chen-hai 鎮海

Chen-nan-kuan 鎮南關

ch'en 臣

Ch'en Ch'i-t'ai 陳啟泰

Ch'en Hsüeh-fen 陳學棻

Ch'en Lan-pin 陳蘭彬

Ch'en Pao-ch'en 陳寶琛

Cheng Kuan-ying 鄭觀應

Cheng-te 正德

chi 即

chi hsing tiao-hui pien-chieh

即行調回邊界

Chia-ching 嘉靖

Chiang Kai-shek 蔣介石

chien-kuan 諫官

Ch'in Chung-chien 秦鍾簡

Ch'in Kuei 秦檜

Ch'ing, Prince 慶親王

ch'ing-i 清議

Ch'ing-i pao 清議報

Ch'ing-liu 清流

Ch'ing-yü 慶裕

cho-ting 酌定

Chou Chia-mei 周家楣

Chou Te-jun 周德潤

Chu 船頭

Ch'un, Prince 醇親王

Chung-kuo i ch'ing-i wei-ch'ih

ta-chü 中國以清議維持

大局

Ch'ung-hou 崇厚

Ch'ü Te-lin 區德霖

Cochin China 南圻

Dan-Phuong 丹鳳

E-le-ho-pu 額勒和布

Fan Chung-yen 范仲淹

Fan Kung-hsü 樊恭煦

Feng Tzu-ts'ai 馮子材
Feng Ying-shou 馮應壽
fu-che 附摺
Fu-k'un 福錕

Hai-Phong 海防
Han Wu-ti 漢武帝
Hanoi 河內
Ho Ching 何璟
Ho Ch'ung-kuang 何崇光
Ho Ju-chang 何如璋
Ho Kai (Ho Ch'i) 何啟
Hsi-chen 錫珍
Hsi-chün 錫鈞
Hsi-yüan 希元
Hsiao-che 孝哲
Hsiao-ch'in (Tz'u-hsi) 孝欽
Hsien-feng 咸豐
Hsü Chih-hsiang 徐致祥
Hsü Ching-ch'eng 許景澄
Hsü Keng-shen 許庚身
Hsü Shu-ming 徐樹銘
Hsü Yen-hsü 徐延旭
Huai 淮
huan-ch'ü 寰區
Huang T'i-fang 黃體芳
Huang Tsung-hsi 黃宗羲
Hué 順化
Hui Yen-pin 惲彥彬
Hung-Hoa 興化

I-hsin (Prince Kung) 奕訢
I-huan (Prince Ch'un) 奕譞
i-i chih-i 以夷制夷
Ito Hirobumi 伊藤博文

jo-kan li 若干里
jun 閏
Jung-lu 榮祿

K'ang-hsi 康熙
K'ang Yu-wei 康有為
Keelung 基隆
Kep 良甲
Kuang-hsü 光緒
Kuei-hsien 貴賢
K'un-kang 崑岡
Kung, Prince 恭親王
kung-lun 公論
K'ung Hsien-chüeh 孔憲穀
Kuo Sung-tao 郭嵩燾
kuo-t'i 國體

Lai Ch'eng-yü 賴承裕
Lang-Son 諒山
Lao-Kay (保勝) 老街
Lei Chen 雷震
li 里
Li, Prince 禮親王
Li Feng-pao 李鳳苞
Li Hung-chang 李鴻章
Li Hung-tsao 李鴻藻

243

Li Jo-nung 李若農

Li Lien-ying 李蓮英

Li Tuan-fen 李端棻

Li Tz'u-ming 李慈銘

Li Yang-ts'ai 李揚才

Liang Ch'i-ch'ao 梁啟超

Liao Shou-heng 廖壽恒

Ling-kuei 靈桂

Liu Ch'ang-yu 劉長佑

Liu En-p'u 劉恩溥

Liu K'un-i 劉坤一

Liu Ming-ch'uan 劉銘傳

Liu Yung-fu 劉永福

Lo Feng-lu 羅豐祿

Lu Ch'uan-lin 鹿傳霖

Lung Chan-lin 龍湛霖

Ma Chien-chung 馬建忠

Mao Tse-tung 毛澤東

Nam-Dinh 南定

Ni Wen-wei 倪文蔚

Ningpo 寧波

nu-ts'ai 奴才

P'an Ting-hsin 潘鼎新

Pao Ch'ao 鮑超

Pao-t'ing 寶廷

Pei-yang 北洋

p'eng-t'u 朋徒

P'eng Yü-lin 彭玉麟

Po-yen-na-mo-hu

伯彥訥謨祜

Saigon 西貢

Shang-hsien 尚賢

shang-i fu-ch'i 上意負氣

Shao Yu-lien 邵友濂

Shen Shang-i 申尚毅

Shen Yüan-shen 沈源深

Sheng Hsüan-huai 盛宣懷

Sheng-yü 盛昱

Shih Ching 詩經

Shu Ching 書經

Shun 舜

Son-Tay 山西

Sun I-yen 孫衣言

Sun Yat-sen 孫逸仙

Sun Yü-wen 孫毓汶

Ta-t'ung Shu 大同書

Taewongun 大阮君

Tamsui 淡水

tang 黨

T'ang Chiung 唐炯

T'ang Ch'un-sen 唐椿森

taotai 道臺

Teng Ch'eng-hsiu 鄧承修

Thai-Nguyen 太原

t'i-tu 提督

T'ieh-pi 鐵壁

244

t'ien-hsia 天下

T'ien Kuo-chün 田國俊

t'ien-tzu 天子

Ting Chen-to 丁振鐸

Ting Jih-ch'ang 丁日昌

Ting Pao-chen 丁寶楨

Tongking（東京）北圻

Tsai-ch'un (T'ung-chih Emperor)
載淳

Tsai-t'ien (Kuang-hsü Emperor)
載湉

Tsai-yüan 載垣

Ts'en Yü-ying 岑毓英

Tseng Chi-tse 曾紀澤

Tseng Kuo-ch'üan 曾國荃

Tseng Kuo-fan 曾國藩

Tso Tsung-t'ang 左宗棠

Tu-Duc 嗣德帝

T'ung-chih 同治

T'ung-wen kuan 同文館

Tuyen-Quang 宣光

tzu-chu 自主

tzu-hsiao chih jen
字小之仁

Tz'u-an 慈安

Tz'u-hsi 慈禧

Vietnam 越南

wai-ch'iang chung-kan
外強中乾

wai-fan 外藩

Wan P'ei-yin 萬培因

Wang Wen-shao 王文韶

Weng T'ung-ho 翁同龢

Wu Hsün 吳峋

Wu Ju-lun 吳汝綸

Wu K'o-tu 吳可讀

wu-li 無禮

Wu Ta-ch'eng 吳大澂

Wu T'ing-fen 吳廷芬

Wu Tse-t'ien 武則天

Yao 堯

Yen Ching-ming 閻敬銘

yen-lu 言路

Yen-mao 延茂

Yüan Shih-k'ai 袁世凱

INDEX

An Te-hai, 215
Army
Chinese: in Tongking, 54, 55–56, 59, 68, 71, 95, 101, 170–172; presence in Tongking admitted, 58, 87n; denied, 61; size of, in Tongking, 85, 101; withdrawn from Tongking after Treaty of Hué, 95; withdrawn from Tongking during Patenotre Negotiations, 139, 153, 162; first resist French openly, 96–97; members of punished, 102, 171; casualties, 172; conditions of, in Tongking, 113, 170–171, 196, 199. *See also* China
French: size of, in Vietnam, 85, 101; operations of, 50, 87–88, 97, 101–102, 125, 169, 171–172; casualties, 172
Arrow War: French participation in, 32
Authority: defined, 2n; and power, 5
Ayers, Thomas William, 26n, 27n, 208n

Bac-Le Incident: described, 125; French reactions to, 125–126, 130–131; responsibility for, 132–136, 207; effect of, in China, 136
Bac-Ninh: importance of, 101; French capture of, 102
Barthélemy St. Hilaire. *See* St. Hilaire, Jules Barthélemy
Billot, Albert, 79, 81, 88, 103
Black Flags: dominance in Tongking, 46–49, 67; size of, 48, 101; Chinese officials' view of, 48n, 64, 91, 99; French enmity toward, 67, 110, 120; kill Rivière,

73; military operations of, 87–88, 96–97, 102, 116, 162n, 171; relations with Chinese government, 89, 90, 96, 101, 119, 138n, 141n, 170. *See also* Liu Yung-fu
Blockade: of Taiwan, 166–167, 174, 189, 196; of Ningpo, 169; of rice to North China, 169, 189
Book of Poetry, 44
Bourée, Frédéric Albert: personality of, 57; discussions with Tsungli Yamen, 58; angered by dismissal, 65, 67; proposes policy for China, 67–68. *See also* Bourée Negotiations
Bourée Negotiations: described, 59–63; clauses of Convention, 60; Chinese opposition to, 61, 64, 81; France rejects Convention, 64–66; consequences of, 66–69, 70
Brière de l'Isle, Louis, 172

Campbell, James Duncan, 188
Challemel-Lacour, Paul, 79, 85n, 86, 88
Chang Chih-tung: revered tradition, 16n; and Ch'ing-liu, 26, 28, 208n; and Northern Party, 28; letter from Li Hung-chang, 75n; militancy of, 98, 104, 195, 197–198; criticized by Li Tz'u-ming, 28, 148, 208; sent ships to Foochow, 157; Tz'u-hsi indebted to, 215n
Chang Chih-wan, 149n
Chang Fang, 23n
Chang P'ei-lun: and Ch'ing-liu, 26, 27n, 28, 208; and Northern Party, 28; and Li Hung-chang, 81, 90, 161; militancy of, 81, 90,

247

INDEX

Hart, Robert: background, 92; advises China, 82, 92–93, 142, 146, 148; and Detring, 110; Tsungli Yamen view of, 142–143; distrusts British and German aims, 177; and peace protocol, 188–189, 193–194, 202
Herbinger, Paul Gustave, 172n
Ho Ch'i, 204
Ho Ju-chang, 52
Ho Kai, 204
Hsi-chen, 148n, 149n; praticipant in negotiations, 138n, 201
Hsiao-che, Empress, 215n
Hsiao-ch'in. See Tz'u-hsi
Hsiao, Kung-chuan: quoted, 107n
Hsieh, Pao Chao, 214
Hsü Chih-hsiang: reputed member of Ch'ing-liu, 27n; and closing of yen-lu, 191–192
Hsü Ching-ch'ing, 189
Hsü, Immanuel C. Y., 26n
Hsü Keng-shen, 148n, 149n
Hsü Yen-hsü, 99, 102
Hsü Yung-i, 148n
Hu T'ieh, 23n
Huang T'i-fang, 26
Huang Tsung-hsi, 206, 213n
Hui Yen-pin, 181

I-hsin. See Kung, Prince
I-huan. See Ch'un, Prince
I-k'uang. See Ch'ing, Prince
Ili Crisis, 26, 82
Indemnity: French demand for, 111, 120, 138, 139, 142, 144, 145, 146–147; Chinese opposition to, 119, 139–140, 141–142, 144–145, 150–151, 165, 207; offered by Tseng Kuo-ch'üan, 143; French drop demand for, 175; China waives claims to, 187
International law: translated into Chinese, 41; Chinese understanding of, 41–43, 56, 147, 163
Ito Hirobumi, 198, 200

Japan: and Korea, 14, 185–186, 187, 196–197; stops Ryukyuan

tribute mission, 25; and France, 185–186, 198; relations with China, 184, 185–186, 196–199, 200
Jung-lu, 215

K'ang-hsi, Emperor, 217
K'ang Yu-wei: and Ch'ing-i Pao, 23; response to war, 204
Kaplan, Abraham, 216
Keelung: French bombardment of, 145, 152; French occupation of, 166, 169
Korea: and China, 14–15, 56n, 167; and Japan, 14, 185–186, 187, 196–197; riot of 1882, 15; coup d'état of 1884, 167, 196–197; and Russia, 184, 198
Ku Hung-ming, 16n, 27n
Kuang-hsü, Emperor, 8, 215n
Kublin, Hyman, 42n
K'un-kang, 148n
Kung, Prince (I-hsin): absence from Tsungli Yamen, 12; response to Franco-Vietnamese treaty of 1874, 33–34, 40; and Li Hung-chang, 82n; dismissal of, 102–105
Kung-lun, 17n, 213
Kuo Sung-tao: criticized by ch'ing-i, 24–25; quoted, 143, 208, 213
Kwangtung: nationalistic riots in, 165

Lang-Son, French capture of, 171; causes Ferry's resignation, 189
Lasswell, Harold D., 216
Lei Chen, 220
Lespès, Sébastien, 110, 112, 145
Levenson, Joseph R., 5n
Li, Prince (Shih-to), 103, 149n
Li Feng-pao, 153, 155, 163, 177
Li-Fournier Convention. See Fournier Negotiations
Li Hung-chang: background, 11; and Tseng Kuo-fan, 11; goals of, 15–16; regional base of, 15, 100; power and influence of, 11–13,

250

INDEX

Sun I-yen, 27n
Sun Yat-sen: response to the war, 203–204
Sun Yü-wen, 149n

Taewongun, 56n
Taiwan: French blockade of, 166–168, 174, 189, 196; fighting in, 169, 199
T'ang Chiung, 95n, 99
Teng Ch'eng-hsiu: member of Ch'ing-liu, 26, 28, 208; member of Tsungli Yamen, 148n, 149n; and closing of *yen-lu*, 193; and Treaty of Tientsin, 201
Throne: bases of rule, 4, 214, 216; and Confucianism, 4, 7; and policy formation, 5, 72, 210, 211; and officials, 5, 6, 10, 115–116, 118, 160, 211, 212–213. *See also* Tz'u-hsi
Treaty: of Kanghwa, 41n
  Franco-Vietnamese, of 1874: provisions of, 33; and French claims, 52, 57, 71; Chinese responses to, 33–34, 41, 45, 56, 77; violations of, 44–45; basis of Tricou Negotiations, 76
  Franco-Vietnamese, of 1883 (of Hué): concluded, 57, 87; Chinese responses to, 89, 91, 95, 98
  of Tientsin: terms of, 200–202; assessed by Hart, 202
Tributary system: Chinese concepts of, 35–44; French view of, 40, 57; and international law, 41–43, 56; and Chinese intervention in dependency, 56. *See also* China
Tricou, Arthur. *See* Tricou Negotiations
Tricou Negotiations: described, 76–78; results of, 79–83, 85
Tsai-ch'un. *See* T'ung-chih
Tsai-t'ien. *See* Kuang-hsü
Tsai-yüan Conspiracy, 9
Ts'en Yü-ying: military operations of, 91, 95n, 101; reports on mili-

tary situation in Tongking, 113, 162n, 170–171, 196; opposes peace protocol, 195
Tseng Chi-tse: protests French activities in Tongking, 51, 56, 68, 71; relations with French government, 56–57, 85, 86, 110–111; view of tributary relationship, 38n, 39; and Tricou Negotiations, 80, 81, 83, 84, 86n; not truthful, 87n, 91; and September 15 Memorandum, 88–89; loses influence, 95, 113; and Li Hung-chang, 111; mentioned, 25, 52, 53, 163, 186, 189
Tseng Kuo-ch'üan: background, 140; refused aid to Foochow, 157, 159–160; and Taiwan relief expedition, 167–169; reports French blockade of Taiwan, 174. *See also* Patenotre Negotiations
Tseng Kuo-fan, 11, 24, 140
Tsiang, T. F., 42n
Tso Tsung-t'ang: Sinkiang expedition opposed by Li Hung-chang, 15; war advocate, 25, 130, 149–150; influence of, 107, 130, 134, 149–150; military command in Fukien, 150
Tsungli Yamen: members of, 148n; authority of, 12–13, 53n, 71, 83; seeks advice of high officials, 52–54, 64; peace advocates, 106, 148, 195, 198; not truthful, 87n; and Bourée Negotiations, 58, 62–63; mentioned, 96, 112
Tu-Duc, Vietnamese Emperor, 45, 57
T'ung-chih, Emperor, 9, 215n
Tz'u-an, Empress Dowager, 8, 104, 105, 215
Tz'u-hsi, Empress Dowager: gains power, 9; goals of, 9, 212, 218; alleged immorality of, 9, 215–216; concern for Peking, 12; power of, 104–105, 107, 154, 160, 213–217; and policy vacillation, 107, 130, 153, 210–217; militancy of, 105, 129–130, 133–

HARVARD HISTORICAL STUDIES